The Collapse
of the
Dale Dyke Dam
1864

THE COLLAPSE OF THE DALE DYKE DAM 1864

Geoffrey Amey

CASSELL · LONDON

CASSELL & COMPANY LTD

an imprint of
Cassell & Collier Macmillan Publishers Ltd
35 Red Lion Square, London WC1R 4SG
and at Sydney, Auckland, Toronto, Johannesburg

and an affiliate of The Macmillian Company Inc., New York

First published 1974

ISBN 0 304 29362 8

Printed in Great Britain by
Northumberland Press Limited
Gateshead

F. 474

For David

Contents

Illustrations

All illustrations are from the Sheffield City Libraries' collection (and
permission to reproduce them is gratefully acknowledged), with the
exception of the portrait of William Leng, which is reproduced by
courtesy of *The Morning Telegraph*, Sheffield.

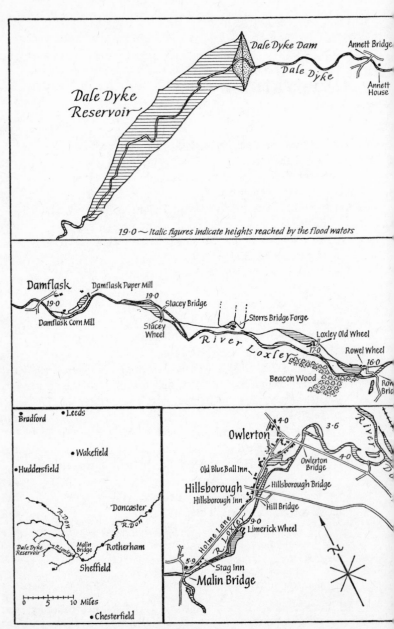

Dale Dyke Dam

Annett Bridge

Dale Dyke

Dale Dyke
Reservoir

Annett
House

19·0 ~ Italic figures indicate heights reached by the flood waters

Damflask

Damflask Paper Mill

19·0

Stacey Bridge

Storrs Bridge Forge

19·0

Damflask Corn Mill

Stacey
Wheel

River Loxley

Loxley Old Wheel

17·0

Rowel Wheel

16·0

Beacon Wood

Row
Bri

•Bradford •Leeds

Owlerton

4·0

3·6

River D

•Wakefield

Owlerton
Bridge

4·0

•Huddersfield

Old Blue Ball Inn

Hillsborough

Hillsborough Bridge

Doncaster•

Hillsborough Inn

R. Don

R. Don

Hill Bridge

Dale Dyke
Reservoir

R. Loxley

Malin
Bridge

Rotherham

9·0

Limerick Wheel

Sheffield

Holme Lane

R. Loxley

5·9

Stag Inn

0   5   10 Miles

Malin Bridge

•Chesterfield

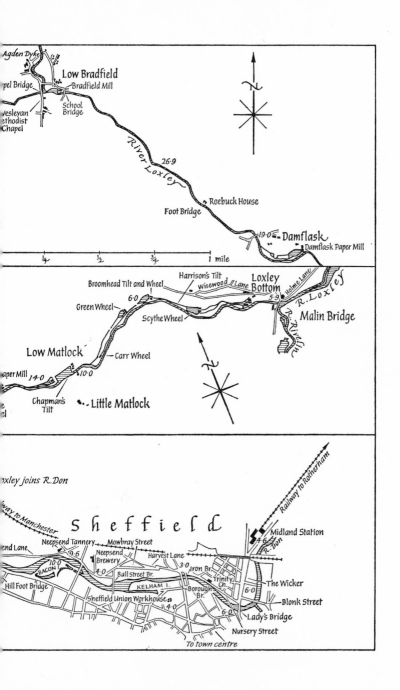

'The work was done in a few minutes, but in that space was a world of horrors, domestic tragedies without end, feelings more dreadful than shall ever be expressed and results more capricious than any tale would ever tell'—*The Times*

Introduction

The collapse of the Dale Dyke dam, which unleashed several hundred million gallons of water on to a vulnerable population, is almost certain to remain forever the most tragic event of its kind in Britain. Modern technology will see to that.

In the middle of the nineteenth century, however, the increasingly urgent need for larger reservoirs threatened to overtake the development of the techniques required to build them, while speedy forms of communication were non-existent. Thus, perhaps, did danger and inadequate means of warning constitute a fatal combination. In March 1864 an unforeseen flood left a winding trail of more than eight miles looking like a battlefield; except in war-time, few towns in this country can have sustained as much damage as did Sheffield during that stormy night. In terms of loss of life, human suffering and material destruction, the disaster is arguably the worst to have occurred in Victorian England.

It is not now a 'popular' catastrophe like, for instance, the Tay Bridge failure, and yet it was infinitely more dreadful. Nevertheless, since the actual period of the tragedy (when graphic eye-witness accounts shocked the nation), surprisingly little has been written about the dam that burst with such frightful consequences. Indeed, it is my guess that outside Sheffield very few people have even heard of it.

So far as I know, only one book hitherto has been devoted exclusively to the subject and that was written, printed and first published shortly after the calamity by Samuel Harrison, editor-proprietor of *The Sheffield Times*. It retains the freshness and impact of first-hand narrative and, although necessarily limited in scope, the volume is an invaluable source and can be regarded as something of a minor classic. Inevitably, there is an almost irresistible temptation for a modern writer to look through Harrison's perceptive eyes, but I have tried not to stare too hard. I have had also the advantage of distant hindsight—a luxury denied to Harrison and his journalistic contemporaries.

Descendants of victims and survivors treasure their own tales, handed down like family heirlooms, of what grandfather and great-aunt did during the Great Flood of Sheffield and, as with most anecdotes, they have probably gained and lost a little in the re-telling. Although such incidents are essential to a comprehensive picture, I have tried to avoid repetition and, instead, to include a selection of the countless individual happenings. For much of that on-the-spot material I have drawn upon accounts written by the newspaper reporters of the day; where conflicting stories have arisen I have had to make a choice or, in some cases, to com-promise with an amalgam.

Soon after the disaster a list of fatalities was issued by the Chief Constable of Sheffield (John Jackson); some name-spellings and ages differ slightly from those cited in this book because, in some instances, I have tended to rely upon information to be found in census records, death registers, etc. My drastically truncated version of the coroner's inquest on 23 and 24 March 1864 is based largely on the transcription of notes by John Farrell of Sheffield, an official shorthand-writer at the hearing, and appended to the report prepared and presented to Parliament by Robert Rawlinson and Nathaniel Beardmore (engineers appointed by the Government to investigate the failure of the dam).

As the whole drama stemmed from the breakdown of a man-made structure it is logical, where the general story demands, to refer to the dam's design and construction, but this book does not repre-sent any kind of technical or analytical study of civil engineering. I have tried to reflect, as honestly as personal bias allows, the thoughts and expressions of those who were there at the time. In short, my aim has been to present a readable account of the actions and reactions emanating from a great industrial town in the throes of a major disaster. It all happened a long time ago and my allusions to conditions in Sheffield in the 1860s should be in no way construed as referring to the modern, go-ahead city of today. For too long has Sheffield suffered unfairly from its image of bygone years.

I believe this book contains by far the most detailed story of the Dale Dyke dam tragedy yet published. I could not have written it without much generous assistance and encouragement, particularly from the following: Miss Mary Walton, formerly on the staff of Sheffield City Libraries and the author of what has become a standard work on the city's history and achievements; Mr L. T. C. Rolt, a writer of distinction on engineering and other subjects; Mr John Bebbington (city librarian), Mr J. M. Olive (local history librarian) and the ever-helpful staff of Sheffield City Libraries; the staff of The British Library Newspaper Library, Colindale; the staff of my own 'local', the Guildford Public Libraries; Mr A. B. Baldwin (formerly general manager), his successor (Mr G. T. Calder) and the supply works engineer (Mr G. Brewin), of Sheffield Corporation Waterworks, which is scheduled on 1 April 1974 to cease in its present form and to become part of the Southern Division of the Yorkshire Water Authority, of which organization Mr Baldwin has been appointed chief executive officer. On a more personal note, I am greatly indebted to my friend, Bryon Butler, for his unfailing enthusiasm and support, and to two grand old ladies, Miss Phyllis Williams and Miss Ida Birtles, for their hospitality and kindness in allowing me to use their comfortable home as a kind of Sheffield 'headquarters' during my research work.

My thanks are also due to the Controller, H.M. Stationery Office, for permission to use extracts from official correspondence between Robert Rawlinson and Sir George Grey (Public Record Office: Home Office Papers—H.O.45); to Sheffield Newspapers Ltd for allowing me to quote from certain articles; to Penguin Books Ltd for permission to use two excerpts from *Victorian Engineering*, by L. T. C. Rolt (Allen Lane, 1970); to Peter Davies Ltd for permission to quote from *A History of Dams*, by Norman Smith; and to the Hamlyn Publishing Group Ltd for permission to quote from *Victorian Cities*, by Asa Briggs (Odhams Press).

Happily, I required no permission from my wife Jean who, with characteristic equanimity, has suffered my erratic movements and temper during the writing of this book. Indeed, had it not been for the care and understanding shown to me by her and also by my old friend, Roy Boswell, I might not have had the opportunity of embarking upon it. To both, I am especially grateful.

Geoffrey Amey

Guildford
November 1973

1   The Admiral's Warning

The wind came in from the west and, during that overcast Friday in March 1864, grew stronger. After ploughing through smoke, which hung like canopies above the mill towns of Lancashire, it swept to gaunt heights where the tail of the Pennines is formed by the High Peak district near the Derbyshire-Yorkshire border. It was severe on those moorlands in winter and shadow-grey farmhouses, hugging the sanctuary of dipping cloughs, could be cut off for weeks when the snow came. Melting drifts had been followed that year by prolonged periods of rain and now the dark hillsides, to which clung heather, cotton grass and twisted trees, felt the full force of a gale. Gusts thumped against dry-stone walls and storm clouds scudded overhead as the wind roared across the uplands of millstone grit overlooking Sheffield.

Eight miles from the steel-manufacturing capital of England, it concentrated upon a stretch of water about a mile long, more than 400 yards wide in some places and lying in a hammock of hills close to the picturesque village of Bradfield. Shimmering patterns whipped over the surface, ridges of off-white foam appeared and the immense body of water slapped its enclosing barriers as if some geological giant had been suddenly immersed in it. The Bradfield reservoir was bounded on three sides by natural elevations and on the fourth, overhanging the green vale of the River Loxley, by a massive dam which had taken more than five years to construct. In fact, the work was not yet quite finished, but the embankment was now called upon to withstand the tremendous pressure of over 700 million gallons of water being churned up by the fury of the wind.

The reservoir, which reached a depth of nearly 100 feet, covered some 78 acres, while the high ground from which the water was gathered extended for over seven square miles. It was one of a series being built to serve the rapidly growing industrial town and was the pride of the Sheffield Waterworks Company. Only two days previously, the Town Council had heard from the company's directors that the Dale Dyke dam (as it was known) was almost complete and that millowners in the Loxley Valley, in particular, and the residents of Sheffield, to a lesser extent, would soon benefit from the new water-storage project.

CUT-AWAY CROSS SECTION AT CENTRE OF DAM

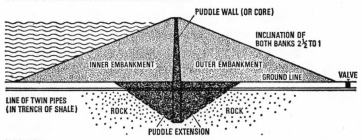

Height: 95 feet
Thickness: 500 feet (base); 12 feet (apex)
Width of puddle wall: 4 feet (apex); 12 feet (base)
Total depth of puddle wall: 155 feet
Capacity of reservoir: 712 million gallons

The man-made barrier was impressive by the standards of those days, towering to a height of 95 feet and measuring 418 yards long. The apex of the dam was 12 feet across and the whole structure, containing more than 400,000 cubic yards of stone, clay, shale and earth, sloped gradually from the top on either side so that it was 500 feet thick at the base. The timorous were assured by the company that it would remain firm against the strongest of nature's onslaughts. Not all the locals were so confident, however, and there had been some private misgivings about the vast amount of water penned in above their heads. The work, started on New Year's Day, 1859, should have been executed within a couple of years, but that optimistic estimate proved to be well wide of the mark. Due partly to 'hidden' springs which permeated the area, it had been extremely difficult to construct the watertight core of the embankment and two pumping engines operated almost non-stop for many months to keep flooding to a minimum. There had been talk in the village about minor subsidences during some stages of building the outer wall and it was also suggested that insufficient time had been allowed for the natural 'settling' of the constituent materials.

Low Bradfield, Damflask and Loxley were hamlets situated along the valley for some four miles from the dam towards Sheffield and inhabitants there had expressed doubts among themselves, but derived some comfort from the thought that the experts ought to know what was what. Several winters had passed without serious incident and the embankment certainly looked safe enough. This time it was different, however. Until a short while ago the reservoir had contained only a small amount of water. Now it was almost brimming over. The outlet pipes had been closed the previous June to allow the great bowl to fill, but everything was carefully regulated. From time to time the valves were opened to release water and the level was not permitted to get very high. Heavy rain and melting snow had combined to bring about a dramatic rise during the past fortnight, however, and for some reason it was not considered necessary to free more water at that stage. Consequently, the water was now just inches below the level of the semi-circular bye-wash (or waste weir), incorporated into the southern end of the dam, built of masonry and 64 feet round, from which any overflow was to fall through a spillway 24 feet wide. The 'escape' channel was partly stepped before sloping steeply to a point below the valve-house outside the embankment. The efficiency of the bye-wash was never put to any practical test, but it was later held to be inadequate for its intended purpose. The official capacity of the reservoir was 712 million gallons, at which volume the water should have been about five feet below the top of the dam.

The navvies got on with their work. Only a few of the original labour force of hundreds remained, for there was little left to be done, and many had been transferred to build the Agden dam up in the hills a mile or so away. Those at Dale Dyke toiled in the wind. As they saw it, their job was to dig, extract, hump and tip (using pick, shovel, barrow, cart and railway wagon for the purpose) and nothing more. They were not paid to offer advice on engineering techniques. In the main, the navvies were tough, ill-educated men who lived rough. Some had helped blast the routes of railways through tunnels and cuttings and over ravines and marshlands during those pioneering decades; sweating and swearing, they had rioted and randied their energetic way across Britain, laying the iron road as they went. A handful at Dale Dyke had probably helped construct the Woodhead tunnel three miles through the Pennines between 1839 and 1845, a feat of engineering which made possible the forging of a rail link between Sheffield and Manchester. It had claimed lives and numerous men were maimed. By comparison, the damming of the Dale dyke was a gentle operation, but it was not without dangers for the foolhardy. The navvies could give tongue to every known epithet when it suited, but they also knew just when to keep their mouths shut. A discrepancy discovered in the building of the embankment, for instance, would mean delay while the matter was investigated and might result in a temporary laying-off of labour, a contingency none of them could afford. It did not behove them to point out faults, unless it was to their advantage. That came strictly within the province of the engineer, contractor or foremen. Let them worry about it.

The landscape had changed in five years. Before the creation of the dam, the Dale dyke had trickled from the hills and was but one of a number of pretty, innocent streams which converged a mile or so down the valley to form the River Loxley running quietly between tree-studded slopes of outstanding beauty. At intervals along the banks of the river stood small mills relying on water-power to turn the wooden wheels which operated grindstones, tilt hammers and other machinery inside the buildings. These independent manufactories had their own storage dams into which water was diverted via a narrow channel and, thence, regulated by a shuttle (or sluice-gate) on to a slatted revolving wheel, before returning by a tail-race to the river.

While many factories were turning increasingly to steam-power, the millowners on the Loxley continued to utilize natural resources to carry on their crafts, as had generations of their forefathers. The peaceful valley had been associated with the cutlery trade since the sixteenth century and, whatever their shortcomings, long-established traditions die hard, so that when the Sheffield Waterworks Company announced their intention of damming the headwaters of the Loxley there was determined opposition from the millowners whose very livelihood was at stake. The company got their way, but at a price. Included in their 1853 Act, which gave the necessary sanction, were stringent clauses compelling the provision of compensation water and, for the privilege of drawing from the gathering grounds high up on the moors, the company had to guarantee a supply to the mills of 10 cubic feet of water per second, round-the-clock, six days a week. Any surplus would go to the people of Sheffield.

Like other industrial towns in the middle of the nineteenth century, Sheffield had to look farther afield for additional water to satisfy the demands of a booming commerce, the attendant rise in population and an improvement in the standard of living. The Pennines presented an obvious target, cradling, as they did, a number of natural sites eminently suitable for impounding water. The waterworks company also enjoyed the added economic advantage of utilizing the sharp gradients down which to run the supply over several miles without having to invest in costly pumping equipment. Sheffield had endured water problems for years. Ever since a man named Barker founded the town's first artificial reservoir for public use in *circa* 1630, there had been seldom enough to go round. In Barker's day, and for a long time afterwards, the inhabitants collected their water in buckets and barrels from the Pool, which was itself supplied from adjacent wells. Occasionally, for cleansing the streets and in cases of fire, water was released from the primitive reservoir and ran down a narrow channel to the centre of the town. The site of Barker's Pool is perpetuated by the broad street of that name outside the present City Hall.

By the time the Pool finally closed in 1793 a number of more ambitious reservoirs had been, or were being, constructed in various parts of the town, notably at Crookes Moor, not far from the centre. The overall supply, carried via wooden pipes, was still far from satisfactory, however. With the exception of those living in large houses, most inhabitants had to rely on communal taps or pumps placed in courtyards and, because of the erratic distribution, were forced to store their water in barrels or tubs, and it was not long before it became polluted. Incorporated in 1830, the Sheffield Waterworks Company purchased the existing system for £41,802; they began with capital of £100,000 (raised in £100 shares) and had borrowing powers of up to £30,000. To their credit, they wasted little time in getting to grips with what were extreme difficulties; such was the vast expansion of industry and population, there seemed little chance of meeting the correspondingly greater call for water. By 1864, the company had increased their capital to £450,000 and had built a number of new reservoirs. Between 1830 and 1860, the number of houses to be supplied with water rose from 12,000 to 36,000, the daily requirement from about one million gallons to four million and the total rate levied from £3,600 to more than £25,000. During that thirty-year period, something like 107 miles of iron pipes had been laid. Between 1854 and 1863, nearly £177,000 had been spent on fresh schemes, while the laying of urgently needed additional mains was costing in the region of £3,000 annually. Those figures were soon out of date, however, because of the constant demand for more water.

During their reign, the company had built three reservoirs (completed in 1836, 1849 and 1854) at Redmires, on the western outskirts and linked to the Hadfield service reservoir at Crookes Moor by a mainly open conduit about four-and-a-half miles long. Two other impounding reservoirs, the Rivelin Upper and Lower, which were mainly for compensation water, had been finished in 1848. Even with these and several minor projects, the company had been unable to give anything like a continuous supply to the town and there were protracted 'dry' periods. Nevertheless, the directors seemed fairly happy with their record, placed much confidence in their newest works (either under construction or on the drawing board) and stood by their somewhat questionable claim that Sheffield was well supplied and low-rated compared with other industrial towns.

By obtaining the necessary permission, under a 1853 Act of Parliament, to build reservoirs at Dale Dyke, Agden Brook and Strines (all three in the same area about eight miles to the west of the town), the directors felt they had achieved something of a major advance towards solving what was undoubtedly a serious problem. Anyway, they were confident enough to promise a constant water supply to the whole of Sheffield when the Bradfield scheme, as it was known, became fully operational. There was much preparatory work to be done and funds to be raised and it was not until 1 January 1859 that the first shovel turned the soil to begin the construction of the ill-fated dam of Dale Dyke.

The usual method of making an earth-fill dam at that time involved the use of rock, shale and earth to build up a thick, sloping embankment either side of a core of puddled clay (i.e. clay mixed with a specific quantity of sand, wetted and 'kneaded' into an amalgam which is impervious to water). The technique was to set the heavier material on the outer wall of the embankment and the better-binding ingredients on the inner which was in contact with the reservoir water. It was essential to construct the embankment in uniformly thin layers, each being well compacted before another was laid upon it. In this way, it was possible to produce a solid structure and also to minimize any natural tendency of the materials to sink. The puddle wall in the centre was not required to have much inherent strength, its sole purpose being to prevent the water seeping through; it was imperative, of course, that the mixture of suitable clay and sand was accurately dispensed, because a leaky core would prove fatal to the whole embankment. The specifications for the Dale Dyke dam followed broad principles accepted for many years and which, in essence, were those employed (on a much smaller scale) by the eighteenth-century canal builders. Since then, however, reservoirs and dams had increased greatly in volume and size and, even by the second half of the nineteenth century, comparatively little was known about soil mechanics and hydraulics. As the works became bigger, so did the danger.

Mid-Victorian Sheffield was prosperous. It was also dirty. The smoke represented a barometer of trade, for the more it billowed the more likely it was that business was booming. Batteries of chimneys, poking upwards from acres of huge, barn-like buildings of black corrugated iron, could be seen from almost any part of the town. The area occupied by many of the major steelworks was interwoven with railway lines—the final links of the transportation chain of raw iron from Sweden and Russia and, similarly, after conversion into steel and metal products, the first stages of dispatch to markets throughout the world. Most of the growing number of workers drawn to Sheffield by the prospect of better wages lived near their employment in what Arthur Raistrick, in *West Riding of Yorkshire*, described as a 'wilderness of tightly-packed rows of minimum standard housing'. In contrast, Sheffield was surrounded (and still is) by some of the most beautiful countryside in England and, even within its boundaries, there were a number of pleasant open spaces. Most of its more attractive features were overshadowed by the dictates of industrial development and resultant material riches, however. Britain's flourishing commercial success in the 1860s also tended to highlight that far less edifying aspect of manufacturing towns—poverty. Sheffield was no exception. Sadly, its gilt-edged image was tarnished.

It is not difficult for a modern author unwittingly to paint too dismal a portrait of nineteenth-century Sheffield, but an inescapable impression remains that for a large proportion of inhabitants it was not an agreeable place in which to live. In fact Charles Reade, the novelist, dubbed it 'the most hideous town in creation' and, although that description could be literary exaggeration, there was not much about its outward appearance in which to glory. Nevertheless, it possessed a compelling, gritty character of its own and a kind of vibrant awareness of its part in the scheme of things. Outside London, Sheffield (with a population of about 200,000) ranked the fifth largest town in England. It was predominantly radical in outlook but its dogged adherence to independence, praiseworthy though it might have been in the past, in some respects hindered its progress. For instance, while other towns were enjoying the benefits offered by the Local Government Act of 1858, Sheffield's aldermen and councillors were still dallying and debating whether or not to adopt it. Vital services and amenities were controlled by a number of different organizations, often in competition, and this led to the overlapping of interests, inaction and inefficiency. For want of an effective overall authority, municipal development was slow and piecemeal. There was little visual relief from the grim reality that in Sheffield was concentrated a large powerhouse of industry. Almost everything, it seemed, was geared towards that end.

Much of Sheffield was black, or at best, grey. Some of the worst quarters were crammed with a conglomeration of dingy alleys and courtyards, fractured hump-backed streets and rows of uninviting back-to-backs. In the poorest districts, families lurched from day to day, hope and enthusiasm having been long since killed by apathy and despair. Decrepit dwellings huddled together, often around unpaved yards where the contents of overflowing middens (in some cases, one to twenty households) were trodden into a putrid morass in winter and trampled to crusted pathways during the summer. The stench of excrement, as well as the fall of sulphurous soot from the chimneys of the ironworks, caused windows to be kept permanently shut. The average back-to-back terraced house (there were 38,000 of them in Sheffield in 1864 when, incidentally, further building of these houses in the town was banned) comprised a ground-floor living-room (paved with flagstones and used for dining, cooking, washing and drying), a first-floor bedroom, a cellar and an attic. Into such cramped spaces crowded a workman, his wife and family and, perhaps, a lodger or two. It is hardly surprising that the bottle provided a temporary means of escape for so many.

The percentage of population living near the centre of the town was drastically lower than it had been a couple of decades previously, for increasing numbers dwelt close to their work at the factories. These, because of the large amount of land required, had been erected progressively farther out. The death rate in Sheffield was high—28 per thousand, compared with the national average figure of 22—and the incidence of child mortality a horrifying feature. One town councillor reckoned more than a thousand people died annually 'for the want of the commonest sanitary arrangements' in the town. Effluent was discharged untreated into the rivers, which surged foully through high-density areas, and the air was polluted by industrial smoke. At night, a fiery red glow spread across the north-eastern sky like a choking sunset.

Some of the giant steelworks were strung along Savile Street, Brightside Lane and Attercliffe Road—edging out towards Rotherham. There were the world-famous names like John Brown and Co., Thomas Firth and Sons, Naylor and Vickers, Cammell and Co., William Jessop and Sons, Spear and Jackson, and Sanderson Brothers. In those mills, as in many others dotted throughout Sheffield, the activity was almost continuous. Day and night echoed to a noisy metallic symphony as white-hot iron and steel were beaten and rolled. It was nigh on perpetual motion incarnate. Some of the broad-chested men would disintegrate into wheezing consumptives as they laboured to keep the furnaces fed, the molten metal flowing and the Nasmyth hammers pounding. Workers toiled in the knowledge that their wages, though meagre enough, were substantially higher than those of their counterparts elsewhere in the country. Indeed, conditions generally were better. The trade unions, of which Sheffield was a recognized stronghold, claimed the credit for that.

The men who made the real money—those autonomous monarchs of the steel industry—were not obliged to live under the pall which blotted out the sun, but could afford to move to the newly emerging districts reflecting opulence and social prestige on the opposite side of town, such as Ranmoor, Endcliffe and Tapton. Their big houses, surrounded by fields and parkland and enjoying fresh breezes from the high moors of Derbyshire, were symbols of material prosperity. Most of the rich businessmen were generous in some form to the town and many of the institutions, recreational facilities, civic parks and streets in the modern smoke-free Sheffield bear their names. For all their public magnanimity, some of those bosses of Victorian industry could be stern taskmasters and hard-headed traders; they had to be, for only the toughest survived for long in that fiercely competitive commercial world.

Some of them, like John Brown and Mark Firth, were largely self-made successes, having risen to the top of their trade from comparatively modest origins by hard work, persistence and perspicacity. Brown, born the son of a Sheffield slater in 1816, went to school in a garret where he sat opposite little Mary Schofield who was to become his wife. From his early days as an apprentice, young Brown showed much promise and a willingness to learn, though not necessarily to follow, the traditional tricks of the trade. Before he was thirty, Brown was making his own cutlery steel in a small factory in Orchard Street, in the middle of the town, and it was not long before he moved to larger premises where he concentrated on manufacturing steel, railway springs and files. When he patented a conical spring buffer for wagons, orders poured in from many railway companies. Business flourished and in 1854, when he was thirty-seven, Brown looked around for partners. He found them in two young men from Birmingham, John Devonshire Ellis and William Bragge, and, in 1856, the firm moved to Queen's Works in Savile Street. The premises were renamed the Atlas Works and it was there, with a fast-growing work force, that Brown was to win a considerable fortune and an international reputation. John Brown, initially reluctant but urged on by the persistent enthusiasm of Ellis, was the first seriously to adopt Bessemer's new process of steel manufacture—a method which, by means of a converter, cold-blasted the impurities from pig-iron—and he used it to make some of the heavy products hitherto regarded as being exclusively within the province of wrought-iron. That versatile inventor, Henry Bessemer, whose experiments with steel had been greeted with scorn by most of the manufacturers, took the fight to the 'enemy' by himself setting up a factory in Sheffield in 1859 to develop his creation and to demonstrate its potential. When Bessemer began producing his steel at £20 a ton less than his rivals', it did not go unnoticed by his next-door neighbour, John Brown.

By 1864, the Bessemer process had been taken up by nearly all the steel-producing countries and, by having faith in it (after a few false starts) early on, Brown had achieved a head start in the manufacture of steel rails. Hull-born Charles Cammell, who was said to have arrived in Sheffield in 1830 as a young man of twenty and with only five pounds in his pocket, and who now controlled the renowned firm of that name at the Cyclops Works, was the next to utilize the new method. He was followed, in 1862, by Samuel Fox. Bessemer steel could not compete with crucible steel for cutlery and tools, for which Sheffield was famed, but Brown and his partners foresaw in it an opportunity to break into the market of railway tyres and axles and also to establish new outlets in the spheres of armaments and other heavy engineering. It was the production of armour-plate that won for Brown his greatest honours.

Mark Firth also rose from relatively humble beginnings. His father was once head melter at Sandersons and a steel-maker of some skill, the firm of Thomas Firth and Sons being formed in 1842, when Mark was twenty-three. The father died six years later and, from that point, Mark Firth was virtually the right arm of the organization, which was moved to the Norfolk Works in Savile Street in 1849. Under his dynamic leadership, the firm grew into one of the largest and most famous of its kind anywhere. Business rivalry between Brown and Firth must have been further sharpened when Brown devoted much of his energy to making armour-plate, while Firth specialized in ordnance. In their book, *A History of the British Steel Industry*, J. C. Carr and W. Taplin referred to a 'leap-frogging contest for supremacy between artillery and protective armour, stimulated by the emergence of the ironclad'.

Brown and Firth were among the most influential men in Sheffield, each serving as Mayor and as Master Cutler and playing a prominent part in public affairs generally. Like many self-made men, they could be as tough as the steel they produced; on the other hand, they retained a homely touch: Firth, for example, often eating in the workshop for his midday meal a meat pie prepared by the wife of one of his workmen. As men who had come up a comparatively hard road, Brown and Firth were also proud of their independence, proud of their achievements and, to some extent, proud of the power they held over thousands. They demanded a long day's work from their employees, some of whom were boys between ten and fourteen years old. As masters in their respective domains, the steel bosses of Sheffield looked unkindly upon anything approaching insubordination and probably viewed with suspicion the spreading trade union movement.

John Brown was once faced by Robert Applegarth, the Hull-born union pioneer, then in his twenties and secretary of a small craft society in Sheffield. Applegarth admitted he was on union business and Brown, who stood no nonsense from anybody, snapped: 'Well, I shall cut you short.'

The young union official, who later claimed he never had a cross word with any employer, replied sweetly: 'Please don't; I'm only five foot two and that's short enough.'

Brown and Firth were regarded as good employers by the standards of those days when indignities and outrages were often perpetrated in the name of employment. For instance, they and other manufacturers made some effort to encourage their workers in basic education. If they were not always loved by their employees, Firth and Brown were respected, not least because they worked so hard themselves. Brown, for example, personally supervised the construction of all the firm's home-made machinery and also planned every inch of his factories. In 1863, he had installed a hydraulic press of 2,000 tons for bending giant armour-plates and it is an intriguing thought that, only yards away, Firth was perfecting a 12-ton cannon, with rifled steel tube, capable of firing a 250-pound shot.

In March, 1864, the square-shouldered Firth, resolute and looking 'wilful enough to win his way in any company', lived in an impressive mansion known as Oakwood, at Ranmoor. John Brown lived at Shirle Hall, but, later that year, was to move into Endcliffe Hall, described as 'a Chatsworth in miniature' and which he had spent a great deal of money building. While nearly all the prosperous heads of Sheffield industry dwelt in luxury and clean air and drove to their factories in horse-drawn coaches, the workers who had helped to provide that affluence trudged to their labours and back again in clunking boots and, even when they emerged from the inferno of the mills after a shift, many found no escape at home from the fall-out of the sickly smoke. That, however, was the way of things—even in mid-Victorian Sheffield which held jealously to its belief in radical independence.

There was nothing unusual about the morning of Friday 11 March 1864. The slated roofs of the back-to-backs were smeared with grimy drizzle and, in the blurred light of dawn, the nightworkers slouched homewards, their coat collars pulled up to touch dirty caps pulled down. A chilly, rain-flecked breeze blew down the narrow streets and gas-lamps flickered before a man with a long pole arrived to snuff them out. Early morning trains puffed yet more smoke into the asthmatic atmosphere. The Victoria Station, on the Manchester, Sheffield and Lincolnshire line, was elevated and stood at the end of a viaduct which crossed the broad thoroughfare of The Wicker. Not far away, at ground level, between the fork of Savile Street and Spital Hill, was the Midland Station for trains to Rotherham, where one changed to travel to London; surprisingly, Sheffield was not yet on a main line to London, though a direct route via Chesterfield was in the offing.

As light began to filter through, the majority of inhabitants awoke to peer out of windows running with condensation. Horse-buses clattered over the cobbles and passengers, perched insecurely on knife-board seats on the top deck, held on for dear life. Private coaches jostled for position while pedestrians, not without considerable risk, picked their way nimbly between gigs, shays and carts, as well as the occasional brougham or clarence. The town was coming to life (not that it every really slept) and the dawning heralded for most Sheffielders another day much the same as yesterday and the day before that. For some, it would be their last.

In Division Street, at its junction with Carver Lane, near where the City Hall now stands, lived John Gunson. He dwelt in comparative comfort, was a man of some means and the father of three grown-up sons and a daughter. He breakfasted quietly with his wife, Charlotte, who, at fifty-six was a year his senior. As was his custom, he glanced at the columns of his morning newspaper. Indeed, he was fairly set in his ways—punctilious, conscientious and loyal almost to a fault. He folded the paper neatly to a fresh page and looked at the weather intelligence. What he saw not only made him think, but also changed the whole course of his day and, indeed, affected the remainder of his life. There was a Fitzroy forecast of a gale sweeping in from the west. Vice-Admiral Robert Fitzroy, superintendent of the Board of Trade's meteorological department, had two years previously instituted a system of storm warnings—the forerunner of daily weather forecasts. Fitzroy had packed a lot into his life which was to end tragically in April 1865, when he cut his throat. He had joined the Navy when he was barely fifteen and, before he was thirty, became commander of the famous survey ship, *Beagle*, in which sailed a twenty-two-year-old naturalist, Charles Darwin. Since then, Fitzroy had been M.P. for

Durham and a Governor of New Zealand. Afterwards, he devoted much of his time to studying the elements; he was a Fellow of the Royal Society, the inventor of a barometer and an author of books on the weather. In short, Admiral Fitzroy knew what he was talking about when it came to gales. His reputation was such that John Gunson read no more, left his paper on the table, kissed his wife farewell and went to his office at the headquarters of the Sheffield Waterworks Company.

Gunson was the company's resident engineer. He could have been hardly more 'resident', for his house was next door to their premises. It was as a young man of twenty-two that Gunson, a native of Hunslet, joined the company and, by diligence and long hours, had risen to the rank he had now held for many years. He knew he was not destined for promotion, either with that company or elsewhere, and accepted the situation with equanimity. Although he was proficient and an expert with figures, it is possible he lacked that spark of personality that impresses the hierarchy. Nevertheless, he was highly thought of, not least because his long service had enabled him to build up an almost unrivalled knowledge of the company's affairs. He was reserved by nature and, because of his willingness to work was, perhaps, inclined to be put upon but, he reflected, he was happy with his lot. Despite his apparent shyness, he never shirked responsibility and, as he was to demonstrate, he possessed deep reserves of physical and moral courage.

As resident engineer, Gunson's duties included the supervision of the reservoirs and he had intended that day to make a routine inspection at Redmires. The prospect of a high wind from the west caused him to alter his plans, however, and he decided instead to visit the nearly completed Dale Dyke dam. Possibly he had a nagging doubt about its stability under the combined pressure of strong winds and water, but that seems unlikely for he had been intimately connected with the work from the beginning. It could equally well be argued, of course, that because of his familiarity with the structure he did have some misgivings about its strength. He appears not to have been unduly worried at that time, however.

The consulting engineer was John Towlerton Leather, who lived in style near Leeds. He had drawn up the plans for the Dale Dyke and had, in fact, designed most of the company's other reservoirs. Leather had been the company's engineer-in-chief from 1830 until the early 1840s, since when he had been retained in a consultative capacity. Even so, that aspect of his profession had for years taken second place to his more remunerative business as a contractor, so Gunson had seen remarkably little of him during the building of the dam. There had been some discussions and Leather had been over a few times to look at progress, but liaison was intermittent.

Gunson busied himself with office work that morning, which suggests he was not deeply perturbed about the state of the dam. He told a colleague of his proposed whereabouts that afternoon and, after a meal, he climbed aboard his gig and gently coaxed the horse through the hilly centre of the town and in the direction of Bradfield. There seemed to be no reason to rush and the animal jogged along at a comfortable trot. It was pleasant to escape from the town for a while and Gunson, his topcoat buttoned up against the wind, was soon out in the valley of the Loxley. Shortly it would be aflame with colour, with banks of wild flowers rippling under the greens and browns of leafy trees, but now the oaks and elms stood skeleton-like and darkened by misty rain. It was still preferable to the steely starkness of Sheffield. Gunson had touched the village of Hillsborough (a name now renowned as the home ground of Sheffield Wednesday Football Club), turning left after crossing the bridge into Holme Lane and then passing through the growing community of Malin Bridge. He reined in his horse to conserve its energy for the long climb to the reservoir, which was hidden in the gloom more than four miles away.

Now he was in open country, inhabited only by the hamlets of Loxley and Damflask—'sylvan nooks of rare loveliness', a contemporary writer called them—and, as he followed the road cut into the slope of the valley, he again reflected upon the tranquillity of the rural industries down at the river's edge. Some of the little mills, with their dams and water-wheels, were fringed by neatly cropped grass and Gunson could hear the screech of grinding coming from within the buildings. The pretty and apparently restful scene screened from view the grim life of a grinder, who was often a 'veteran' at thirty-five and considered semi-senile at forty—if he lived that long. When he was at work, the grinder sat astride a wooden 'horse' (a narrow seat), rested his elbows on his knees and bent his head over the grinding stone which rotated towards him. To fashion and sharpen blades, therefore, he was in that cramped position for hours at a time and frequently toiled in badly ventilated 'hulls' (workshops). It was a hazardous occupation. If a spinning stone broke it could kill, and, more often than not, there was no fan to disperse the injurious dust which a grinder could not avoid sucking in continuously. Chest and lung complaints, notably silicosis ('grinder's disease'), were common. So, too, were early graves. Few grinders took much notice of personal cleanliness and almost invariably ate their meals at work without washing their stained hands and licking from their fingers particles of food with, of course, metal dust as well. There was some old wives' tale that drunken grinders lived longer, but the opposite was in fact the case.

Dr J. C. Hall, senior physician at Sheffield Public Hospital, gave a graphic account of a grinder's working life, which could begin when he was a child of seven. 'There is no more melancholy object,' he declared, 'than a fork-grinder looking prematurely old and dying from the dust inhaled in his trade, no object more deserving of our pity as we see him often crawling to his hull to labour when altogether unfitted by the grinder's disease for his calling; his poverty and not his will consents. In this condition, a day or two a week, he grinds for a few hours, inhales additional dust and, in order to obtain bread, increases the disease which is already rapidly destroying him.'

Conditions varied greatly from mill to mill and those 'Wheels' in the country, in the Loxley Valley for example, were generally considered to be less dangerous to health. It was purely a matter of degree, however, for there were precious few factories where the set-up was anything like ideal. This applied to both heavy and light manufacturing premises. In 1864, inspectors appointed by the Children's Employment Commission reported some appalling cases of ill-treatment and exploitation of youngsters in industry and Sheffield came in for a share of the condemnation. In fairness, a number of employers in the town were humane and far-sighted enough to realize the benefits to be derived from providing good conditions for their workers. It was found that mills installing fans had fewer casualties from respiratory diseases and, consequently, the work-rate improved. Most of the trouble occurred in the large number of small workshops where employers were unable, or unwilling, to buy the equipment, which they regarded as unnecessary expense. Proprietors of larger concerns (particularly in Sheffield where trade unionism flourished) realized that it paid them to have healthy employees. Not that everything was an industrial bed of roses. It was far from that, but at least here was recognition that much remained to be righted.

The world of the grinder was far removed from that of John Gunson. He also had his share of problems as the servant of a company constantly being reminded of the need for an unfailing supply of water to the town. The completion of the Dale Dyke reservoir, and of the other projects in the area, would help, but the company were always losing the fight to keep up with domestic, municipal and industrial demands.

Gunson flicked the reins to enliven his horse and continued up the valley. Knots of cottages graced the slopes and an inn or two merged into the hillsides, which became closer together and steeper as they neared the site of the dam. It had taken Gunson about an hour to reach Low Bradfield, which was situated about a mile from the reservoir; from that angle, the embankment appeared to fill half the sky and, such was its size, Gunson must have wondered why he had entertained even the slightest twinge of uncertainty about its stability. Spots of water hit his face, but he was unable to decide if they came from inside the dam or were drops of rain. Soon he was at the site; he clambered down from his gig and walked forward to meet an approaching figure. It was around three o'clock on that blustery afternoon.

George Swinden, one of the company's overseers, was used to Gunson visiting the dam three or four times a week, but he had not expected to see him that day. Gunson assured him it was just a normal call, saying he merely wanted to find out how the high water and the top of the dam reacted in a strong wind. On that exposed height, the gusts were powerful and the coats of the two men flapped wildly. Gunson nodded to some of the navvies and then went about his work. The dam, faced on the outside by large blocks of smoothed stone, stretched across what had been a 400-yard gap between the hills. On the inside, the water was within a few feet of the top and, every now and again, flurries of spray flipped over. Gunson was not perturbed, however, for the water was still some 15 inches below the level of the waste weir and, anyway, he had seen waves several times as big at Redmires. He could see no movement in the mass, nor did he observe any signs of a fissure. Near the waste weir, the navvies struggled in the wind to put the finishing touches to a portion of the embankment at the southern end. It was virtually all that remained to be done.

Gunson would probably have liked to have inspected the core of puddled clay. Of course that was impossible for it had long since been covered by the massive banks of rock, shale and earth. Anyway, he felt confident enough about it. Admittedly it had caused some trouble in the early stages when the puddle trench had frequently become flooded but, in order to make it unusually safe, the core had been taken down as far as 60 feet below ground level until it had made contact with impervious bed-rock. From top to bottom, therefore, the puddle wall measured as much as 155 feet. Gunson inspected the outer wall of the dam to see if there was any seepage from within, but he found nothing. Then he looked at the discharging end of the two 18-inch diameter outlet pipes which, cocooned in puddled clay and set in a trench of shale, ran beneath the embankment. Had water 'crept' along the outside of the pipes it would have been discoloured and easily recognizable. Again, Gunson saw nothing. He went to the valve house and then walked up to the bye-wash; in fact, he found himself making an extensive tour. He discovered no flaw which suggested any danger.

Gunson spent much of the afternoon watching the effect of the increasing wind on the water and stood for a long time at a point level with where the water touched the inner embankment. He saw not the slightest depression in the structure. One thing he did not do was to walk across the embankment which, he explained later, was 'on account of the spray that was blowing over'. At about 5.30, most of the navvies knocked off work and Gunson himself left the dam and drove back down the valley towards Sheffield. He passed familiar, homely sights and, for the last time, as it happened, admired the fine farmhouse standing close by the river at Malin Bridge. It was the home of James Trickett, who lived there with his wife and three children and who was sufficiently well off to have servants. Lights twinkled from inside as Gunson drove past and into the dimness of dusk.

Shortly after Gunson had departed from the dam one of the workmen, William Horsefield, was crossing the embankment to get home for his supper. The gale pulled at his clothing and, to get some protection, he walked along the outer wall a few feet from the top. He could see flickering lights from the mills and cottages down the valley and, pulling up his collar and hunching his shoulders against the storm, he saw something else. He stopped and peered down the slope of rock. There was a crack, not very wide but long enough to cause Horsefield some alarm. Making certain his eyes were not playing tricks in the semi-light, he hurried off to tell of his discovery. It was possible the thin crevice was just a surface blemish, caused perhaps by frost, but some of his colleagues to whom he related his story were not so sure and one of them told Samuel Hammerton, a farmer, who was in the habit of using the embankment as a short cut to get to part of his land on the opposite side of his home. He could not recollect having seen a crack before and set off to inspect it for himself. What he found worried him and he immediately sent word to George Swinden, who lived in the vicinity. Swinden needed no second bidding and, joined by some of the navvies, hastened to the scene. Meanwhile, Hammerton had called on Joseph Ibbotson, the proprietor of a corn mill in Low Bradfield alongside the River Loxley. Other locals, too, rushed to the dam where they found Swinden, lantern in hand, and a small group already pondering over the crack which ran across the outer face about 10 feet from the top. It was barely large enough to get one's fingers into and there were arguments as to whether it was a superficial scar or something more serious. By now, it was after seven o'clock.

Among those on the spot was a man named Fountain, one of the contractors for the works; he dispatched his son, Stephenson Fountain, on horseback to fetch Gunson and also Craven, another of the contractors. Lights danced as more workmen arrived at the dam and awaited orders; voices were raised in the teeth of the gale and were heard some way down the valley, word quickly spreading that something was amiss. The fears of the local inhabitants seemed confirmed when the horse carrying young Fountain, whose head was bent low, galloped through the darkness. The rider shouted as he went, but there was confusion as to what exactly had occurred. When Fountain reached Damflask, the horse's saddle girth broke and he called in at The Barrel to repair it and doubtless to quench his thirst. He mentioned his mission, casually it appears, to the landlord, Jonathan Ibbotson, before setting off once more, but at least his enforced stop had served to give some warning in the hamlet, some two miles from the dam. In the event, all too few people received any intimation of possible disaster, but some of those who did were sufficiently convinced to prepare to evacuate themselves and their livestock.

Fountain's horse clattered to a standstill outside No. 14, Division Street, and Gunson, who had not long finished his supper, was summoned to the door. On being apprised of the situation he wasted no time and, harnessing his horse to a carriage, collected Craven and was on his way. It was a tricky operation to follow the narrow, uneven roads by night, but Gunson pressed his horse to the limit into the fury of the storm.

At the reservoir meanwhile, Swinden had ordered the workmen to open the valves of the outlet pipes in order to lessen the pressure of water against the embankment. It was no easy matter. Five men took almost an hour to raise the sluice-gates in the two pipes by means of a screw and, such was the force of the released water, the pipes vibrated alarmingly and the ground shook. There was a fearful noise as something like 30,000 gallons a minute leapt through, but it was obvious from the start that even that amount of water was not going to do much to ease the weight of 700 million gallons pressing upon the dam. It was also disconcerting to see that although the level of water was still not sufficiently high to flow down the bye-wash, plenty was now flying over the top of the embankment in the wind. It was raining as well.

By the time John Gunson arrived, it must have been nearly ten o'clock. He and Craven had been told by a labourer down the road that it was a false alarm, but they carried on. At the embankment, Gunson found a little crowd of workmen and local residents waiting for him and they quickly pointed out the crack. He was breathless after the hectic drive and, although he had done his best to reassure people on the way that nothing was untoward, he was most likely worried. He noted with satisfaction that the valves had been opened, but he also realized that further measures had to be taken. It was essential to free more water and he instructed the navvies to blast a gap in the wall of the bye-wash. Chilled hands set to work to lay the charges, but the gunpowder was apparently damp and would not explode. The men tried again and yet again. All the time, the wind was whipping up the reservoir water and driving both it and the rain horizontally.

Gunson returned to the crack; and, in such weather conditions, his next action was hardly that of a man who sensed any calamity and who had lost faith in the efficiency of the structure. Crouching in the comparative calm of the leeward side, he closely examined the slender fissure. He was joined by others and, after listening to what they had to say, reached a conclusion that, due to the storm, part of the inner embankment had subsided slightly, 'pulling' the outer wall a few inches towards it and thus causing the thin crack. The theory did not sound very convincing but, at that stage, the defect was regarded as nothing more than minor. Hopes brightened a little. Gunson was unable to locate any leaks, although it was difficult to distinguish very much at all by lantern light. Occasionally the new moon appeared briefly from behind careering clouds before returning to the blackness. Gunson and Swinden, sometimes advised by shouts from the men above, discernible to them only as leaden outlines, stuck to their task. The outlet pipes appeared to be in good order. Perhaps there was nothing to worry about after all; certainly Gunson, who must have felt there was no danger, thought it unnecessary to send a general warning down the valley.

After half an hour or so Gunson and Swinden, together with some of the workmen, again went back across the embankment to get an idea if the crack was above or below the surface water in the reservoir. The crack appeared not to have spread but, when he stood up, Gunson was appalled to see at the top of the dam 'water running over like a white sheet in the darkness' and it went 'right under my feet and dropped down the crack', Gunson edged his way down the embankment and entered the valve-house to get an idea of the amount of water running there, but Swinden, feeling that something was radically wrong, shouted to him to keep clear. As he emerged, Gunson looked up and saw a breach in the crest of the dam about thirty yards wide—'just as though a river had been placed in the bank'. A mass of water heaved through with a crash and, as it struck the outer wall, geyser-like jets flew high into the air. Just as Gunson scrambled to the top of the embankment, there was another tremendous crash and, in his own words, 'then, of course, I knew it was all up'. Ironically, soon after the water had begun to charge through the broken barrier, the gunpowder went off and blew a hole in the side of the bye-wash. By then, however, it was much too late.

What went through Gunson's mind as he stood numbly by as the immense volume of water, frothing and foaming, thundered into the night, we can but imagine. His own life had been saved by the quick-thinking Swinden, but what of the others who slept innocently in the valley below? Even Gunson, with his engineering know-how and head for calculations, cannot have conceived the horror that was about to unfold. For five years, the Dale Dyke dam had been his professional preoccupation. Now, inexplicably to him, it had collapsed—spectacularly and decisively. Estimates of how much water tumbled into the valley that night vary from 200 million gallons to the whole of the 712 million stored in the reservoir. This figure must be incorrect, for the basin did not empty entirely, while the former total is very much on the low side. Something in the region of 650 million seems more likely.

Despite his shocked state, Gunson displayed considerable presence of mind in the crisis. Although he could not then have appreciated the futility of it, he did what he could to raise the alarm—albeit belatedly. After sending horsemen down the valley to shout the news, he whipped his own horse into action and, with the wind at his back, drove furiously to Low Bradfield to rouse the residents. Fortunately, most of those living near the river had heeded their private forebodings of an impending catastrophe. They had watched pinpoints of light and listened to distant voices coming from the embankment and had moved, or were ready to depart, to higher ground. By so doing, they preserved their lives. They lost their homes and most of their belongings, however. Some hint of the danger passed feverishly down the valley, but it did not get beyond Damflask. Before would-be rescuers could get far, the flood overtook them and washed away parts of the roads. As it was put later: 'The velocity of the flood was something awful and, after the dam burst, not even a Derby horse could have carried the warning in time to save the people down the valley.'

The collapse of the dam appears to have occurred in two distinct stages, the second following quickly upon the first. The colossal weight of water, abetted by the wind, finally established a gap in the top (the newest and, presumably, weakest part) of the buckling dam and through it rushed thousands of gallons within a few seconds; the fierce action of the escaping water then caused a much more devastating rupture: the eventual chasm measured about 300 feet wide at the top, tapered to a width of some 60 feet at the base and was approximately 80 feet deep. The giant bite represented something like a quarter of the entire embankment. It was just half an hour before midnight when the dam broke and the roar, accompanied by a loud hissing, increased in intensity as the flood swept for itself a path of annihilation. The seething waters hurtled down the hillside and, in the confined space of the valley, licked up everything in the way.

One of the workers (his name was not revealed) later claimed that, while efforts were being made to explode the gunpowder, he noticed the water level in the reservoir was dropping considerably faster than it would have done passing solely through the outlet pipes. Upon investigation, it was found to be pouring over the dam. 'I saw the water boiling through,' he said. 'Then the top fell in, which appeared to stop the water for a minute or two until the water ran over the top in sheets of foam. An immense gap immediately opened and the bank where I stood began to incline towards the water which was washing through.' Considering the speed with which things happened and the extreme danger involved, it was miraculous that none of those on the dam that night sustained even a scratch.

In Sheffield and the neighbouring communities of Loxley, Malin Bridge, Hillsborough and Owlerton, most inhabitants slept soundly. Others were preparing for bed; some lay awake listening to the wind rattling windows and doors. Night-shifts kept the steelworks alive, while their masters slept in their comfortable houses. Working people huddled together in modest, crowded homes alongside the River Don; the poorest curled up in hovels, drawing about them extra sacks to keep out the cold. John Gunson did not sleep. He spent the night in a house in Bradfield, his mind paralysed by the overwhelming tragedy. His head still echoed to the roar of the unleashed flood, but, agonizingly, there was nothing more he could do.

For nearly two hundred and fifty people in and around Sheffield, that night was to be their last on earth. An awesome avalanche of water was on its way.

2 The Desolated Valley

Joseph Ibbotson, the corn miller, stayed at the dam until after John Gunson arrived. Then he went home. At Low Bradfield, his neighbours were understandably anxious and, despite his assurances that officials believed things were not as bad as at first feared, some families in cottages near the river remained frightened and were prepared for a quick getaway. It was still raining and blowing hard.

Ibbotson, whose house was well up the side of the valley and above the roof-level of his three-storey mill at the water's edge, retired to bed. His brother, William, who lived nearby, did not. He had also been at the dam, but was unconvinced that all was well. 'Danger or no danger,' he told some villagers, 'I don't go to bed tonight.' So, fully clothed, he sat downstairs and kept the front door slightly ajar. It was as well he did. Just after half past eleven, above the sound of the wind, he heard some shouting and, almost instantaneously, a great roar. He ran outside, yelling and banging on doors and windows, to be joined by others doing the same. There was precious little time for warnings now, however. The unleashed torrent had already hit the head of the valley and was rushing down the slope at frightful speed.

The nearest property below the dam and in the line of the flood was Annett House, about a thousand yards away. There lived a farmer, Joseph Empsall, his wife, their three young sons and a lodger, William Rose, who was employed by the waterworks company. Empsall had also been up to the embankment that evening, but soon returned home after being persuaded that the defect was nothing more than a frost crack. Nevertheless, he felt uneasy and stayed up while the remainder of the household went to bed.

At about 11.30 a labourer, Tom Fish, who must have had a fair start on the actual bursting, ran down the valley shouting 'It's coming, it's coming.' Empsall roused his family—who had no time to dress—then managed to rescue a cow and two calves. They all got clear. 'The night was dark, very windy and very cold,' he recalled. From the sanctuary of higher ground, the group could but watch helplessly as the huge wave carried away a solid stone bridge and splintered the farmhouse and barns.

After launching itself from the dam, the water generated an incredible pace and, initially, was travelling at getting on for 30 feet a second. Within the narrow restrictions of the valley, it gouged out the lower parts of the hillside and obliterated the natural course of the river. Boulders, each weighing several tons, were hurled into the air as if they were corks and descended with a monstrous splash yards farther on. Some were catapulted clear of the racing waters to land with a deadened thud on ground already made soft by the rain. One rock, estimated at more than thirty tons and 'in dimensions not unlike the largest stones at Stonehenge,' was whisked along for two hundred yards before it sank. Above the dreadful gurgling of the water could be heard an almost incessant series of cracks, like a fusillade of musket fire, as trees were snapped off at ground level. Many too were torn up by the roots. Bridges were severed from sturdy foundations and, in some cases, disintegrated. Everything in the way of the flood's progress at that stage was swept away and it was about forty-five minutes before the water subsided sufficiently to return to within the banks of the swollen river.

It took something like three minutes after the burst for the flood to reach Low Bradfield. Aroused from his uneasy sleep, Joseph Ibbotson went to his bedroom window and, in the diffused light of the moon, saw what looked like 'dirty fleeces of wool tumbling over each other' moving towards him. Never did he forget the unearthly sound made by that high wall of water. 'It seemed as if the bowels of the earth were being torn up,' he was quoted as saying later, 'or as if some unheard-of monster were rushing down the valley, lashing the hillsides with his scaly folds, crunching up buildings between his jaws and filling the air with his wrathful hiss.' At one moment, he noted, the water was running through his mill weir in the normal way and his manufactory and adjacent bridges were still standing. By the time he had thrown on a coat and gone outside, they were in the process of disappearing. First, the chapel bridge was engulfed. The corn mill on the ground floor, sturdily constructed of ashlar, held for a few seconds before it was borne away, breaking into a hundred pieces as it was bored and battered by the flotsam of trees, rocks and other objects accumulated upstream.

As Ibbotson watched, another stone bridge was thrown upwards. Nearby, and racing for their lives, were Thomas Nicholls, the local schoolmaster, and his wife, Jane. They had been undecided whether or not to go to bed, for Nicholls had also been up at the dam earlier to examine the crack; in fact, only five minutes before the arrival of the flood he went out to look at the level of the river and, finding it normal, returned to tell his wife there was no cause for alarm. He had barely finished speaking when William Ibbotson hammered on the door and shouted at them to run. The couple dashed outside and, as Nicholls went back to get his topcoat, his wife shrieked when she saw the approaching flood 'many yards high'. Nicholls re-emerged safely and he and his wife, their faces dripping with muddy water, got clear. As they turned, they were just in time to see the newly built Wesleyan School and their adjoining home reduced to rubble. A smithy was swallowed by the maelstrom, as were a number of cottages which, tossed into the wind, returned to the water like so much gravel being flicked into a whirlpool. A wheelwright's shop, though seriously damaged, hung in parts to the foundations, but Martin Hawke and his family suffered the sad sight of their farmhouse and outbuildings being lifted into the darkness.

Two more houses were gutted, the occupants managing to smash through the roofs, leap into the water and scramble to firm ground. One woman threw her baby into the outstretched arms of her husband before jumping from the eaves of their home; another, Elizabeth Oakes, was injured attempting an equally spectacular escape and was lucky to be pulled out of the water. Only shouts and occasional light from the moon guided the rescuers and rescued. And there were some strange happenings. Richard Ibbotson had removed his five children to safety earlier that evening because, it was said, his wife had 'a very peculiar' dream the previous night that she was in a flood. In the event, she and her husband got away from the real thing with seconds to spare.

Joseph Dawson was a tailor and lived in a cottage at Low Bradfield. Only two days before, his wife had given birth to a son. When news came that the dam had collapsed, Dawson told his brother to take the elder child, aged four, to Joseph Ibbotson's house on the hill. Dawson, who believed he could not carry both his wife and baby safely, went outside for help. None was available and he hurried back inside. His wife, with nothing on but her nightdress, picked up the infant and Dawson wrapped them both in blankets. He succeeded in lifting them downstairs and outside. Then the first human tragedy occurred. A wave of water knocked them down and, as he struggled to his feet and started to carry the pair back towards his home, 'the flood caught us again and washed the blankets and my child away and left my wife naked in my arms'. It was the first of many fatalities. Dawson and his wife pushed through the rising water and reached the bedroom, from which they escaped by a ladder brought back by his brother and another local, Thomas Robinson.

The wave, which according to one eye-witness reached a height of 50 feet in some parts, roared on with unabated fury. More bridges were torn away and flipped aside, mills were erased or ruined and hundreds of trees bobbed along like matchsticks. The next hamlet was Damflask, a mile or so downstream from Low Bradfield. There had been some warning of a possible disaster, but it was not treated very seriously by all the inhabitants. That was not altogether surprising, for none could have envisaged just what devastation the water from a broken dam almost three miles away could cause. As at Low Bradfield, the portions of Damflask in the vicinity of the river were virtually razed to the watery ground. The Barrel public house disappeared, cottages were cast aside and the Damflask Wire Mills almost demolished, machinery being wrenched from floor boltings. A boiler was later found a quarter of a mile away, embedded deeply in mud. Four men were swept from the mill and drowned.

The bridge at Damflask was destroyed. All the occupants in a house nearby had heeded a warning and got out—bar one. The exception, a navvy who lodged with Thomas Kirk and family, was known officially as Henry Burkinshaw, but familiarly as 'Sheffield Harry'. Despite screams from the women and shouts from the men, he refused to budge from his bed. He worked at the Agden reservoir and had to be up early, he said, so he needed a good night's rest. What was more, he reportedly added, he had been employed on the Dale Dyke embankment and it was his considered opinion that 'there isn't water enough in Yorkshire to burst that dam'. He wasn't going to move for anything and turned over to go back to sleep. 'Sheffield Harry' did not survive the night. Mrs Kirk almost paid for her own rashness when she went back into the house to collect her cat, a rescue act which cost her no more than a sopping nightdress. It appears she had the luck of the foolish.

Joseph Hobson, on the other hand, suffered the misfortune of the provident. He was a miller and spent a couple of wearying hours transferring sacks of corn and flour from the ground floor of his granary to a higher storey. If there was to be a flood, then he would not be caught napping. His modest self-congratulation did not last long. The whole mill was wrecked. Rowel Bridge, a mile and a half from Damflask towards Sheffield, was washed away; so, too, were two nearby 'Wheels', in one of which William Bradbury, apparently alone, was working overtime. He was carried off and never seen again, leaving a young widow, Esther, and two infants to mourn his sudden departure. The mills employed 60 men and this absolute destruction of the premises and loss of tools meant unemployment for many of them. At least they still had their lives.

Joseph Denton lost his life. He was only a youth and his father was head of H. Denton and Co., renting premises at the Old Wheel. Joseph was at work that night with his younger brother, John, and a man named Robert Banner. They must have experienced a living hell as the water poured in. Banner managed to escape by way of a shaking chimney and some beams, but the two boys were dragged under a mass of machinery and timber. Joseph did not re-surface. John Denton did and saved himself by clambering up a pole, where he remained until the water dropped about half an hour later. It was found that a haystack, hardly a stalk out of place, had been deposited in the mill weir, having travelled more than a quarter of a mile from a farmer's field. The flood had pushed into the mill itself a cart which, laden with three tons of coal, had been seen shortly before outside a house some distance away. W. D. Tallent, then a nineteen-year-old apprentice with Samuel Newbould and Co., Sheffield Moor, the firm which owned the forge rented by the Dentons, recalled forty-eight years later how he was in a party sent to look for the missing young man, whom they found, after moving 'huge blocks of stone', near one of the hammers in the forge. That was on the Monday following Friday night's disaster. Tallent also remembered seeing holes in one of the roads leading out of Sheffield 'big enough to put a horse and cart in'; they had been made, he said, 'by the swirl of the waters washing the soil away and leaving pits, as it were'.

At Little Matlock, there had been no warning. The valley began to open out at that point (more than four miles from the reservoir) on the left-hand downstream bank of the river. Having attained maximum speed down the preceding narrowness of the terrain, the waters leapt across the lowlands and took a terrible toll. Villagers were awakened by a deep-toned roar and a strange swishing as the flood devoured life and property. Before they could do much more than shout in terrified disbelief, it was upon them. In this hamlet occurred the first of whole-family tragedies. Daniel Chapman, his wife Ellen, their two sons, aged six and three, as well as a seventeen-year-old domestic servant, Alathea Hague, and two apprentices, John Bower and George Clay, both seventeen, who had lodged with the family for three years, lived in the second of a row of houses which stood at right-angles to the river. The uninhabited end-house was sliced away and as the water, now filled with a ghastly array of debris, lunged forward, the Chapman home was inundated and all the occupants drowned. Chapman, who was twenty-nine, was worth about £450, then a handsome sum, particularly to one so young. It suggested that the firm of Thomas Chapman and Co., steel tilters and forgers, where he had worked with his elder brother, Thomas, was flourishing. At least it had been, for after the flood had struck the premises there was not much to be seen. Thomas Chapman lived nearby with his family and seeing his son, William, aged fifteen, in danger of being sucked by the water through a window, he managed to seize hold of the lad. A falling beam dropped on the father, who lost his grip; poor William was drowned.

The water, fizzing with froth, swept through Harrison's Tilt where two young workmen, Walter Booth and Joe Gregory, disappeared amid a whirl of bricks and iron. Several factories within a short distance of each other were ruined and heavy machinery flung into the air. Abel Wain, who heard a noise 'like thunder', peered out of his bedroom window and could 'discern, though inadequately, the destruction around me'. He fled with his family to an adjoining wood, up the hillside, from where he 'gazed with horror upon the scene'.

Until now, the flood had met little opposition. It had run riot through lightly populated rural communities and, compared with what was to happen, the loss of life had been mercifully small. The wall of water now fanned outwards, approaching higher-density districts at an irresistible power and speed. And it came without warning. First to feel the impact was Malin Bridge, a growing village about two miles out of Sheffield. There the River Loxley joined the River Rivelin and, even without that additional volume of water, it was a hazardous place. Houses were closely grouped and some of them crudely built. Malin Bridge was a sitting target that night, positioned at the lethal end of a giant water-chute. Commented one observer: 'A bombardment with the newest and most powerful artillery could hardly have proved so destructive and could not possibly have been nearly so fatal to human life.' Some homes were set prettily upon tongues of land jutting towards the river, a delightful picture in normal circumstances but now an ideal lay-out for a life-and-death struggle. It was estimated more than a hundred people lost their lives in Malin Bridge and Hillsborough in about twenty minutes. Hundreds more lost their homes and belongings. Not all the bodies were recovered, let alone identified.

James Trickett was forty and had worked hard to become a successful farmer, building up a handsome dairy herd and having a remunerative sideline in pigs. His commodious house, surrounded by a cluster of outbuildings and a well-tended garden, was a feature of Malin Bridge. The property was perched on a small peninsula right in the path of the advancing flood. The Tricketts had endured recent family bereavements; a child had died two months previously and, only that Wednesday, Mrs Trickett's mother had been buried. Her father, seventy-year-old Thomas Kay, had moved into the household. His arrival presented something of a space problem and meant that Joseph Barker, who had lodged with the Tricketts to be near his work, would have to move out. Barker, a fairly wealthy young man of twenty-seven, the son of a Sheffield butcher, was co-proprietor of the Limerick Wire and Rolling Mill, and due the following morning to leave the farmhouse for fresh accommodation. As it tragically transpired, that night was the last for all the occupants: James Trickett, his wife, Elizabeth (aged thirty-six), their three children, Thomas Kay, Joseph Barker and three servants. Whether they slept into death or experienced a few seconds of terror could not be ascertained, but neighbours spoke of seeing lights in the house just before it was swept away. Mrs Corbett, who lived nearby, said the flood approached 'like a mountain of snow'. The farmhouse was smashed and, when the waters subsided, a chasm, and an ash tree stripped of its bark marked the site. A substantial barn survived, having served to divert the water even more fiercely upon the doomed house. Elizabeth Trickett's body was found the next day at Rotherham, about eight miles from her home, while that of James Trickett, junior, was not recovered until three weeks later. An indication of the strength and size of the flood in the vicinity of Malin Bridge can be gleaned from the fact that heavy tree trunks were jammed among rocks 40 feet above the normal level of the river and that a thick stone wall, some 50 yards from the left-hand downstream bank, was demolished.

Close to the Trickett house was a line of three cottages; of their twelve inhabitants only two, Henry Spooner, and Charles Wood, escaped. They were shot clear when their home folded and were lucky to scramble to safety; Spooner's widowed mother, Hannah, her brother-in-law, Benjamin, her son, Jonathan, and her seven-year-old granddaughter, Sarah Ann Spooner, were trapped and drowned. Their next-door neighbours suffered a similar fate: John Hudson would forge shear-steel no more; he went under with his wife, Eliza, and their two children, Mary and George. In the third cottage died James and Mary Bagshaw, a married couple in their fifties. Virtually no trace of the homes remained. Just across the road Thomas Spooner, a thirty-eight-year-old collier, his wife, Selina, and their seven children, whose ages ranged from two to sixteen, also perished—a total of thirteen members of one family within a few feet of each other.

The stone bridge at Malin Bridge was battered and borne away, after which the flood divided into two principal courses of destruction. Just a few yards from where the Spooners died was the Stag Inn, of which little was left standing. The landlady, Eliza Armitage, an elderly widow, was drowned along with her son, William, an anvil-maker of thirty five, his wife, Ann, and their five young children; next door the younger son, Greaves (twenty-eight), who followed the same trade as his brother, died with his wife, Maria, and their two little daughters, aged three years and four months. So departed twelve Armitages in a matter of seconds. That inn also proved a death-trap for Elizabeth Crownshaw, a seventeen-year-old domestic servant, for Henry Hall (a guest there that night) and for James Frith, a scythe-grinder, who lodged there and was survived by his wife and five children who were living at Eckington. In houses near the Stag, the deaths were reported of Thomas Bates, his wife and three sons, and of Thomas and Sarah Bullard, a married couple, whose bodies were found more than a mile away the next day. Within hailing distance, a whole row of houses collapsed like a pack of cards and, it was said, about twenty people succumbed in the shambles. Joseph Crapper who, at thirty-nine, had built up a reputation as a fine shoemaker, drowned with his wife, Elizabeth; among others who did not live until daylight were Ann Mount, a well-known local shopkeeper; William Sellars, an ageing coal-miner, and his wife; Joseph Goddard, his wife, daughter and two grandchildren; four Jepsons and three Barratts.

Almost opposite the Stag stood the Malin Bridge Inn, apparently better known locally as the Cleakum public house, the front of which was ripped out by the raging torrent. George Bisby, who was forty-two and doubled as innkeeper and carter, was swept to his death as were his wife, Sarah, and five children. The body of Bisby and that of his eldest daughter, Teresa, who was fourteen, were found four days later at Sheffield; those of the other five Bisbys were never identified. Whole families were being wiped out. There were also some remarkable family escapes. When the water rose in one house, destroying much of it in the process, Henry Whittles succeeded in getting his wife and five children on to a floating bed. Holding on to it with one hand and clutching the mantelpiece with his other, he displayed that kind of ingenuity and courage deserving of the luck which went with it. The house tottered and, after the ordeal, little was left of the room but the corner in which the frightened family survived. Whittles recalled after the drama: 'The water smelt awful, like a grave that had been newly opened.' A filesmith named Robert Graham, his wife and six children, had a similar experience when they found muddy water slopping about in their bedroom. A wall fell in, but Graham, showing considerable pluck and skill, somehow held on to two buoyant beds upon which huddled his family. A recollection upper-most in the memory of most survivors was the speed with which the water rose; within a minute or two it was up the eaves of some houses.

The havoc wrought by the flood, now bolstered by a flailing mixture of timber, iron, bricks, slates and sodden filth, was enormous. The bodies of men, women and children were borne along with those of horses, cows and pigs; some were badly mutilated and limbless, while others looked as if they were dozing serenely on the surface. The gruesome carrion was tossed about by the water, which pursued relentless routes through, around and over the houses, shops and inns of Malin Bridge and Hillsborough. The flood carved a 'river' across a sloping field and, transforming itself into an artificial waterfall, poured into the Limerick Wheel where William Bethell, labouring through the night, was mangled and buried beneath machinery and falling masonry. His body was not uncovered for five weeks. The works were hopelessly damaged and a partly built extension obliterated. It will be recalled the co-proprietor, Joseph Barker, died with the Tricketts; later it was reported that his partner, Johnson, financially ruined, had emigrated to the United States to start a new life.

Some householders escaped by sitting it out on rooftops, watching the water rushing along a few feet below. It was a touch-and-go risk, however, and several who sought the uneasy sanctuary of slippery slates and chimney stacks were hurled into the depths when houses broke up under them. It was said that one house, sheared off at its foundations, travelled a quarter of a mile in perfect order before settling itself on a new site. It was strange, too, how houses on one side of a street got away with little more than a wetting, while others only yards away were smashed to smithereens. Although it can have been of only academic interest at the time, it was also noted that brick-built structures generally stood up better than those made of stone; indeed, some bricks were so well secured by mortar that entire walls were pushed along and defied all the flood's attempts to break them into pieces.

Two days earlier Sarah Price, the twenty-eight-year-old wife of Edward Price, had been delivered of a son, a brother for Charles John, aged two. Also staying in the house was a relative, Hannah Hill, a pretty girl of nineteen, who was helping Sarah, and an apprentice grinder, Walter Damms, who lodged with the family. They all died, as did Edward Price's parents, Charles and Elizabeth Price, who ran a flourishing hardware store at Malin

Bridge. William Pickering, landlord of the Freemasons Arms, was swept away with his wife and twenty-three-year-old sister, Elizabeth, who had the misfortune to be visiting that night.

At Malin Bridge and Hillsborough, such was the extent of devastation that even some locals lost their way in the streets without familiar landmarks to guide them. Situated in the main firing line between Malin Bridge and Owlerton, a distance of less than a mile, were about 250 houses occupied by 1,260 people. According to one land agent, 50 of those dwellings were wholly or partly destroyed and 57 more rendered uninhabitable. The population was reduced by death and departure to other districts to 800. That is what the flood did in one small area, the physical, mental and material effects being catastrophic. An idea of the ferocity of the water can be gauged from the fact that, having travelled more than five miles from the reservoir, spread out and slowed up, it still retained enough power to flatten sizeable factories and to topple houses. The worst damage occurred during the first fifteen minutes or so after the flood's arrival. Having wrought destruction in one place, it moved quickly on, leaving a trail of dirty, bubbling water, wrecked homes and a thick layer of mud out of which stuck bodies and bits of machinery at grotesque angles.

The end-house of Brick Row, Hillsborough, a terraced line of three-storey back-to-backs, was battered as if by a giant sledgehammer. At the back of the house crowded the Dyson family. Joseph Dyson was reliable and industrious, and he also held down a £200-a-year job as head man at a wireworks factory. His home was neat and well furnished and, like the others in the row, had been built in 1853-4 at a cost of £70. The owner, William Haden, considered Brick Row to be a 'better class' of cottages and let to 'good tenants'. On that tragic night, the house was occupied by Dyson, who was thirty-four, his wife, Mary, their two sons and three daughters (their eldest child, Selina, was staying with her grandmother on the other side of Sheffield), his brother, Vincent, and two apprentices. With the exception of Vincent Dyson, all lost their lives.

In the other half of the end pair of houses lived William and Margaret Styron, their three children and Styron's brother-in-law, Joe Hyde, who was jerked from his sleep by a noise like a 'hundred engines letting off steam'. Lighting a candle, he went to investigate, believing the house to be on fire. He quickly revised that opinion, however, for he was not half-way down the stairs when a torrent ripped off part of the gable of the house. Then the party wall, which separated the Styrons from the Dysons, collapsed and Hyde nearly fell into the turbulence below. The candle blew out and Hyde, who had fractured a finger saving himself from tumbling, returned to the other occupants, who were extremely afraid and kneeling in prayer. He joined them for a while but, perhaps thinking the Almighty helped those who were prepared to contribute something themselves, he hit upon an idea.

Tearing off a bedpost and, calling upon the others to follow him, Hyde climbed to the garret of the shuddering house and smashed a hole in the wall between them and the adjoining house. Scrambling through this escape hatch, the family were soon joined by equally frightened neighbours. They managed to keep their feet as the building wobbled and, looking back, Styron saw that his own house had almost disappeared. Fearing a fatal chain-reaction, the Styrons and neighbours, led by the enterprising Joe Hyde, broke through another intervening wall, and another, collecting more families as they went. They were also met by Vincent Dyson who, having forced his way through the top of his brother's ill-fated house, had crawled along the windswept roof. Hyde and his companions crashed through no fewer than five walls and, by the time the dramatic journey ended, 'their number had accumulated to thirty-four, of both sexes and all ages'. Dressed only in their scanty night clothes, they remained beyond the reach of the flood until the water diminished. A few yards away, seven Atkinsons drowned. Pitiful screams and sobs penetrated the cold night air.

Both the bridges at Hillsborough were badly hit. A nearby toll-house was wrecked and the elderly collector, Thomas Winter, died. A large rolling-mill, belonging to George Hawksley, was seriously damaged, but his comfortable home was saved to a large extent by the fortuitous fact that a mass of debris lodged against it and acted as a protective wall. The stone and iron fencing in front of Hawksley's house was washed away, a summer shelter flung across the road and his garden covered in deep mud, from which protruded 'a pretty statue of praying Samuel'. The Hillsborough Inn suffered when water cascaded into the cellars and 'blew up the flooring and burst out of the doors and windows'. Nearby, the Shakespeare Inn was also damaged, as was the surgery of Dr Roberts and, to a great degree, the grocery shops of Cockhill Woodcock. Subsequently, Woodcock claimed compensation not only for the material injury to his premises but also for loss of trade brought about by the 'departure' of so many of his customers. John Cowton Appleby, a widower of thirty-six, also a prospering grocer in the district, lost not only his stock but also his life. Appleby, together with his sixty-three-year-old mother, Mary, and her granddaughter of the same name, fought vainly to get out of their crumbling home. Mrs Appleby's body was recovered from the river at Rotherham.

Some of the houses in Malin Bridge and Hillsborough were poorly built and the flood revealed what superficial attention had been paid to their construction. Something much less than a flood would have damaged them, remarked one resident, adding that 'a good smith's hammer would have smashed all before it'. There were five-inch walls put together with dabs of mortar, 'floor joists like clothes-props, and boards more like plasterers' laths than flooring'. Much laid bare by the water illustrated more graphically than could any social reformer just what was required (or, more precisely, not required) in the way of some housebuilding. One writer, referring to similarly poor houses in Sheffield, declared: 'They are breeding places of ill-health, bad manners and bad habits. They deaden the sense of decency, encourage recklessness and imprudence, and drive the occupants from their dirty and cheerless rooms anywhere —to beershop or ginshop—so long as they can get out of the sight of the misery which they are compelled to endure.' In the flood, some homes curled up like soggy cardboard and the pinchpenny policy of some speculative builders undoubtedly caused a greater loss of life than there might otherwise have been. In too many instances, homes became coffins. In one, the clock had stopped at 27 minutes past midnight.

The cries for help were heart-rending and, in most cases, nothing could be done. Peering into the gloom, it was sometimes possible to distinguish a figure bobbing in the flood but there was no chance, for instance, of saving a man who went by 'sitting bolt upright in the water'. William Watson, an anvil-maker by trade, broke the surface with his wife, Sarah Ann, two youngsters and his father-in-law, John Oakley, all clinging to each other. The group was split by the surging flood, but Watson managed to hold on to his wife and little son, George. Then, as they were dashed against a wall, Watson alone survived and floated close to a bedroom window through which he was dragged by a man called Widdowson.

The Great Flood had its share of what would have otherwise

have been comical incidents as well as a number of bizarre episodes. When the water bounded into the modest home of a Hillsborough tailor called Joseph Chapman, he promptly clambered into a wooden box and pulled the lid over himself. Thus enclosed, he floated around for a while until some neighbours hauled him clear of danger and Chapman, used to creating items of sartorial elegance, stepped out triumphantly—in a state of near-nudity. Then there was the story of a domestic row which saved two others from drowning. A man, frustrated by his wife's nagging about his drinking habits, decided to return to a late-night concert hall to submerge his sorrows in ale. The wife, not to be outdone, followed him and kept up her carping commentary. When they finally returned to their home, only half of it was still standing.

Stranger still was the case of a man who, earlier that day, had attempted to commit suicide by throwing himself into the river. He was fished out and locked in a cell at Hillsborough police station, pending an appearance in court. When the flood rushed into the building and began to rise alarmingly he no longer relished the idea of sudden departure by immersion and shouted to be let out. Inspector Thomas Smalley and his wife, Victoria, sleeping in a room above the lock-up, were aroused by the commotion and, by the time the policeman got to the screaming prisoner, the water was up to his armpits. With difficulty, Smalley rescued the man who by now was trembling and appeared to have abandoned all thoughts of a self-inflicted demise. The inspector, who spent the remainder of that night and the following few days assisting the many sufferers in the area, caught a chill. He confided to his wife and his doctor: 'I got my death on the night of the flood and shall never get better.' His premonition was sadly accurate. He also contracted typhus (probably through swallowing dirty water) and died two months after saving a man who, for a time at least, had not wanted to live.

Destiny dealt more kindly with John Corbett, an unmarried steel tilter of twenty-one, who lived just beyond the reach of the flood as it sped down the Loxley Valley. For a young man, he had a strongly developed sense of duty and self-discipline. He was on night-shift that week and would normally have been walking through Malin Bridge on his way to work at the time of the disaster. He awoke and started to dress when, for some unexplained reason, he changed his mind and got back into bed. It was the only time in his life he was late for work and, to his dying day, some sixty years later, he declared he never knew what prevented him from following his customary routine. Being a devoutly religious man, he doubtless attributed his good fortune to the Almighty. His workmates, at least, had given him up for lost.

Having reduced parts of Malin Bridge and Hillsborough to rubble, the flood reached Owlerton—a point near which the Loxley runs into the River Don. Owlerton Paper Mills, where old John and Susannah Turton died, was seriously affected and tons of expensive stock rendered useless. William Robert Marshall, head of the papermaking firm, had just congratulated himself on surviving a bad recession in trade and that business was picking up again when the flood devastated one mill and damaged another. The unfortunate Mr Marshall also owned a number of nearby cottages which, along with his own house, had been hit by the water and, to add to his troubles, his whole family went down with scarlet fever. Water tore into the Royal Hotel, dashed against a group of solid-looking houses and rebounded with enough force to wreck a factory in which wire was made. Not far away, Herbert Gravenor Marshall, aged two, the son of a Sheffield pawnbroker, was sleeping overnight with Isaac Turner, his wife and two children. All were drowned. Of the Turners, only the man of the house was later identified.

A youth named Joseph Dean, sleeping with his brother, awoke to find himself pressed against the ceiling, the bed having risen on the water. In an effort to push himself away, the lad fell out and drowned. His brother survived. Fortunately, the loss of life in Owlerton was small compared with the amount of damage. Mrs Proctor, who was up late reading, testified to hearing a 'great roaring noise' at about 12.30 a.m. She escaped upstairs. The main course of water, after spreading through meadows, was drawn into the route of the Don which flowed directly into Sheffield itself. The flood, now some six miles from its birthplace on the moors, had lost a little of its earlier impetus but, augmented by the Don, prepared to launch itself with renewed fury upon the last mile or so into the near-centre of a large industrial town. As the water reached the densely populated districts, so the death-rate and injuries again increased. Having run swiftly over some low land, the great wave rebounded from a ridge of rising ground with such a brutal back-lash that several factories either side of the river were seriously damaged. A silver mill sustained a crushing broadside and much costly metal in the process of being rolled was lost, the workers scattering to get clear of the advancing tide.

To all intents and purposes, the Don disappeared. A wide stream extended well beyond its banks, transforming the network of streets into fast-flowing rivulets. Waterborne trees became battering rams. A solid wall enclosing army barracks was breached near the NCOs' married quarters and a guard narrowly missed death. Paymaster-Sergeant Foulds was awakened by his wife and, jumping out of bed, found himself in water which was coming in through the window. 'Good God,' he yelled, 'the world's breaking up.' When at last he succeeded in opening the door a torrent swept in and he and his wife were knocked over. They grabbed their baby from a cot and got out, but when Sergeant Foulds returned to rescue his other children, Isabella aged five and John aged three, the door was jammed and the room full of water. The bodies of the infants were recovered when the flood went down. Crashes and shouts had alerted other occupants and half-dressed soldiers shepherded their families to the safety of upper floors.

The water punched its way through the mill of Marchington and Makin, pitching out machinery and leaving a semi-built masonry weir in pieces. William Simpson and a boy named Capper were working in the forge and almost drowned where they stood. The lad climbed to a beam, from where he watched the water rise to a height of 15 feet; shaking with fear and cold, there he remained for several hours before being helped down. He was badly shocked, but physically unharmed. Simpson was less fortunate. Having hauled himself to the top of a boiler, he must have felt comparatively safe. He had reckoned without the strength of the current, however. The boiler was sucked out and, although he was able to 'ride' it for a while, he was eventually tipped to his death. His wife was left at home to bring up six children aged between sixteen and three. Along one street metal railings, attached at intervals to pillars of iron, were twisted into a fantastic filigree. Nearby, a row of houses crumbled and the body of a man was found wedged between branches fifteen feet up a bark-stripped tree.

The ghastly experience undergone by so many was expressed by one householder: 'I was completely bewildered by the frightful sound that fell upon my ears; it has never been truly described, nor can it ever be. The nearest definition is *hissing thunder*. I was so stupefied by this horrid sound that I did not see the wild waters immediately before me, nor did I dream of the nature of the calamity by which I was threatened, until I actually stepped in water at my garden gate. I at once mounted the railings and was terrified by the sight of the rushing flood.... For anyone to brave the flood with the design of rescuing some whom it threatened to engulf, would only be to rush to certain and sure destruction. This being my feeling, I could only wait and pray that the Almighty would bare his arm and save. When the flood invaded, it rose rapidly but, when it retired, it seemed to sink slowly, very slowly.'

That man's house was on fairly high ground. Water ran into his living-room but he and his family, though frightened, were in comparatively little danger all the time they stayed upstairs. What of the many others who dwelt close to the normal edge of the river? From that area came plaintive calls for assistance. Some of them did not last long.

3 Sheffield Under Water

The finale was frightful. Loaded with garbage, the water rumbled out of the darkness to submerge unsuspecting families in the town houses of Sheffield. Plumes of muddy spray shot into the air as the torrent dashed against buildings while streams, swirling through side-streets, collided with tributaries driving in from different directions. Trees, propelled and rotated by eddies, pierced brickwork and sheared off cornerstones to bring down walls from above. Within minutes, several regions were inundated, those on low-lying land up to a depth of nearly twenty feet. Hundreds of people were marooned in upstairs rooms, sometimes to their hips in water.

Slithering swiftly along Neepsend Lane, which runs close to the River Don for half a mile or so, the flood caused some of the worst havoc. The fronts of some houses were torn away, revealing people gasping and threshing about; in a number of single-storey dwellings, said to be scarcely larger than pig-sties, entire families floundered and drowned. Between the river and the embankment of the Sheffield-Manchester railway line about 900 acres were laid out as gardens, 'cultivated in small plots by industrious artisans residing in adjacent parts'. On those allotments (for that is what they would now be called) were some whitewashed cottages, a number being used as tool-sheds but others lived in by modest working-men who rented the plots. The gardens were swamped and homes smashed. Thomas Petty, who was employed by a firm manufacturing stove-grates, met his death along with his wife, Margaret, and their three children. The same was reported of four Websters, five Midwoods and Alfred and Sarah Hukin and their twelve-year-old niece, Alice Jackson.

The story of the Midwoods was recounted fifty years later by

Mrs Harriet Nicholson, when she was sixty-nine. Joel Midwood, an apprentice to a master builder, lived with his parents, John and Phoebe Midwood, his two younger brothers, Dawson and George, and his little sister, Fanny. After the flood hit their home, Joel Midwood got on to the roof and pulled up his mother, father and sister. He saw nothing more of his brothers. Sitting astride the roof, the four were swept along by the current and 'heard the voices of stricken people pleading for mercy, imploring the Almighty for aid, praying and singing'. After a while, Midwood's parents and sister 'slid from the roof and perished before his eyes'. Joel Midwood was also shot into the water, but managed to keep afloat and became caught in debris piled against a bridge. Although 'numbed and exhausted, he groped his way over the wreckage, got on to the parapet of the bridge and stumbled along to a house where the light was shining'. He was put to bed and the following day went to hospital to have a large metal nail removed from his foot. That injury soon healed, but there was nothing to mend the horror of his memory. Such experiences were all too common.

Terrified souls snatched at anything projecting above the water-line to save themselves or thrust out an often unavailing hand to rescue others being pulled along by the racing tide. Thomas Peters, a leather dresser, was working at Lincoln when the flood came and returned home to find his wife had managed to save only one of their four children. Thomas Albert, a skinner, threw his eldest son on to his shoulders and waded to safety but, before he was able to get back to the house, his wife and their two children had been overcome. Another skinner, William Needham, and his wife, each carrying a child, got away from their flooded cottage and reached a neighbour's house. They hauled themselves up the stairs only to find the bedroom door stuck by the pressure of water. Eventually the door panels were smashed from inside and Mrs Needham dragged through; by then, however, her infant had been drowned and carried away. Her husband also lost hold of their other child and only saved his own life by dog-paddling to a window where helping hands plucked him from the water. The bodies of John and Martha Needham, aged four and two respectively, were later found nearby.

John and Sarah Ann Glover, a married couple, both twenty-five years old, stumbled and half-swam to a house on higher ground, but the effort was too much for them; they were clawing their way up a staircase towards safety when weakness and water overcame them. Thomas Wilkinson had 'been in a flood before' and, when water drove him from his bedroom, he climbed on to the roof. A light cart floated close and Wilkinson clambered into it and held on to an edge of his house, from which vantage point he persuaded neighbours to remain in their garrets and on no account to attempt to 'make a dash for it'. Thomas Wilkinson knew about such things and a number of people survived, thanks to his cool thinking and comforting advice.

Three Coggin children, whose parents were away overnight after attending a family funeral at Wakefield, were entombed. Four members of the Bright family, together with Edward Cross aged fifteen were trapped and slowly drowned, while two other occupants effected a getaway by wriggling up the chimney. A butcher, John Mayor, his invalid wife, Elizabeth, and their daughter perished in a downstairs room. Such tragic incidents, against a background of cries, crashes and rushing water, were repeated along the whole melancholy route. A girl of eleven, signing herself 'S. J. G.', wrote to her grandmother in Leeds describing what it was like being in the flood. Her aunt woke up her uncle and told him: 'Oh, John, the world's at an end.' The uncle replied: 'Nay, lass, it cannot be.' The water rose in the house and, wrote the girl, 'just then, the gas went out and we only had about half a candle. Aunt and I gave ourselves up for lost, but uncle said if the water came any higher we should be obliged to get on the roof'. After what must have seemed an eternity, the uncle announced that the flood was going down. 'O, how thankful we were when we heard that,' added the girl.

Thomas Elston was only thirty-four, but illness threatened to bring his job as a blade grinder to a premature end. He was a victim of inflamed lungs and his doctor had prescribed a period of rest in the clean air of the countryside. Elston lived modestly in one of the Neepsend garden houses and, like so many of his colleagues suffering from 'grinder's disease', was reluctant to give up his work, even for a short time. He could not afford it and was resigned to the fact that respiratory troubles were an accepted hazard of the trade. He was ill, however, and finally convinced himself there was no real alternative to the physician's advice. He sent his crippled son, William, aged six, to stay with his grandmother in another part of Sheffield and Elston himself was due to depart for his 'cure' on the day before the flood. Only twelve days previously his wife, Elizabeth, had given birth to a son, who was called Thomas after his father. Perhaps mother and child were going to travel with Elston; possibly he postponed his trip until they had gained in strength. At all events, he put off his 'holiday' for forty-eight hours. It proved a fateful decision. The flood covered the cottage by the river and the three Elstons inside never stood a chance.

The gasworks at Neepsend were extensively damaged; retorts, boilers and engines were wrested from their fixtures and the water carried away a thousand tons of coke and a large quantity of timber. More bridges broke up, houses staggered and fell and a tall chimney folded, showering hundreds of bricks into the vast stream. At the end of one row of cottages lived John Gannon who, on his small wage as a labourer, provided for his wife, Sarah, and six children. They shouted desperately for help when the waters came, but in vain. As Joel Midwood had done, Gannon smashed through the slates and hauled his family up after him on to the roof. There they sat and shivered, clinging to each other for comfort and safety and, perhaps, blessing their luck that they had got beyond the reach of the flood. However, the top part of their home was detached from the remainder and whisked along like so much balsa wood. The Gannons held on grimly as what was left of their cottage pitched along like a storm-tossed ship. Soon it fell apart and all eight were drowned. It was the biggest family loss from one house in Sheffield: John Gannon was listed as being thirty-six-years old, Sarah (thirty), Henry (eleven), John (nine), Peter (five), William (four), Sarah Ann (two) and Margaret (four months).

The water was further charged with 200 gallons of oil flushed from a file-making factory, where 20 workers had only minutes before knocked off for supper. Pelts and hides were added to the hideous paraphernalia when the flood prised open two tanneries, carrying away the stock and destroying machinery. Hardly a house or mill, shop, church or stable, within two hundred yards either side of the River Don, evaded damage. Neepsend Lane, Mowbray Street, Harvest Lane, Nursery Street, Bacon Island, Kelham Island, Cotton Mill Walk, Long Croft and The Wicker were but a few of the many places badly affected and they became nationally known names after the flood.

John Parkes, who lived in Harvest Lane, heard cries of 'Make for the tip' (railway embankment) and, in the confusion, imagined his house to be ablaze. When he opened the door water rushed in, bringing with it a dead grey horse. Together with her husband, Emma Parkes strove to get out with their son, Alfred, who was five, and baby Emma, aged three months. The wife cried: 'I can't stand, I'm going.' That was the last Parkes saw of his family. He remembered no more, but was told later he had floated out of a window and dragged himself by a shutter to the roof of his house. Another reported version of the tragedy was that Parkes was bedridden and remained safely upstairs, but his wife, presumably panic-stricken, leapt through a window with her two children and into the seething waters. The first story, though less dramatic, sounds the more feasible.

Several people in the same area were quickly overcome by the sudden influx of water. Mary Crump, a septuagenarian, and her son, Samuel, who was thirty-eight, were discovered lying in sodden beds; next door Elizabeth Green, a manglewoman, also died in a poky single-storey home. John Vaughan and his wife, an elderly couple, did have an upstairs room but had let it to lodgers, who escaped unharmed. The Vaughans, sleeping on the ground floor, experienced the horror of slowly drowning before anyone could reach them.

Police constable No. 150, John Thorpe, was among the officers on duty that night. His hours were long and the pay small—not more than a pound a week—considering the responsibility of his task. He was pounding an uneventful beat, cursing the wretched weather and banging his hands together to keep warm. Before joining the constabulary, he had served with the British Army in the Crimea and in India and had seen some harrowing scenes in his time. Even so, he was staggered by what he witnessed now. It was about half-past midnight as P.C. Thorpe strolled towards the river. Above the wail of the wind, he detected a deep rumble and, close upon it, an extraordinary rushing noise. As it grew louder, he also heard crashes and shouts and, in the darkness, was just able to make out an approaching wave.

At the Shuttle House, situated upon a strip of land wedged into the Don and known as Bacon Island, lived James Sharman. He was forty-nine and, in addition to being a blacksmith, had charge of the sluice-gates through which water was diverted to a couple of mills. He slept soundly with his wife, Mary, his daughter, Emma, two daughters-in-law and four grandchildren, and was unaware of anything untoward until he was awakened by P.C. Thorpe thumping on the door. By the time the family had got up, water was beginning to fill downstairs rooms and they were forced to remain aloft. P.C. Thorpe, who had helped to raise the alarm in the immediate vicinity, returned chest-deep in water and, with the aid of a ladder, assisted the Sharmans to safety. As the policeman and James Sharman, who was the last to leave, struggled through the current, there was a resounding splash and the whole of the house and connecting bridge shattered. The policeman's timely and courageous action prevented a number of deaths that night.

Indeed, there were many acts of bravery, not least by members of the Sheffield Police Force. About fifty officers and constables were commended for their deeds that night and during the aftermath, resulting in promotion and cash awards. John Thorpe became a 'merit-class constable' and received a small financial bonus from the Watch Committee. In addition, grateful residents clubbed together to present him with seven shillings.

Not all those living on Bacon Island were as fortunate as the Sharmans. George Wright, a warehouseman at a nearby steelworks, and his wife, Rebecca, were drowned when the gable-end of the house fell in on them but, by a stroke of fortune, their infant daughter, Anna Maria, was found happily playing in a saturated cot. Alongside, a candle was still flickering. Mrs Wells, who dwelt nearby, was at that time waiting at the Midland Station for a consignment of watercress being forwarded by her husband for sale later that day. As she collected the parcel, she noticed water creeping across the station yard. Because of the flood, Mrs Wells had to make a detour and, when she reached Bacon Island, she was horrified to find great damage and the area still under water. She had left two of her five children sleeping downstairs (so the story goes) and, as she waded towards her home, she saw the other three leaning from the bedroom window. They could only report hearing their brother and sister scream but, because of the water, had themselves become frightened and stayed upstairs. Imagine her joy when Mrs Wells found the 'missing' children alive. With remarkable presence of mind the boy, aged thirteen, had lifted his three-year-old sister on to a high cupboard above the level of the water and had climbed up after her. Their mother spied them fast asleep—on top of the cupboard!

Neighbours called to each other over the dark waters and

rescuers blundered across littered stretches of mud. It was highly dangerous. Some lost their lives attempting to save their animals which, on the face of it, may seem a needless sacrifice, but a pig or a horse was a valuable asset to the working man and often represented the difference between a slightly better standard of living and the pinch of poverty. The destruction continued. A mill producing crinoline wire disappeared without much trace, the tough double doors of a tool-making factory were brushed aside and much damage caused within; and a much-used footbridge was snapped off at one end, leaving the other (which connected with a tannery) 'sloping upon the edge of the weir, bent as if it were a piece of whalebone'. The new works of Becket and Slater, manufacturers of steel, saws and files, were badly hit. Their boundary wall was flattened, a boiler was lugged from its foundations and 'delivered' free of charge to a rival firm more than a hundred yards away, cellars were flooded, 24 newly charged furnace holes destroyed, machines put out of action and goods ready for dispatch borne away. Many houses survived with no more than flooding and damaged furniture, but it was all miserably relative for some sufferers could ill afford to lose even a door-knocker (if, indeed, they had one).

A hole was ripped into the whole length of a wall of a Wesleyan chapel, an underground hot-air flue exploded in one factory and carts and wagons by the dozen passed by together with the mutilated carcasses of animals. On the town side of Bacon Island stood a flour mill and steel manufactory, the scene of a mass escape. Men, humping sacks of grain to an upper storage-room, scrambled aloft themselves and, from their shaking perch, watched sticks of furniture and lifeless forms floating through the mill below. Some flotsam became stuck between machines, a dead cow spun like a top after clipping the side of a delivery cart, and an expensive-looking piano sped along, twanging as it went. Considering the concentration of industrial and residential development in the area, it was surprising that even more people were not killed.

Thousands of pounds' worth of destruction was wrought at the Philadelphia Steel Works, costly machinery and stocks being tossed into the turmoil. The night-watchman there was William Bonsor, who augmented his fifteen shillings a week by assisting his wife, Sarah, to sell eggs and poultry. He was getting old now and money was short, partly because he had been a bit of a boozer in his day.

His worries were over—ended by the flood. The firm's steel manager, Henry Walker, had rather fewer financial problems. His was a good job and his higher station in life was exposed when a wall on one side of his home, attached to the factory, was ripped out, revealing tasteful furniture and fittings. It was hardly a time to be status-conscious, however. Walker, who was forty-nine, was as frightened as his wife, Emma, and the rest of the family, for the house shuddered alarmingly as the waters wrapped around the lower floor. It was a terrible experience but the Walkers, cold and thankful, remained in the bared safety of their bedrooms until the flood subsided. Not far away, the front wall of terraced homes—known as Waterloo Houses—collapsed, the floors of some bedrooms tilting to a steep slant. Although all the houses were occupied only one person, Ann Cooke, who was eighty-seven, died. She had been sleeping in a bottom room and, when the water came in, her bed, with her in it, floated out. Mrs Cooke was believed to be the flood's oldest victim and her body was not recovered until 3 April—near Rotherham. Less tragic, but nevertheless sad for beer drinkers, was the fact that a nearby brewery was inundated and barley and malt saturated beyond use.

The Sheffield Union Workhouse, an 'unsightly edifice', originally a cotton mill, stood severely in Kelham Street. About 1,200 inmates were there at the time. The water forced its way up through drains and burst from under the floorboards into ground-floor rooms, including the smallpox, venereal and children's wards. One of the first to notice it was a simpleton called George, who was considered to be of sufficient intellect, however, to be in charge of the boiler house. He shouted and whistled and, instinctively sensing danger, climbed on to a low roof out of harm's way.

Meanwhile the matron, Miss Rebecca Frances Day, was awakened by the crashing of two heavy entrance gates which had been secured by iron bars. James Wescoe, the workhouse master, was also jolted from his slumber. The flood swept into the downstairs bedrooms and offices of that austere place and the matron, shouting warnings as she went, proceeded to the boiler house where she found George, apparently unperturbed, still whistling loudly and merrily. The room was fizzing with steam and the dull-witted, though happy, young man was enticed from his temporary haven. Miss Day and Wescoe continued to sound the alarm—not a moment too soon. Some of the women's quarters and lunatics' wards were on the ground floor and, as the water surrounded them, the inmates began to wail. Some beds floated. Able-bodied men were summoned to carry the females to higher floors. There were some anxious moments when the water rose to a height of five feet but, astonishingly, considering the incapacity of some patients and signs of panic, not a single life was lost. The rescue operation took place to the accompaniment of piercing shrieks from the women, the shrill chorus being emulated by the wide-eyed, uncomprehending mental cases. The under-master, who had started his duties only a week previously, very nearly went under for good. He awoke to the sound of water lapping around his bed and, still drowsy, somehow got into a tub in which he paddled around for a while. Then he was up-ended. Now fully conscious and soaking wet, he decided it was perhaps easier to effect a conventional escape through his bedroom door. This he achieved without much difficulty and went to help in the general task of removal. The food stores of the workhouse were saturated and the master's office, furniture and library left in a chaotic state. In one room, the water climbed to within a few inches of disturbing corpse-filled coffins, set high on trestles and awaiting burial. Large quantities of quicklime and whitewash were required to restore much of the ground floor to habitable conditions.

The streets around the workhouse were racing with water when Sidney Varney, the son of a shopkeeper, was returning on horseback to his home in Kelham Street. The animal bucked when it met deep water and was knocked down by a whirling tree. It struggled to its legs again. Sidney Varney did not. He was eighteen.

Kelham Island, a sliver of land protruding into the river, caught the full impact of the flood. A thick, protective wall, capable of withstanding any normal rise of the river, was washed down. John Eaton, a forty-eight-year-old machine supervisor employed by a firm of saw manufacturers, left his house to rescue his pig. His wife, Keziah, followed him. The stubborn animal refused to budge and neighbours shouted in vain for the Eatons to get clear. The water smothered pen, pig and owners. Poor Eaton was flung cruelly against the wall of a mill and, for a time, held there by the flood; he was seen in the moonlight, unable to move and crying for help, until another swell put an end to his suffering. His body was recovered two miles away while that of Mrs Eaton was found just a few yards from their home, which was little damaged.

A dramatic impression of the bursting of Dale Dyke dam—from a sketch
by W. Nicholson

A view of the broken dam from inside the reservoir. This illustration was appended to the official report on the dam's failure prepared and presented to
Parliament by Robert Rawlinson and Nathaniel Beardmore, engineers appointed
to investigate the disaster

The ruptured embankment

All that was left of the Wisewood Rolling Mills, near Malin Bridge

At Kelham Rolling Mills, the men had just finished their mid-night meal when water began pouring in through the windows. They succeeded in climbing on to the roof and one of the men, who first raised the alarm, saw his own bed and other furniture from his home in Malin Bridge floating by. Subsequently, it was said, he discovered his wife and children had drowned. The story sounds preposterous enough to be true. Stranger things have happened. In the mill that night was B. T. Barstow, a young worker, who described what occurred when the flood burst in: 'We made a rush for safety but, before we had gone many yards, we were up to our waists in water. We got on top of the engine house. The water had risen to something like 12 feet. We heard a policeman calling for help and we saw one climb a lamp-post only to be washed away with the post. When the water had gone down we tried to get out of the gate but, to our surprise, found our way blocked by the Bow Street Bridge. Then my uncle and I started for Attercliffe; it was pitch dark and we fell over all sorts of dead animals and we were up to our knees in mud. When we got to the old toll bar, which stood near the Twelve O'clock Inn, one of the posts had been washed away and I fell up to my neck in water. We continued our way home and got there about half past three.' That reminiscence was recounted by Barstow half a century later. It was a memory forever fused into his mind.

The flood rolled relentlessly on and only the natural elevation of land prevented the very centre of Sheffield from being inundated. Even so, the water got close enough and swept through a number of highly populated districts. By now, warnings were being given at full cry by constables, night-watchmen and residents, but it was impossible to avert further loss of life. Happily, it was no longer so great. An iron footbridge, which had stood the test of time since 1795, was demolished by baulks of timber being thrown against it, although it had been sheltered for a while by the infinitely stronger Borough Bridge which arrested a heaving mass of wreckage. The fall of the iron bridge was timed at one o'clock on the Saturday morning. The streets alongside the river were said to have resembled a 'manufacturing Venice' and, the observer added with considerable understatement, 'gondolas could have been rowed about with the greatest ease'.

Some homes were closely packed into low-lying yards and, in one, a poor old man named Dennis McLoughlin died with his sleeping companion—a donkey. The water just toppled in on them. Christopher and Mary Calton, and nephew Christopher, aged four suffered a similar fate, the pressure of water preventing them from opening the door. Nearby Mrs Ryder, her eight-year-old daughter, and her son, Robert, who was eleven, at least succeeded in getting out. The mother waded exhausted to a lamp-post, hanging on to it with one hand and gripping the little girl with the other. Robert, clenching with frozen hands his mother's clothes, was suddenly swept away in a rush of water and never again seen alive. In an effort to save him, Mrs Ryder let go of the post and she and her daughter were dragged along by the current. Luckily, they were spotted by some men, who tugged them clear. Generally, the families in that area who remained in first-floor bedrooms survived, although it was a dreadful ordeal as houses shook and bricks fell. Of course, some people had no upstairs retreat; for them, it was touch-and-go. A widow, Emma Wallace, awoke to discover her house in Cotton Mill Row awash and had rushed outside before realizing her two children were still asleep inside. As the water rose, she screamed for help and a neighbour threw down a knotted sheet. Mrs Wallace hung to it for a time, but her strength ebbed and she was borne away to die. Ironically, her children were rescued from their bed.

Henry Wall worked at a local tannery as a skin dresser. He was twenty-eight years old and each week earned twenty-five shillings on which he kept his wife, Louisa, and their three children. When the flood reached their little home in Green Lane, the family got on to the roof and were exposed to the cold for a long time. Wall, normally a healthy man, was shivering so from shock and damp that he was unable to move and had to be assisted down. He became ill and died within three months. That was just one of many similar cases that would not be included in the casualty lists. As a direct result of the flood, a regrettably large number of people contracted diseases brought on by exposure or immersion in filthy water, or sustained permanent injury, leading sometimes to death.

The wrought-iron fencing in front of Holy Trinity Church, Nursery Street, was buckled by blows from floating debris and, according to one onlooker, the water burst down the doors and 'poured with a sacrilegious rush into the sacred edifice'. Pews were submerged, while hassocks and prayer books bobbed about in the unholy water. On the other side of the river, the home of the Rev.

Charles S. Wright, curate of St Philip's Church, was bounded by a brick wall eight feet high. During the early hours, he was disturbed by strange sounds. Peering through his bedroom window, he was startled to see his garden covered in thick mud, out of which stuck a horse, in semi-squatting position, whinnying and flailing the air with its forelegs. When it was eventually dug out, the animal was found to have been attached by a rope to a heavy, rough-hewn stone. There was little doubt that the horse had been washed from its stable, together with its weighty tether, and tossed over the solid wall by the force of the water.

The large steel manufacturing plant of Naylor and Vickers extended along the riverside between Borough Bridge and Lady's Bridge, on the town centre side, for about three hundred yards. The business was headed by Edward Vickers, a former Mayor of Sheffield, who was in partnership with his father-in-law, George Naylor. Although now eight miles from its source, the flood was still strong enough to cause considerable mischief. One can hardly imagine the chaos had those works had to face the first mighty onslaught of water in the Loxley Valley. Barely a minute after receiving a warning, the men on night duty saw water splashing across the yard. Some leapt a wall and reached higher ground; others climbed on to the roof of the rolling mill but, before doing so, sounded a large bell to alert people in the neighbourhood. The works suffered substantially, melting-pots being ruined and valuable machinery in the rolling mill and casting shops badly damaged. From their vantage point on the roof, the steelworkers saw lights blinking in many houses and screams told them something of the terror being experienced. They could also hear the yells from would-be rescuers as well as the agonized shouts of the dying and the injured. One of these came probably from Richard Hazlehurst, who scraped a living retailing coal and was known locally as 'Old Dicky'. He lived in a low shed (in which he also stored his coal) and slept in a wooden box in one corner. His body was located later that morning some way off in the Tinsley Road.

At Lady's Bridge, which crosses the Don as the river starts what is virtually a U-turn away from the heart of Sheffield, flotsam piled up against the stonework. The whole mess rocked and slopped and a great volume of water broke away and flowed deeply along the wide thoroughfare of The Wicker. Racing under the arches of the high-columned viaduct of the Manchester, Sheffield and Lincolnshire Railway, the flood swept into the Midland Station, which served a rival line. It forced open the double gates of the coal yard, where a clerk on night duty (though probably asleep) was drowned, ran over the platforms and on to the railway track. An engine turntable was transformed into an ornamental pond, while the goods yard became a macabre collecting-point for the flood's 'spoils'. Many shops in the areas of Lady's Bridge and The Wicker were flooded and, as a result, a number of small retailers faced ruin. Part of the enclosed cattle market vanished.

The visibility during the night of the Great Flood must have varied a great deal. Some survivors spoke of 'complete darkness' and 'black as tar', while others were absolutely certain of what they had seen, often in remarkable detail. One young man, who knew nothing of the flood until the following morning, but who had been on Lady's Bridge about an hour before it arrived, was a certain Joseph Dyson. Many years later (and one must make allowances for lapses of memory), he recalled that he had travelled by train from Wakefield and alighted at Sheffield's Midland Station at about eleven o'clock. It was moonlight, he said, when he walked up The Wicker. Looking over the bridge, he noticed the water which, 'white and bright under the moon rays, seemed to dance over the weir'. Although tired, he put his arms on the parapet and 'rested awhile, enchanted with the splendour of the night'.

Little more than an hour later deep water was flowing down The Wicker and into Savile Street, but there were definite signs of the pace dropping. For the most part now, damage to buildings was confined to flooding, although a few suffered structurally. The gradually dispersing streams pushed on towards Brightside, Attercliffe and Tinsley—*en route* for Rotherham—and reached larger areas of open ground. Only one more death—in geographical sequence, that is—was reported. The melancholy distinction went to Thomas Gill, who was on duty at a chemical works, near Brightside Lane. Despite his cries, nobody was able to get to him in time because he was encompassed by 'a waste of waters boiling like the sea'.

In the region of Savile Street East, smoke mushroomed from the chimneys of the steelworks. Water infiltrated the yards and cellars as well as some of the workshops of those giant complexes, and workmen's cottages were flooded. The first indication of trouble inside one plant came when water spurted from the boiler holes, quickly extinguishing the fires. Alarm spread rapidly, for there was no way of knowing what was happening. Fortunately, the water soon went down. Although damage was done to most of the works in that area, there were no reports of casualties.

Farther along Brightside Lane, with the railway embankment on the left and rising ground towards Attercliffe on the right, much of the water found a slight hollow in which to settle as an artificial lake a quarter of a mile across. It was a long time before it soaked away. A large portion of land in that vicinity was not built up but, due to physical necessity for industrial expansion, a number of firms had already established themselves there or were in the process of erecting new works. Stanley and Co., G. W. Hawksley and Co., and Humphrey Turner and Co. were among those with premises near the railway while, on the other side of Brightside Lane stood a factory of Sanderson Brothers. Slight damage was caused to the partly built new premises of Naylor and Vickers, near the village of Brightside, but the extensive layout of William Jessop and Sons was more seriously affected. Water rose to about four feet in the yard and to about half that depth in several workshops. Some 160 cases of steel, packed for export, were badly damaged, and seven furnaces (each charged with 24 pots) had just been fired, only to be put out by the water. Some recently completed sheds, not yet in use, were wrecked, so the damage at Jessops was considerable.

It was apparent that the size and speed of the flood had greatly diminished and much of the water was flowing back into the distended Don. The flood had run itself out, leaving in its wake widespread grief and destruction. In addition to the deaths and injuries, thousands were without homes or work. Some factories and shops never reopened; in a number of instances, nothing remained to reopen. Bodies were being found weeks afterwards, while others were never traced. In material terms, an accurate balance sheet was virtually impossible (although various valuations were attempted). In human terms, the damage was incalculable.

What can be regarded as official returns differed. According to statistics issued soon after the tragedy by Chief Constable John Jackson, 238 people (made up of 138 males and 100 females, between the ages of two days and 87 years) lost their lives. Of that total, 35 bodies were found but not identified and a further 27 unrecovered. About 130 buildings (houses, factories, shops and inns) were destroyed, some 500 'partially destroyed or damaged' and nearly 5,000 flooded only; 15 bridges were swept away and six others badly damaged; 700 animals (horses, cows, donkeys, pigs, fowls and tame rabbits) were drowned. The General Relief Committee, established almost immediately after the disaster, reported that nearly 800 houses had been destroyed or abandoned and another 4,357 flooded.

Whether or not those returns were absolutely correct (and the chances are they were not) does not really matter. They serve to give a broad picture of the immensity of the horror and devastation brought about by the failure of the Dale Dyke embankment— an occurrence that remains Britain's worst dam disaster. Happily, it is unlikely to be repeated, or even approached, such is the safety factor provided by advanced technology—not to mention modern communications.

Almost before that dreadful night of 11/12 March 1864 broke into dawn and, tauntingly, a day of clear skies and sunshine, questions were being asked. Why had it happened? Who was responsible? Could there be another calamity? Was it manslaughter? Why wasn't adequate warning given? Who was going to pay?

As things turned out, there were serious misgivings about some of the answers....

4 A National Disaster

When the flood rolled remorselessly into Sheffield, the town's two daily newspapers—*The Sheffield Daily Telegraph* and the *Sheffield and Rotherham Independent*—were going to press with their latest editions. Reporters were rounded up and dispatched to the 'river' and it says much for their skill that, without the modern means of communication we take for granted today, they were able quickly to collate an extremely commendable summary of what had occurred and to meet hastily arranged deadlines.

It was about 12.30 a.m. on Saturday, 12 March, when newsmen received the first intimations of an 'unknown' drama. In the dank darkness of the small hours, they gleaned what information they could and their fragmented messages were shaped into a coherent story in the editorial offices. The printing departments, too, were kept at full stretch. Many special editions were produced as additional information arrived and, for several days, the machines were seldom silent. Both newspapers could have sold their maximum output ten times over. Indeed, their offices were besieged by struggling Sheffielders clamouring for the latest intelligence. The *Independent*, apologizing to distant agents for being unable to cope with demand, feared that some dispatched parcels had been 'stolen in transit'. Reports in the *Telegraph* and the *Independent* were reprinted in newspapers throughout Britain, as well as in some overseas countries, and were also used as a basis by other reporters sent from a number of centres to cover what was rightly adjudged a national disaster.

The *Telegraph*, though obviously unaware at the time of anything like the full extent of the tragedy, declared there had been 'one of the most terrible calamities that has ever visited this part of the country'. That early assessment could hardly have been more accurate. The report continued: 'Houses have been washed down, streets have been turned into rivers, great stacks of timber, mingled with pigs, furniture, beds, carts and trees, have been swept on the banks of the Don.' The newspaper told of damage and death near the town centre, adding that 'owing to the suddenness of the catastrophe and the hurry and excitement of the crowd of people now thronging the scene, we have to take much on credit, but the general belief is that the great reservoir at Bradfield has burst and thrown its immense volume of water into the country'.

Similarly, the *Independent* appeared with a short, yet admirable, initial description of what had happened. Their reporters also understood that the Dale Dyke dam had collapsed and 'the enormous mass of water burst down the hillsides with a roar like heaviest thunder, and its roar was the death-knell of many of the unhappy cotters in the valley who were drowned instantaneously in the house from which they had not the slightest chance of escape.... Appalling accounts of the number of missing were transmitted, but we hope they are exaggerated.'

A disaster provides journalistic jam to the circulation bread-and-butter of newspapers and this one supplied enough for many extra helpings. The sales of both dailies soared. For William Christopher Leng, who had started as joint proprietor and managing editor of the *Telegraph* only 71 days previously, the tragedy represented a timely opportunity to show his professional paces. He developed into one of the most influential of provincial editors and, in the years ahead, was to make his presence felt far beyond the boundaries of Sheffield. Leng was forceful and fluent in his writing, courageous when attacking anything he regarded as against the public interest and an unflinching adversary. As one admirer put it: 'He never truckled to any man or any section of men.' The new editor found plenty of scope for his persuasive pen after the failure of the dam.

William Leng, who had just celebrated his thirty-ninth birthday, began his working career as a chemist in his home town of Hull. Even as a young man dispensing potions, he had clear-cut ideas about social reform and was fortunate in being able to disseminate his views in articles which he wrote anonymously for the *Hull Daily Press*. Happily, the editor had the courage to publish the often strongly worded onslaughts on what the enthusiastic Leng saw as injustices. It was said one of his pieces inspired Samuel Plimsoll to crusade for the introduction of the safety load-line on ships. Leng soon acquired his own business as a chemist, but gave it up in 1859 to move to Scotland where he worked for the *Dundee Advertiser*, of which his younger brother John, an equally forthright journalist, was editor.

With financial assistance from Frederick Clifford, the ambitious William Leng became co-owner of *The Sheffield Daily Telegraph* and the first issue under the new régime appeared on 1 January 1864, when the stated intention was unmistakably plain. The *Telegraph*, he announced, was going to be 'inferior to no newspaper in England in the vigour of its management and the literary ability employed upon it'. Leng kept his word and hauled the paper from its knees, transforming it into a powerful and respected voice in the land. His partner, Clifford, was a barrister and journalist and, for a time, was on the parliamentary staff of *The Times* (of which he became assistant editor in 1877). He wrote authoritative articles on legal matters and also acted as the Sheffield paper's London correspondent. Clifford was content to pursue his profession in the capital city and, although he regularly sent hints and advice to Leng (who treated them with the 'utmost deference'), he appears to have been tactful and unobtrusive. Such an arrangement suited Leng very well, for he was a free-ranging editor and niggling interference concerning editorial policy would surely have been intolerable to him. So the partnership worked successfully. Said one of Leng's friends: 'He never saw a man or an institution or a nation suffering wrong but he ranged himself on the side of the sufferers, receiving blows with them and for them and dealing out such return as his great ability enabled him to give. He sought no man's good opinion first. The consciousness that he might be applauded or upbraided for what he wrote never incited him to write or deterred him from writing.'

In March 1864, Leng was an unknown quantity in Sheffield: after he had written about the flood and its repercussions, he was not. A rare talent was at work. Three years later, he was to achieve a triumph by helping to smash those behind the 'Sheffield Outrages'. For years, rattening (damaging machines or depriving workmen of equipment) had been practised in the town by persons whose identity was hidden by a screen of fear and secrecy, to induce non-members to join a trade union. Coercion and terror were

used to get operatives (particularly those in tool-grinding) to toe
the line; failure to comply often meant the stealthy removal of
some vital item (a wheelband or set of tools) which prevented a
defaulter from earning his living. Once the victim had seen 'reason',
the article was replaced as mysteriously as it had vanished. Then
things got out of hand. In extreme cases, workshops were blown
up, there were shootings, at least one murder, injuries and the ham-
stringing of a horse; in addition, threatening letters were sent to
leading industrialists.

With patient probing and scathing editorials, William Leng (in
some personal danger himself) traced the trail of silence back to
William Broadhead, secretary of the Saw Grinders' Union. Eventually, the Government were persuaded to appoint a Royal Commission of Inquiry into union affairs. It was only by the promise of
indemnity against criminal proceedings and punishment that some
of Broadhead's henchmen were induced to give evidence against
him. Finally Broadhead, also legally safeguarded by a certificate of
indemnity, had little option but to confess to a number of 'outrages'.
Although he remained a free man by law, it did not prevent the
local magistrates from revoking his publican's licence—for Broadhead was landlord of the Royal George, Carver Street, which also
served as union headquarters. Other disclosures of rattening, in
which Broadhead was not implicated, were made to the commission
and 12 of the 60 unions in Sheffield were involved. As for Broadhead, friends raised enough money for him to go to the United
States, but he returned to Sheffield where, in 1879, he died a
'broken-spirited man'. For that, he had largely to thank Leng and
Chief Constable Jackson who, between them, amassed some damning evidence. By no means everyone agreed with the 'trial' of
Broadhead who, it was held in some quarters, was an over-zealous
trade unionist anxious to strengthen the movement and who had
done much to better the lot of the working man. One view was that
he was more misguided than criminal.

Charles Reade's novel, *Put Yourself in His Place*, published in
1870, had rattening as its theme and ended with a colourful description of a dam bursting and the resultant flood. Reade hardly
deviates from the facts of the real disaster when it comes to the
layout and measurements of the Dale Dyke embankment and he
also tells how the waters cause havoc at 'Poma Bridge' (Malin
Bridge) and 'Hillsborough' (Sheffield). In the book, William Leng

is 'Mr Holdfast', a broad-chested man who has 'an agreeable face, a mouth full of iron resolution and a slight, humorous dimple at the corners'. The character, 'Grotait', is based on William Broadhead, and the chief constable who unmasks him is 'Ransome' (John Jackson), a 'very tall man, with a handsome, dignified head'.

The real-life Chief Constable outshone his fictional counterpart. Hailing from the Lake District, John Jackson joined the Lancashire County Constabulary when he was just twenty-three. Serving in a district between Oldham and Manchester, he had a tough apprenticeship during which he helped to quell Chartist riots. He so impressed his seniors that, in 1848, he was appointed Oldham's first Chief Constable. He was only twenty-six and had been a policeman for little more than three years! John Jackson continued to reveal outstanding qualities of leadership, tenacity and courage, and was odds-on favourite to fill the vacant position of Chief Constable of Sheffield. He took up his new, onerous duties on 1 January 1859. By coincidence, it was the same day on which work began on the Dale Dyke dam. Jackson was always remembered for his bravery during the night of the Great Flood and became a minor legend in his own lifetime. He was recalled as having a 'tall, rather gaunt figure, a firm rather stern face, though with kindly eyes, and a profile not altogether unlike that of the Great Duke'.

John Jackson was only thirty-six when he became head of the Sheffield Police Force which, by 1864, comprised about 30 officers and about 180 constables. He was then paid about £400 annually, out of which he was 'required to purchase and keep a horse'. Jackson built the force into one of the most efficient in the land and remained at the helm until death removed him from it on 30 September 1898.

If Sheffield had reason to respect Jackson, it was no more than he deserved. The same went for William Leng. Had he not been in his office in Aldine Court, just off the High Street, when the disaster news broke, Leng would have been summoned (if, indeed, he ever allowed himself to be *summoned*) from his home in Victoria Road, Broomhall Park, nearly a mile away. This man, who once declared that 'I carry the whole journal in my head,' would want to be supervising the biggest on-the-spot story to come his way. He normally worked a fourteen-hour day (often longer) and seemed to possess inexhaustible reserves of energy. By nature, Leng was a kindly man, but he never allowed sentiment to cloud what he saw as his duty nor did he permit it to influence his professional judgement. He expected, and usually got, an all-out effort from his staff and he was not above expressing his appreciation (frequently in tangible form) of competent and loyal service. A journalist who worked under Leng in the mid-1860s recalled: 'He inspired those about him with a sense of comradeship and zeal for the success of his enterprise.... Servility he could not tolerate. There was an air of freedom about the place which made service under such a man singularly pleasurable.'

The building in Bank Street of the *Sheffield and Rotherham Independent* was also the scene of feverish activity that night as the dramatic details were pieced together. The newspaper was controlled, as it was for many years, by the Leader family—at that time by Robert, who was fifty-four, assisted by his sons, John Daniel and Robert Eadon. It was much older than the *Telegraph* (founded in 1855), having been established in 1819 by a printer, Henry Andrew Bacon, from whom Robert Leader's father bought it in 1829. Robert himself was then twenty and an apprentice on the *Sheffield Iris* of which James Montgomery, the poet and reformer, was editor. Leader later joined his father and became sole proprietor of the *Independent* in 1842, eventually handing over to his sons in 1875. Robert Leader contributed much to Sheffield during his industrious lifetime. He entered keenly the public affairs of the town and became an alderman; and his vigorously voiced opinions were greatly respected. His newspaper reflected the predominantly liberal-cum-radical views of Sheffield, but tended to follow rather than lead public thought. The *Independent*, which developed from a weekly to a daily in 1861, lacked the flair Leng injected into the *Telegraph*, but it presented a stolid, reliable face and was probably regarded by its publishers as more respectable than its rival. In a sense, this was strange, for Leng was an avowed Conservative and his paper strongly supported the party, which was not the easiest way to win popularity in the town at that time. There was little professional love lost between the Leaders and Leng, but the battle between the *Telegraph* and the *Independent* resulted in Sheffield having a news service bettered by no other provincial town.

The only other newspaper in Sheffield in 1864, *The Sheffield Times*, made its appearance once a week under the enterprising eye of thirty-seven-year-old Samuel Harrison, son of a Wesleyan minister in Somerset. Harrison had been editor for ten years and, although he was unable to compete directly with the two dailies, he was bright enough not to try and, whenever possible, struck out on his own in pursuit of fresh angles. He was hardworking and inventive and, during his brief life, developed a number of ideas for speeding-up the production of newspapers. For a young man, he had unusual depth of perception.

When he realized he could not hope to emulate Leng and Leader in their widespread day-to-day coverage of the disaster, Harrison shrewdly anticipated that something more permanent would be both acceptable to the public and profitable to him. So, not long after the Dale Dyke failure, he published *A Complete History of the Great Flood at Sheffield* describing it, in a sub-title, as 'A True and Authentic Narrative'. It was based on reports and illustrated by engravings from photographs which had appeared in his news-paper, plus 'many interesting incidents that have never yet appeared in print and a full report of the inquest, lists of the dead and missing etc.'. The publication was 'beautifully printed in large type' and the price of it, 'elegantly bound in cloth', was 2s 6d, while a 'cheap edition' cost a shilling.

Harrison also announced that twenty different views of the flood damage on two large sheets could be bought for 6d and 4d res-pectively, adding that the pictures 'may be had separately' on superior notepaper, or on card, at a penny a time. Samuel Harrison was industry personified, for he seldom stopped working at his business pursuits, although he did find time to beget a large family after his marriage in 1853, six sons and four daughters surviving him. With all those mouths to feed, it is little wonder he rarely rested. He had only one illness in his life and died of it in February 1871 when he was only forty-four.

I have dwelt at some length upon Sheffield's newspapers, and the men who ran them, because they commanded considerable influence and power in the town. Newspapers in those days stood almost unchallenged and appeared to enjoy more freedom than do their present-day national and provincial descendants. They were less inhibited by libel laws and what they had to say was often quoted as 'gospel'. For most people in the mid-nineteenth century, with not much money and outlooks to match, the newspaper was usually the only medium through which they could see the outside world. If they could not read, then they heard the news second-hand from those who could. Those in high places might pretend not to heed what the Fourth Estate said, but an editor could make or break an individual and even topple a government. The incredible John Thadeus Delane, who began the first of his thirty-six years as editor of *The Times* in 1841 when he was only twenty-three, showed just how devastatingly independent of a national administration a newspaper could be; he underlined the lesson when he attacked the Government for its inept handling of the war in the Crimea and, despite threats, continued to publish the revealing dispatches from his reporter at the front, William Howard Russell. In a similar way, the editors of Sheffield mirrored that cherished freedom from official interference and none more so than William Leng (later Sir William), whose military-like figure, dressed in a closely-buttoned frockcoat and sporting a flower, became almost as familiar as his incisive writings.

There was plenty to write about the Great Flood of Sheffield. Long before dawn, parties of rescuers prodded the thick mud and delved into the pools of water for bodies and, less hopefully, for survivors. They worked by lantern, by what capricious light was offered by the moon and by the subdued illumination of those gas-lamps which had not been put out of action. Desperate searches went on in the town and at Malin Bridge and Hillsborough where, not long before, had stood rows of houses and knots of factories. News filtered through to groups of toilers, often unaware of what had occurred in the next street, that the night was hiding a tragedy of tremendous proportions. While many people gave what small assistance was possible in the darkness, others, ignorant of the terrible effects of the calamity but attracted by an intuitive sense of drama, found it exciting just wandering around. As the light improved, a large crowd gathered at Lady's Bridge and were fascinated by the still fast-flowing water and the floating wreckage. From time to time, a body broke the surface. The onlookers fell silent for a moment before finding something else upon which to rivet their attention.

As the waters subsided, so were revealed vast quantities of muck in which were embedded broken bodies, rickety tables and chairs, bloated pigs and horses, machines, masonry, wood and iron. Already, it was beginning to smell. Horsemen rode clattering through the streets, policemen clawed their way into dangerous piles of debris, some of the bereaved were demanding retribution and others had just enough strength to weep outside scarred and sagging homes. There was grief-stricken disbelief at what had happened. Harrison wrote: 'They had no idea that sleeping up above Bradfield, eight miles among the hills, was a power of such terrific potency.... An earthquake, a volcano or a sirocco would have excited no greater astonishment.'

Most Sheffielders slept through that terrible night and many set off for work in the morning unaware of anything untoward. Not for long were they in ignorance as rumours began circulating at an alarming rate. Some of the fallacious tales were not as dreadful as the truth, but each one added to the anxiety. It was firmly maintained, for instance, that one of the reservoirs at Redmires was about to discharge its contents upon the town at any moment and it was not difficult to persuade minds, already troubled and excited, that another catastrophe was imminent. Ironically, some days later, it was found necessary to make a few minor repairs to a dam at Redmires, but the story that it was about to disintegrate was pure fantasy.

As the sun rose above the horizon, the truth was exposed in all its horror. One observer declared: 'In describing a scene of destruction so awful, the mind becomes bewildered by the terrible nature and extent of the calamity. Never has a day dawned on a more complete wreck than are the lower parts of the town this morning.'

Another, correctly judging the worst-hit area to be between Malin Bridge and Neepsend, said: 'A populous district has been almost obliterated from the face of the earth.' He calculated that enough timber had been deposited by the river near the centre of Sheffield 'to build a village'.

Many sufferers had wandered without purpose during the night and, at the police station, a 'little crowd of ill-dressed people' squatted silently around a fire seeking what comfort they could from its warmth. Chief Constable Jackson, who had directed operations as best he could throughout the dark hours, called at early light on the Mayor, Thomas Jessop. Without delay, the Mayor accompanied Jackson to some of the badly damaged districts to see for himself what had befallen so many of his fellow citizens. Jessop, normally a jovial man with a dry sense of humour, was so moved by the experience that he could scarcely refrain from bursting into tears. He was in his sixty-first year and a wealthy steel manufacturer, now heading the business founded by his father, William, in about 1830. Despite his financial and social position (he was also a magistrate and, currently, Master Cutler), Jessop had never lost the common touch. Success had not swollen his head and he was, they said, still the same good old Tommy Jessop he had always been in less prosperous times. He felt a genuine sympathy for the flood sufferers, most of whom were in the artisan and poorest classes: the ones who could least afford the slightest setback. Jessop had a melancholy tour around the area of the The Wicker, now thickly coated with runny mud and which, a little earlier, had been 'an immense river capable of floating a ship of the Warrior class'. As another put it: 'The Wicker was like a dirty disused dry-dock, full of filth and wreckage. The cellars were full of semi-fluids and the fire engines of the insurance companies in the town were employed for many days clearing them.'

Jessop watched men digging out bodies, some almost unrecognizable as such. He noticed that the front of the Manchester Railway Hotel had been stove in and that walls of houses and shops had been smashed and lamp-standards bent to the ground. Picking his way through slime and trash, he looked on as shopkeepers shovelled silt from their doorless and windowless premises, their stock rotting in flooded storerooms below. Every now and again a shout summoned earnest-faced rescue workers to another spot to pull out another bedraggled, lifeless figure. Down at the Midland Station, where early morning trains had been late departing, stationmaster George James was organizing a clear-up operation during which several more bodies were recovered. Some harrowing scenes were revealed in the sunlight of that Saturday morning.

The Mayor chatted consolingly to a number of the afflicted before going to the Town Hall, where he spent most of the remaining day in urgent consultation. He conferred with John Yeomans, the Town Clerk (a position he held from June 1859 until his death in April 1887) and the Borough Coroner (John Webster), he listened to numerous reports and, when news arrived that there had been some looting in the Hillsborough area, he arranged with the officer commanding at the nearby barracks to dispatch a detachment of armed soldiers to patrol the streets. The Mayor also caused a letter to be sent, through the Town Clerk, to the Home Secretary, Sir George Grey, outlining the situation. Yeomans wrote:

Sir, I am directed by the Mayor to inform you that a dreadful calamity has just happened to Sheffield by the bursting of a dam belonging to the Water Works Company.

The dam, which contained 95 acres of water, burst about midnight, and rushing with fearful velocity down the deep valley below, swept everything before it—causing awful destruction to life and property.

One hundred bodies of men, women and children now lie at the Sheffield Union House, but few of them have been identified, for whole families have perished.

Many other bodies have been taken elsewhere and some found as far as Rotherham and even Doncaster, so that at present the number of lives sacrificed is not ascertained.

The Mayor requests me to ask that a Government Inspector be sent down to enquire into the cause of this dreadful catastrophe.

I send you two of the Sheffield papers, which contain other particulars.

During the day, John Webster opened the inquest. It was held at the Union Workhouse, part of which (as indicated in the Town Clerk's letter) was being used as a makeshift mortuary, and the jury had the task of looking at some of the many corpses laid out on fresh straw side by side, in long rows. The victims ranged from infants to the aged, the faces of some reflecting terror, others a serenity associated with contented sleep; some bodies were grossly misshapen and a few had name-tags strung round their necks. Evidence of identification was taken in only four cases, the coroner remarking it would be unnecessary to hear more as 'it is certain that they have all died from the effects of the flood'. The bodies selected were those of Thomas Elston, the ailing blade-grinder, and his wife, Elizabeth, who died with their infant son at home in Neepsend Lane, Keziah Eaton, aged fifty (she and her husband drowned attempting to rescue their pig) and Henry Fairest, a rod-roller of forty-seven, who died while on night-shift at the Philadelphia Steel Works and who was survived by his wife, Ann, and four children. The coroner then adjourned the inquest until 23 March and the jury, of which Henry Pawson was foreman, were told to hold themselves in readiness to visit the site of the broken dam. The following day, Sunday, John Webster went to his office

at 14, St James's Row—overlooking St Peter's Church (now Sheffield Cathedral)—sat at his desk and, on a sheet of bright blue
notepaper, wrote in flowing hand to the Home Secretary:

Sir, A fearful accident has occurred at Sheffield by the bursting of a reservoir belonging to the Waterworks Company. The
destruction of life is terrible—nearly two hundred bodies of men,
women and children have already been collected.

As it is impossible to hold an inquest in each case, as very few
will probably be identified and the cause of death is the same in
all, I have concluded not to hold an inquest, except on two or
three bodies identified yesterday, which will be sufficient for a
full inquiry into the cause of this most dreadful occurrence. I
trust that the course I have taken will be deemed satisfactory.

The jurors wish me to intimate that a Government Inspector
should be sent down to make a careful examination of the works
at the reservoir, and to give evidence at the adjourned hearing
on the 23rd instant, at the Town Hall, Sheffield.

John Webster had been coroner for two years. He was a leading
public figure in the town, where he had been in practice as a
solicitor for nearly thirty years, and was renowned for his straight
talking. Indeed, his sharp tongue sometimes ran away with him and
his acid comments at the resumed inquest were to provoke a storm
of criticism. His honest intentions were never in doubt although
the manner in which he sometimes expressed them was not always
appreciated. Mr Webster was dogmatic. There was hardly a subject
upon which he did not have an emphatic view. 'Even when he was
not found engaged in the duties of his profession,' a contemporary
reflected, 'he could be found expressing his opinions—always clearly,
sometimes tartly and generally positively—on various questions of
public interest.'

On receipt of Webster's letter, the Home Secretary scribbled
a note to his personal secretary telling him to reply that the action
adopted to limit the inquest to a few bodies was satisfactory. It was
as well for, just after the formal opening on Saturday, Webster had
instructed the Chief Constable to have the following notice printed
and circulated:

PUBLIC NOTICE
THE
GREAT FLOOD

I am instructed by JOHN WEBSTER ESQ, CORONER, to give PUBLIC NOTICE that it is not his intention to hold INQUESTS on any of the bodies of persons lying in his DISTRICT who lost their lives in the GREAT FLOOD this Morning, with the exception of those viewed by the Jury at the Sheffield Union House this Afternoon, and their Relatives and Friends will be permitted to move them and make the necessary arrangements for their interment without delay.

It will however be necessary to furnish the Police with the names and ages of all Bodies prior to their removal, and the Persons removing them must give their own names and addresses to the Constables on duty at the places from whence they are taken.

A number of Bodies are at the undermentioned places awaiting identification and removal, viz:

THE SHEFFIELD UNION HOUSE, KELHAM STREET
THE SPORTSMAN'S INN, OWLERTON
MR. ARMITAGE'S BEERHOUSE, OWLERTON
THE SHAKESPEARE INN, HILLSBRO'
THE QUEEN'S HOTEL, Langset Road
DO ROSE INN, near Bottom Barracks Gate
DO NEW BARRACK TAVERN, Bottom Road
DO BARRACK HOSPITAL
DO OLD FLOUR MILL
DO NEW VICTORIA HOTEL
DO YEW TREE INN, Malin Bridge
Town Hall,
Sheffield.   JOHN JACKSON
March 12, 1864   Chief Constable

The posters, printed at the offices of the *Independent*, were promptly distributed and affixed to boards and walls upon which there were already copies of a directive issued by the Mayor:

JESSOP MAYOR
PUBLIC NOTICE
DESTRUCTION OF LIFE
PERSONS are requested to give information to the TOWN HALL

of DEAD BODIES Found, so that they may be removed to SHEF-
FIELD UNION HOUSE for identification, and to wait the Coroner's
Inquest before Burial.

PROPERTY AND GOODS

PERSONS are requested to ASSIST the POLICE FORCE in Re-
covering and Restoring Property and Goods of all kinds to the
Owners.

Persons taking possession of Property and Goods and not
restoring them will be proceeded against.

Persons requiring information to apply to MR. JACKSON, Chief
Constable, at the Town Hall.

Town Hall,

March 12, 1864

THOMAS JESSOP, Mayor

The flurry of announcements and exchange of letters continued,
including the following from the Home Office to the Town Clerk:

Sir George Grey has heard with deep concern of the dreadful
accident which has happened at Sheffield by the bursting of a
dam belonging to the Waterworks Company, and Mr Rawlinson,
C.E., connected with the Local Government Act Office, has been
instructed to proceed at once to Sheffield, and to communicate
on his arrival with the Mayor and Coroner, in order to render
all possible assistance in the enquiry into the cause of this
catastrophe.

In case, after conferring with Mr Rawlinson, the Mayor should
be of opinion that any further assistance is requisite for this
purpose, Sir George Grey will direct another gentleman to proceed without delay, to Sheffield, to be associated with Mr
Rawlinson.

Action was being taken at commendable speed, that letter from
Whitehall reaching Sheffield on the Monday afternoon following the
disaster. That is to overtake events, however, and, back on that
wretchedly confused Saturday, detailed reports were reaching the
town that the River Don had carried its cargo through Rotherham
and on to Doncaster, which is 18 miles from Sheffield. At Rotherham, Police Sergeant Ireland noticed an 'extraordinary' rise in the
level of the river at about 2.30 a.m. He was able to warn those
living close to the banks and the sleepy-eyed residents, more fascina-

ted than frightened, tumbled out of bed and, having surveyed the scene, went back home to collect ropes and long poles. The reason for this was soon apparent: the water was bobbing with articles of all kinds and the inhabitants of Rotherham, some in boats, fished out what they could from the fast-flowing river. Shouts of surprised joy greeted the capture of a table in reasonable condition or of a three-legged chair that could be repaired. The body of a woman, in her nightdress (probably Elizabeth Trickett, of Malin Bridge), was hauled out, as were those of a young girl and a near-naked man. The flood spread over hundreds of acres of low-lying land before reaching Doncaster where the corpse of a woman, wearing earrings and a brass wedding ring, was recovered. It was hours before the Don returned to anything like its normal level.

The craving for news about missing persons was never satisfied. Stories arrived at Sheffield throughout the day, to be exaggerated at every telling, and crowds hung around the Town Hall anxiously awaiting fresh information. Scuffles broke out at the offices of the *Telegraph* and the *Independent* as people strove to snatch copies of the latest editions. The newspapers faced an impossible task attempting to meet an overwhelming demand and, on that Saturday alone, the *Independent* sold 54,000 copies. For their part, the *Telegraph* claimed that had they been able to print a quarter of a million copies it would not have been enough. Before the day was out, hardly a newspaper in the country had not received a report of the disaster. Soon there would be another flood—this time of thousands of sightseers, as well as leading reporters from the nation's foremost newspapers.

The Dale Dyke calamity was being already compared with the dam failure which had occurred at Holmfirth twelve years previously. That tragedy at Bilberry reservoir, some five miles south of Huddersfield, and only about ten miles from the latest collapse, had resulted in 95 deaths. The burst took place at about 12.30 a.m. on Thursday, 5 February 1852, the water pouring down a steep valley to kill, maim and destroy. In that case, the jury had strongly condemned the water board's commissioners, engineers and overseers for culpable neglect and mismanagement and regretted that, because the commissioners constituted a corporation, it was not possible to bring in a verdict of manslaughter. It was ironic coincidence that the chief engineer of the Bilberry reservoir was George

Leather, uncle of John Towlerton Leather, the consulting engineer for Dale Dyke. For a time, a rumour went the rounds that they were one and the same person—an error upon which the *Telegraph*, to the embarrassment of William Leng, based an incisive leading article.

The Sheffield disaster was much greater than that at Holmfirth and it was not long before word was abroad that the works of Dale Dyke had been badly built and that, in any case, there had been ample time to give warning of danger. Inhabitants near the dam now told of their doubts about the structure and of the inadequate means of disposing of surplus water. Some even went as far as alleging that the engineers were 'well aware that the foundation was defective, but they resolved to run the risk as so much money had been expended'. The critical cat had been let out of the bag—and it was spitting. One Bradfield resident rightly pointed out there had been 'five or six hours' between the discovery of the crack and the failure of the embankment. It was equally arguable, of course, that officials had not raised a general alarm because they genuinely foresaw no possibility of the dam collapsing. Most people in the vicinity were in no mood to listen, however. Hindsight was easier and there was a great deal of speculation long before the official inquiry got under way.

Meanwhile, the immediate duty was to help the sufferers. An eyewitness described the plight of people in the Loxley Valley area, a picture repeated in other districts: 'The utterly destitute condition of some of the inhabitants is such as to require the most prompt assistance if a fate even worse than that they have escaped is to be averted—that of starvation. If the unhappy victims of this calamity had been dropped in a desolate desert island, their condition could hardly have been worse. Destitute of resources of all kinds, without homes, food, clothing or fire, their case requires immediate help. Nor can it be other than that for some time to come; they must rely upon the bounty of the benevolent for support.'

A nineteen-year-old girl never forgot what she saw at Malin Bridge, Owlerton and Hillsborough, and recollected years later: 'The country looked like a vast lake, upon which were floating the dead carcasses of cattle and horses, timber, furniture and portions of houses. Here and there the forlorn ruins of what once were happy homes showed themselves above the waters.... The flood caught many families like rats in a trap and death overtook them in their sleep. The water had blotted out familiar features of the district until it was nearly unrecognizable.'

In half-fallen houses, scantily-dressed adults and children strove to make some repair, to salvage furniture from waterlogged rooms and to rid their parlours of stinking silt. Some could stand it no longer and were led away weeping by friends; others left their homes for good and went to live with relatives in unaffected parts of Sheffield. A few sat down helplessly amid the ruins; there was nowhere to go, nothing they wanted to do. There were large gaps where yesterday houses had stood. Some streets were impassable, bridges were down and parts of roads washed away.

Public houses—some of them damaged—were converted into temporary resting-places for the dead. Relatives went inside to retrieve their kith and kin and, as often as not, emerged empty-handed. As some bodies were recovered miles away, there was little chance of their being located by families and friends. Lists were published, it is true, but how many men, for instance, could have fitted the description 'medium height, light-coloured hair, between 35 and 45', or something as vague? Even then, some bodies were so disfigured as to present identification problems. It is a macabre thought, but how many were buried mistakenly for someone else? The Sheffield Union House was the principal reception centre and, within a few hours of the flood's first on-slaught, more than a hundred bodies were taken there. It was a sickening sight, although efforts had been made to clean off mud and blood and each victim had been partly covered by a sheet. Sobbing and screaming broke out as relatives filed past hoping, and yet dreading, to recognize a face.

Whatever misgivings there were about the failure of the dam and some aspects of the aftermath, the response to calls to aid the sufferers was swift and laudable. Mayor Jessop sent letters to the town's leading citizens inviting them to a meeting on the Monday morning to consider how best to give help. He also wrote to mayors throughout the country asking them to encourage the in-auguration of subscription funds. During the next few weeks, thousands of pounds were contributed by high and low; there were also many gifts of clothing, offers of practical assistance from businessmen and the donation of a day's pay from hundreds of workmen. Quick action was taken by the boards of the Sheffield and the Ecclesall Guardians, who sliced through normal red tape and instructed their officers to dispense relief to *bona fide* sufferers whether or not they lived within the regions maintained by the authorities. As things turned out, problems arose because so many organizations were attempting, in all good faith, to administer charity. Inevitably, some 'victims' cashed in two or three times, while a number of genuine cases missed out altogether. Some disgruntled applicants remonstrated and called after departing officials: 'You'll know where to come when you want the poor rates.' There were, too, a few fraudulent claims, but on the whole the errors made by the authorities were of commission and not omission.

In the churches and chapels on Sunday the favourite text was 'Who is thy Neighbour?' and sermons incorporated appeals for the giving of kind and kindness. Far greater 'congregations' were out looking at the devastation. Thousands of eagle-eyed visitors came by train, carriage, cart, horseback and on foot from many miles around. Local bus proprietors were not slow to capitalize on a unique opportunity. Nor were they the only ones. Enterprising freelances, remarkably well equipped with coaches and donkey-carts, were prepared (for a price) to convey sightseers to the desolated districts. Destination boards, announcing the departure of transport to 'Hillsborough and the Ruins', were on display. Photographers did brisk business selling views of the damaged areas; one character disposed of copies of hymns hastily composed for the occasion at 'remunerative prices' and hotels and beerhouses did a roaring trade. The visitors got their money's-worth, for there was plently to see—real-life drama performed in their very presence. They were passed by despairing men and women travelling in the opposite direction and towing carts loaded with mud-spattered remnants. Many day trippers found it necessary to take away souvenirs—a wedge of timber, a broken brick or, perhaps, a child's toy—but the military were at hand to prevent serious looting.

The first batch of journalists from out of town had arrived the previous day. Among them was a representative of *The Newcastle Daily Journal*, a man toughened by reporting tragedy. Still painfully clear in the memory were those sorrowful scenes of January 1862 at the pithead of Hartley New Colliery, Northumberland, when, deep down in the coal mine, two hundred entombed men and boys slowly died after the shaft had been blocked by the collapse of a pumping engine. Even this newspaperman was shocked by the extent of the Sheffield disaster and remembered that when he stepped from the train on to the 'wet and slimy' platform at the Midland Station, he was aware of an atmosphere 'more than sufficiently dismal'—and he wasn't alluding to the smoke. The reporter had been dispatched following the receipt of a telegram telling of a flood sweeping down upon Sheffield 'with the irresistible fury of an avalanche' in the course of which 'hundreds of lives were lost'. Whatever doubts the *Journal* man may have entertained vanished and he recorded: 'Dreadful as this vague statement was, I regret to state that it does not exceed the truth.'

'Wherever you go,' he wrote on Sunday morning, 'it is impossible to fail to observe more or less the effects of the inundation. The whole of the town is in a state of intense excitement, numbers of persons having been patrolling the streets nearly all night. Business of every kind appeared to be at a standstill yesterday, except that connected with the sale of special editions of the newspapers.' In a later message, he said that on the Sabbath, too, 'the whole population appeared to be out of doors, congregating at the various points where the loss of life and property had been the greatest'. The reporter added that some visitors 'conducted themselves in the most unseemly manner, considering the solemn event that had brought them there'.

The sudden invasion of Sheffield by so many newspapermen stretched the resources of the Post Office to the very limit. The small telegraph staff, inadequately equipped, experienced considerable difficulty 'in getting through the wires the vivid descriptive articles forwarded to the papers'. The general postal staff also had their problems, for the mail was much heavier than usual.

The first of the funerals took place on Monday morning. Unclaimed bodies presented the Board of Guardians responsible for the Sheffield Union House with a tricky situation. For health reasons alone, it was obvious the corpses could not remain on the premises for long. Such was the public demand for the 'decent treatment' of the dead, however, that the utmost diplomacy was essential. The board's chairman, Alderman George Lemon Saunders, and his colleagues decided that bodies unidentified by Tuesday would have to be interred in the General Cemetery. It was to be done with dignity and separate graves were dug in various spots to eliminate any suggestion of a mass burial. In the event, the funerals of the 'unknown' attracted very few onlookers. Relatives could never be certain whether or not their loved ones had been committed to the earth, however, and pathetic advertisements appeared in the 'Lost and Found' columns of the local newspapers. Anxious pleas from the bereaved for information of missing fathers or daughters were interspersed with inquiries about lost terriers and tabby cats.

Despite the hundreds of homeless and jobless, life had to go on and it did so not only beneath an umbrella of industrial smoke (which seemed not to have lessened) but also under a cloud of some confusion and criticism. The very soul of Sheffield had been subjected to severe shock from which it would take a long time to recover. The seemingly impossible task of clearing the rubble and rubbish began, but in some places it was weeks before much difference was apparent. Repairs and reconstruction took months. In some cases, it was never attempted.

A fear existed that disease would add to the miseries if roads were not soon cleansed, cellars dried and sewers unclogged. Interiors of some damaged houses contained unsavoury remains of animals, while soggy timber, carcasses and heaps of muck accumulated in the streets. It was more than just unsightly: it stank. The Town Council's Health Committee, who were not always the most efficient body in mid-Victorian Sheffield, arranged for the distribution of chloride of lime and quicklime to inhabitants with printed instructions as to their use. Similar measures were adopted to deal with piles of wreckage being collected on open land. Fire appliances were used to flush out choked sewers. The Highway Board and Improvement Commissioners, taking 'prompt and efficient measures', detailed a hundred carts for the removal from the streets of 'an immense quantity of mud and sand', some of which had been shovelled from houses. Other organizations rallied round and carried out valuable work, but one is left with the impression that the operations lacked central control. One of Sheffield's undoubted handicaps was that there were too many fingers in a crumbly civic pie. By adopting the Local Government Act a few weeks later, the Town Council gained the power to improve matters considerably as they were then able to control more of what we today accept as public services and facilities.

Thomas Jessop lost no time in keeping his promise to help those in distress. He presided at a meeting of the town's most

influential manufacturers, merchants, bankers and 'gentlemen' and
at once had their wholehearted support. Although there was a
strong and understandable temptation to discuss possible causes
of the dam failure and to impute blame, those present showed
admirable restraint. Samuel Roberts and George Hounsfield, two
of the waterworks company's directors, displayed courage by attending the meeting for a short while. Having been advised that they
could not make a donation on behalf of the company, they had
come along (said Hounsfield) as individuals to demonstrate their
approval of the worthy cause, to make personal subscriptions and
publicly to express their sorrow and sympathy for what had
happened. It was not in their power (added Roberts) to comment
on the reason for the accident, because they did not know it, but
'every explanation shall be given to the town at large as soon as
possible'. The two men then hastened to a gathering of their
fellow directors.

The public meeting, meanwhile, which had been punctuated by
cheers and applause as various financial gifts and offers were
announced, was adjourned until the next day, when further
promised contributions quickly raised the total to a staggering
£12,000. That was only a start. During the ensuing weeks, sums
ranging from a few shillings to a thousand pounds poured in from
city, town and village. Each of the major steel manufacturers in
Sheffield gave £200, George Hadfield (one of the town's two M.P.s
and a substantial shareholder of the waterworks company) donated
£500, Queen Victoria £200, the Home Secretary £50, the Duke of
Norfolk and Earl Fitzwilliam £1,000 each, and Lord Wharncliffe
and the Mayor £200 each. The dam's consulting engineer, J. T.
Leather, sent £100. From rich and poor, from affluent businessmen
to schoolchildren, from the Archbishop of York, the Prince of
Wales and Florence Nightingale—the money flowed in. The mayors
of other towns organized relief funds, church dignitaries preached
on Sheffield's need of succour, and the newspapers allowed no one
to forget the tragedy.

The Mayor, in addition to presiding over meetings of the General
Relief Committee, was made honorary treasurer of the fund. An
executive committee was elected, as was a sanitary committee;
also formed were 11 district committees, the duty of whose members
was to tour distressed areas and prepare lists of those in urgent
need. Yet another committee was to ascertain the number thrown

out of work due to lost tools and to help them to find other jobs. The call for aid was being magnificently answered.

Other meetings held in the town were concerned with less altruistic, though equally realistic, actions. Millowners and proprietors of other factories who had suffered material damage wanted to know just what compensation they were going to get—and when, where and how. They had in their possession what they regarded as a watertight clause in the Act of Parliament obtained by the company in 1853. It read: 'That the said Company shall and they are hereby required from time to time, and at all times for ever hereafter, to pay and make good to the owners, lessees and occupiers of all mills, manufactories, buildings, lands and grounds, and to every person whomsoever all loss, cost, charges, sum and sums of money, damages and expenses whatsoever, and for all injury of what nature or kind soever, as well immediate as consequential which such owners, lessees, or occupiers, or other persons, may suffer, incur, pay, expend, or be put into by reason of, or in the consequence of, the failure or giving way of reservoirs, embankments, watercourses, or other works of the said Company.'

The jargon was impossible, but it boiled down to the unmistakable fact that the company were called upon to pay for any damage or injury caused by a defect in any part of their reservoir or dam. There were no doubts in the minds of those at the meeting that the company were liable; it was written in black and white. A committee was elected, with Edward Vickers as chairman, to act on behalf of all present. Within twenty-four hours the committee met to consider a reply from the waterworks company which stated, in effect, that the directors were anxious to discover if the company were liable to pay for all damages caused by the flood and that a case was being submitted to a 'high legal authority to determine this point'. The property owners must have been nonplussed. It seemed things were not so cut and dried after all. What, they asked, were the company up to? Surely they were not trying to evade their responsibilities or to obscure the issue? The committee (not the only one in Sheffield with similar problems) decided to seek legal advice themselves and their faith was somewhat restored when they heard from Sir Hugh Cairns that, in his view, the company were liable to compensate all who had suffered damage and loss. They felt distinctly better, for Cairns (later Earl Cairns) was regarded by many as 'the first lawyer of his time'.

The House of Commons had been officially informed of the Sheffield disaster as soon as possible by John Arthur Roebuck, the town's other M.P., who, apparently unaware of correspondence between Whitehall and Sheffield Town Hall, asked the Home Secretary if he would send an inspector to investigate the cause. Sir George Grey replied that he had already made the necessary arrangements, adding that he had read of the tragedy with 'deep concern'.

Roebuck, who was temporarily to lose some of his popularity in Sheffield because of his tendency to side with the waterworks company after the flood, was ebullience personified. He was a grandson of Dr John Roebuck, of Sheffield, who founded the Carron Iron Works in Scotland who had befriended and financed James Watt. Roebuck, J. A., was only thirty-one when he first entered the House as M.P. for Bath in 1832. From the outset, he declared himself an 'independent member' and, such was his outspokenness, he quickly earned the nickname of 'Tear-'Em'. He could never be charged with physical or moral cowardice and once, in one of his weekly political pamphlets, Roebuck strongly criticized the equally uncompromising John Black, editor of the *Morning Chronicle*, who smartly issued a challenge to a duel with pistols. The unlawful tragi-comedy took place on 19 November 1835, when each man fired twice and missed (Roebuck was said to have done so on purpose), while their seconds almost became embroiled in an ungentlemanly punch-up.

After his rejection by Bath, Roebuck became M.P. for Sheffield in May 1849, being returned for further terms in 1852, 1857, 1859 and 1865. He was defeated in 1868, but regained the Sheffield seat in 1874 and held it until 1878 when the Tory Government made him a privy councillor.

Roebuck, whose bluntness and volatile style appealed to Sheffielders, achieved his biggest political triumph in 1855 when he successfully moved a resolution calling for an investigation into the Government's inept management of affairs in the Crimea and, as a result, brought down the Prime Minister, Lord Aberdeen, and his administration. Although he frequently disregarded logic, Roebuck had supreme confidence in his own ability, had a gift for oratory and was a stern denouncer. His steamroller tactics were not always welcomed in the House, however, and Lord John Russell once said of him: 'His speeches began with a strong exordium and ended with an admirable peroration, but lacked proof or substance in the middle'. By 1864, the little firebrand had lost some of his earlier combustion and he had become a little dull at the edges; for all that, he was still a force with which to be reckoned and could sway audiences with the compelling magic of his personality. Roebuck's fellow M.P., George Hadfield, had been first returned by Sheffield (his native town) in 1852. For years, however, he lived in Manchester where he was in practice as an attorney for nearly half a century. He had grace and wealth; Roebuck was less well off. Both died in 1879, Hadfield leaving almost £250,000; Roebuck, £1,500.

At about the time that Roebuck was asking the Home Secretary to send an investigator to Sheffield, the man already appointed was preparing to leave London. He boarded an express train which pulled away at five o'clock on the afternoon of Monday, 14 March, and was met that night at Sheffield's Midland Station by the Mayor, the Town Clerk and the Deputy Coroner, W. W. Woodhead. At fifty-four, Robert Rawlinson was among the country's foremost civil engineers. He had cut his early professional teeth on dock projects at Liverpool, had served under Robert Stephenson in supervising the construction of part of the London-Birmingham Railway and was thoroughly conversant with water supplies, reservoirs, sewerage and public health.

After the Crimean War, during which he won respect and praise for his work as head of a sanitary commission sent to the field by the Government, Rawlinson became chief engineering inspector at the Local Government Act Office. Only the previous April he had been sent by the Prime Minister, Palmerston, to Lancashire to organize relief employment for thousands of redundant operatives following the interruption of cotton supplies from America because of the Civil War.

This, then, was the man who was to look into the Dale Dyke failure—Robert Rawlinson, thorough, persistent, charming, dedicated and humane. He shook hands with the Mayor and his companions and, after glancing towards the orange-tipped smoke suspended above part of the town, climbed into the waiting carriage, which jerked its way into the gloom. The man upon whose report reputations might depend booked in at the Royal Victoria Station Hotel.

5 Cynosure of All Eyes

It registered with John Webster that he was the unenviable centre of attraction. The dam disaster was big-headline news and, as Borough Coroner, he had inherited a heavy responsibility. Until the jury returned their verdict, every move he made would be noted and every official utterance recorded in the cold, indelible ink of print. Law required that jurors make the final decision but, in practice, it was obvious they would be influenced by what a coroner had to say. A nation awaited the outcome and, despite his experience in public life, Webster must have felt a little daunted by the unsought limelight surrounding him. He had a reputation for fairness and frankness, but even men of the highest integrity have been genuinely swayed by the views of 'experts' and by public opinion. Webster found himself in a controversial cleft stick and, with the country looking on, was to make some rash statements. It was quickly noted that he was not afraid to speak his mind.

Although he had the Home Secretary's approval of his intention to conduct the inquest on a few representative bodies, he was urged to take care that 'the inquiry which is to take place shall be full and complete'. Webster was pleased to have that approval but, for all practical purposes, he was out on his own. What he lacked in diplomacy he made up for in diligence and, so far as the inquest was concerned, he was to make a passionate attempt to get at the whole truth. His main fault was the bulldozing way he went about it. Webster, who was fifty-four, had been a bright young man in his mid-twenties when he settled in Sheffield to start legal practice, having served his articles with a firm from York. He was regarded so highly for his straight dealing that he soon became known as 'the honest lawyer'. He established himself as a respected member of the community, was elected to the Town Council in 1858 and was now an alderman. Webster was a no-nonsense debater, he was condemnatory about the poor sanitation existing in the town and his forthright views and enthusiasm had much to do with the council's adoption of the Local Government Act. He was to be Sheffield's Mayor in 1866 and 1867. In later years, Webster was handicapped by heart trouble; he relinquished the office of coroner in May 1873, and retired from the council the following year. Then, in May 1876, he was appointed a Justice of the Peace for the West Riding.

Before Robert Rawlinson arrived in Sheffield, John Webster and the jurymen went to view the dam. Broken bridges and blocked roads forced them to take a roundabout trip well to the south of the normal approach route and to climb to windswept Hollow Meadows and the even more exposed Strines Moor. As their horse-drawn omnibus was hauled on to the uplands, a panorama of untouched beauty stretched into the blue-edged distance. Hill surmounted hill in a grandeur of grey, green and brown, valleys plunged into deep shadow, and bracken, heather and grasses shimmered in the strong breeze. Dry-stone walls marched across the landscape.

The bus jolted on and the horse struggled up a close-shaven hill, from the top of which the passengers caught a glimpse of the Dale Dyke dam. Despite its fatal flaw, it was an impressive sight. Within a few minutes, the jurors were at the site and marvelling at the size of the structure which had extended for almost a quarter of a mile between two hills. What had once seemed an impregnable barrier now sagged sadly in the middle and water was still trickling through the breach. There was also a considerable amount of water still within the reservoir—up to about 20 feet deep in some pockets —but, as one reporter stated, it was 'as the dregs at the bottom of a teacup'. Pinnacles of bare rock protruded from the bed of the basin, an indication that material had been excavated from inside the reservoir for the building of the dam. Rails, trucks and carts were to be seen on surviving portions of the embankment—a clear reminder that work had not been completed before the disaster— and abandoned puddling equipment stood nearby.

The jury, by no means the only visitors, inspected the dam and adjacent land for nearly four hours and were assisted on technical points by John Gunson, the resident engineer, who, for a time,

A scene of devastation at Malin Bridge, showing (top left) the skeleton-like remains of the Malin Bridge Inn where the landlord, his wife and their five children were drowned

The house in which Henry Whittles saved his wife and five children; they huddled on a floating bed, to which he clung with one hand while holding on to a mantelpiece with the other

Ten people were reputed to have died here: the desolated site of Trickett's Farm

Before the flood, the substantial Hill Bridge here spanned the River Loxley at Hillsborough

was thought to have perished in the flood. His furrowed brow and sunken eyes reflected something of the mental stress he was undergoing. The constituent materials of the embankment appeared to be loose and friable and, although that could have been brought about partly by the abrasive action of the water as it burst through, the jury had to decide with what degree of skill (or lack of it) the dam had been constructed. The make-up of the embankment, therefore, was closely examined, as were the outlet pipes and bye-wash which the coroner and his men may well have thought inadequate in relation to the capacity of the reservoir. As they stood on top of the bank, they could get an idea of the course the flood had taken down the Loxley Valley. A wide, sinuous ribbon of mud, smeared by the bluish-white of puddled clay, reached into the distance as if some giant reptile had slithered down. Looking at the inoffensive stream of water now bubbling from the reservoir, it was difficult to imagine the intensity with which the flood had exploded into the vale.

The Dale Dyke dam was a magnet. Hundreds made the tortuous climb to the moors on foot; others went by horse, cart and carriage. Among them were qualified engineers, for whom the fractured structure proved a rare opportunity to study the dam's composition and likely stresses and, consequently, a chance also to improve on existing dam-building techniques. They speculated and pontificated and, like members of most professions, arrived at different conclusions. On one fundamental point, however, there was almost unanimous agreement: the collapse was due to human fallibility and not to Divine intervention. By far the greater proportion of visitors was made up of laymen, some of whom became overnight authorities on dams and hydrology and, what is more, had no compunction about expressing their opinions. They believed, not unreasonably perhaps, that their eyes could not lie. Had they not seen for themselves a mass of loose rubble with water percolating through it? One impression was that 'a quantity of burnt malt let down a corn shoot could not more possess the spectator with an idea of the granular composition and downpouring appearance of the earth on each side of the chasm'. It was a valid point: certainly the fallen rock and earth now looked as if it had been tipped haphazardly down a chute; it also covered any trace of the core of puddle clay, which caused some know-alls to doubt that such an inner wall had ever existed. One wiseacre, on learning the core had not been made of stone, volunteered his opinion that the 'omission' was unforgivable, adding that the embankment was so weak 'two or three of my lads could have pushed it down'. The laymen, uninhibited by such trifles as burdens of proof, were less circumspect than the engineers and word swiftly circulated that the construction of the Dale Dyke dam was not, to say the least, all that it might have been. Indeed, many minds were already made up.

Sheffield was becoming a 'must' on the traveller's itinerary and, day after day, trainloads of sightseers descended on the town to look at 'the ruins'. One writer said that, apart from the devastation, 'the dirty, grimy town, celebrated for its cutlers and trade unions, has indeed worn a gala appearance'. There was a seemingly endless trek to and from the dam and astute traders seized the golden chance to sell meat pies and drinks, setting up stalls at strategic spots along the route. Youngsters, tugged along by excited parents, would have something special to tell their grandchildren. The noble and the nobodies undertook the lengthy ascent through, or around, the muddied valley.

Lord Alfred Paget and the Honourable Frederick Cadogan, accompanied by John Brown and a Police Sergeant, rode in an open carriage to the dam and, after giving it their closest attention, walked down the valley to Loxley and Malin Bridge. The aristocrats saw the remaining stumps of what had been busy mills and learned from inhabitants a little about the catastrophe that had cut so cruelly into their lives. The grassy banks on either side of the river were daubed with pallid mud, pock-marked by the passage of large boulders and strewn with barkless tree trunks, while higher ground was splashed with slime and pitted with pieces of machinery and household fittings. Paget, it was said, had visited the area at the express wish of the Prince of Wales. He was noticeably affected by what he saw and arranged for a hundred or so sufferers each to receive a parcel of food. Alderman Brown added half a crown apiece. Paget was haunted by the scenes and, after spending the night as guest of the Browns at Shirle Hall, insisted on making another visit to a distressed area, this time around Neepsend, before returning to London. As he pointed out in a letter to *The Times*, it was not only the bereaved who had suffered; but hundreds more in 'the poorer classes are totally destitute of furniture, cooking utensils and clothes'.

Robert Rawlinson was quick off the mark. On the morning after his arrival in Sheffield, he breakfasted early and set off for the Town Hall to meet the Mayor, Town Clerk and Borough Coroner. They soon acquainted him with the principal aspects of the situation and, immediately afterwards, Rawlinson sent a telegram to the Home Secretary. In it he said the three Sheffield officials considered it unnecessary for a second Government inspector to be called in, and added that 'I go up to the site of the embankment at once with the coroner and commence taking evidence.' Later that day, Rawlinson wrote to Grey that he had made 'a full and searching examination of the ruptured embankment, of the sub-strata, of the material, mode of construction and general form of the works. I have also made inquiry and asked for plans, sections and details of the works. This will, no doubt, be forthcoming in due time. The company express the wish to have the fullest possible investigation'.

It did not take Rawlinson long to satisfy himself about defects in the Dale Dyke dam and, in the same letter, written on a double sheet of lined foolscap paper, he went into some detail about the presence of natural springs in the area and referred to the difficulty that had been encountered during construction of the puddle trench. 'For the purpose of making the embankment,' he reported to Grey, 'the engineer has allowed the sandstone rock to be bared on the inside of the reservoir. This rock, as I have stated, is jointed and open, so as to admit water. The coroner and I have seen water rising out on one side of the valley and sinking in on the other side, just within the broken embankment. This is sufficient evidence that the reservoir leaks and, with a great head of water before bursting, must have leaked much more.' Rawlinson had also concluded that the outlet pipes and bye-wash were too small, that the pipes were laid in an 'improper manner' and that the 'material, of which a great proportion of the embankment is made, has been improperly put together ... forming a loose rubble heap through which the river flows at present unchecked.' He included a rough pen-sketch of the dam, but urged Grey to make no use of the information contained in the letter 'until it has been brought out in evidence'. Finally, Rawlinson made it known that he was prepared to 'accept and work with an additional inspector if you consider this necessary to satisfy the public mind', which was probably his way of indicating that he would welcome assistance. Rawlinson undoubtedly had a lot on his plate and, finding it impossible to cope with everything on his own, engaged a local surveyor, Samuel Furness Holmes, to obtain certain details, make various calculations and draw up a number of plans of the dam and adjacent land. For his services, Holmes received £85.

Rawlinson continued his busy programme. He met directors of the waterworks company, to whom he explained what he required in the way of plans, witnesses and relevant information, and also attended a meeting of the General Relief Committee. He suggested to them that, for reasons of health, families in badly damaged houses should be removed by the authorities until proper repairs could be made. He warned: 'If typhus fever is allowed to break out, it may be more destructive to life than the flood.' Rawlinson was taking more than just an engineering interest in the disaster, forming the opinion that 'the whole town is working as one man and the worthy Mayor is untiring'. He dutifully kept the Home Secretary well in the picture and, in a letter dated 16 March, he explained that 'if there had been an open, flat expanse of country immediately below the embankment, the flood waters would have opened out so as to reduce the head and, in proportion, the velocity and power. But it has been pent in and so has traversed the intervening seven miles to Sheffield with the power of a battering ram.... It is in every way a sad, but professionally interesting, inquiry.' In something of an aside he told Grey that 'all the vagabonds in the county and adjoining counties have flocked in to obtain so-called charity' and said he had advised the Relief Committee that a notice in the newspapers urging donors to send their money to the Town Hall, and not give it to ragged-looking callers, would help defeat the aim of the 'importunate beggars'.

Later that week, John Webster and the jury again inspected the dam, accompanied this time by Rawlinson—on the face of it, a strange alliance. Admittedly the jurors had heard something of Gunson's views, but the resident engineer of a provincial waterworks company was small fry compared with a formidable fish like Rawlinson, who had been specially charged by the Home Office to investigate. How much more was his word likely to weigh with the jury and, indeed, the coroner, whose combined knowledge of dam-building was, so far as we know, virtually nil? Although he was 'pumped', Rawlinson did not give much away. According to him, he described the main features of the works to the jury 'but avoided giving decided opinions on any points, stating that they must be guided only by the evidence, using their own judgement to the best of their ability'.

Rawlinson was far more concerned that he had been asked by the coroner not only to give evidence at the inquest but also to act as adviser to him and the jury. He confided to the Home Secretary: 'I foresee great difficulty in such a course and fervently desire to have legal advice to guide me. It cannot be proper for the same individual to advise the coroner as to the questions which may be put to witnesses tendered by the company for examination and then himself give evidence.' He revealed that—and much more—to Grey in a letter, which 'I think had better not be considered official, but private, and be treated accordingly.' Rawlinson also thought 'it can serve no good or useful purpose to attempt to criminate the engineers or the company, but to obtain facts so as to arrive at reliable conclusions for future use'. The company would face 'ruinous claims' and he appeared concerned that evidence at the inquest would be turned against them (presumably unfairly), adding that 'caution is required'. Rawlinson seemed very worried that possibly 'all sorts of evidence will be tendered, feeling will be imported into the evidence, if not checked, and with this I ought not to be mixed up'. Having apparently sympathized with the company's predicament, he continued in unequivocal terms: 'Several grave errors have been committed in designing and executing these works. Some of the errors of construction exist in the other Yorkshire reservoir embankments I have seen.'

He was now in full swing. 'If reservoir embankments cannot be made so as to be absolutely safe, I think power should exist to prevent the construction of such embankments—especially where human life is endangered to so fearful an extent and where property far more in value than the reservoir is involved. As an engineer, I have no hesitation in saying that a safe embankment may be made in the Bradfield Valley—with the proper precautions—as also this embankment might have been. This I will strive to show in my report.'

Robert Rawlinson may have felt he had overstepped the mark, in which case it was hardly surprising that, 'on looking this letter over', he had asked the Home Secretary to treat his comments confidentially. Although he had no doubts in his mind that the company and their engineers were seriously at fault, Rawlinson nevertheless counselled moderation—at least, for the present. His reputation for being humane, it seems, was not ill-founded. Nothing, of course, was known about that letter at the time.

The question of sending another engineer to Sheffield to assist Rawlinson was again raised by the Home Secretary, and Rawlinson, in a telegram dated 18 March, advocated that 'the President of the Institution of Civil Engineers will be the proper person'. The President, J. R. McClean, was overseas; his immediate predecessor, John Hawkshaw, was unable (or unwilling) to go to Sheffield and replied to the Home Secretary that he had tried James Simpson but, as he had been employed by the millowners against the water-works company on a former occasion, it would be 'inadvisable to appoint him'. Grey subsequently wrote to Rawlinson that Hawk-shaw 'has recommended Mr Beardmore as a proper person to be employed for this purpose', to which Rawlinson responded: 'I will act to the best of my ability with any engineer you may send down.'

Meanwhile, Rawlinson was getting to know all he could about the disaster and its aftermath and was obviously intrigued by the whole story of a town's reaction to a major setback. He was full of admiration for what was being done, albeit slowly, which he saw when he walked along the entire course the flood had taken. Characteristically, he kept the Home Secretary well informed about his movements and, once, felt it necessary to say he had seen 'eight dead bodies under one shed—more killed than drowned'.

Nathaniel Beardmore arrived. He was forty-eight and dedicated to his profession, which he had entered as an apprentice when he was only fifteen. Described by his colleagues as 'high-minded, generous and genial', Beardmore possessed a 'ready humour' and an original turn of mind which ensured his popularity in society. Not that he led too much of a social life; far from it. He worked extremely hard and, although handicapped on occasions by rheuma-tism, had established for himself a fine reputation. His early experience had been gained surveying roads and railways and in-specting docks and harbours, but his speciality was hydrology. After helping to improve the service reservoirs of the Devonport Water Company and assisting in a scheme for improving water supplies to Glasgow, he devoted much of his career to the development and drainage of the River Lee—in connection with which he read a paper to the Institution of Civil Engineers, for which he was awarded the Telford Medal in 1854. He now joined Rawlinson and with him went out to visit the dam.

Self-appointed juries up and down the country were reaching their own 'verdicts', often without having been anywhere near the site upon which national attention focused. Inevitably, the 'judges' included newspapers. That the matter was *sub judice* restricted them very little and some hit out boldly at what they considered engineering incompetence—without so much as a mellowing euphemism. Several of the published allegations (however true) would today have resulted in a big bill for defamation.

The leader writer of *The Newcastle Daily Journal* cynically suggested that the Sheffield tragedy would have been 'improved' in hundreds of pulpits and 'its source traced entirely to the hands of that wondrous Providence which moves in a mysterious way and which ever appears to baffle the searching gaze of the keenest eye'. It was all too easy, he told his readers, to shelve awkward questions by throwing the 'whole responsibility on the Supreme Being, but the task which the engineers of the Sheffield Water Company had to perform was not so great as to exempt them from all responsibility for its proper execution.... Mr Gunson, when he undertook the execution of the great work which had failed so miserably, was no bold pioneer of science groping his way along paths never before explored. He had but to follow in the steps of other men. He had to deal with an open foe whose power any schoolboy might compute. He must have been blind and ignorant, indeed, if he could not calculate the accumulated hydraulic force of every one of the bubbling streams which poured down the barren, heath-covered hills into the basin which he had to form. It was his solemn duty to do this and to raise a barrier which the water could not overcome ... but from some cause or other, possibly from a cause over which he, as the engineer, had no control, his precautions have been insufficient'.

As if troubled by faint feelings of guilt, the writer conceded: 'We do not lay the whole load of blame upon the shoulders of Mr Gunson, or upon any single individual. A share of the responsibility belongs to everyone; such catastrophes would not occur were the people generally to take a greater interest in the proper execution of great works of engineering skill like this, in which the mighty powers of nature have to be fought and conquered at close quarters. It is a common thing to represent the careless man as sleeping upon a barrel of gunpowder, but such an act would not show a greater want of caution than that which the people dwelling in the vale all the way from Bradfield to Sheffield have displayed for some months past.'

There was, perhaps, some truth in that. Possibly the local inhabitants could have done more in attempting to dissuade the company from siting the dam at the very head of the valley and also insisting upon more effective safety measures in case of emergency. It is doubtful, however. In 1864, the vast majority of people had no say whatever in what went on and, indeed, knew even less. A few undoubtedly had their suspicions about Dale Dyke, still fewer had much influence and, like Glendower who could 'call spirits from the vasty deep', could not really expect the directorial spirits of the waterworks company to do anything if they yelled at the tops of their voices. For the most part, residents knew precious little about the mysteries of the engineer or builder —a situation that has changed little over the years—and never dreamed of interfering until presented with a *fait accompli*. Apart from some anxiety for a few days before the failure, it appears most of the residents nearest the dam believed (as had the company and their officials) the towering embankment to be impenetrable. Indeed, it is doubtful if many people even thought about it at all. Now the damage had been done, it was not difficult to be prudent.

The fact nevertheless remained that nearly two hundred and fifty lives had been lost, thousands made homeless and thrown out of work. Accusing fingers pointed towards the waterworks company and, to a lesser extent, the contractors, Messrs Craven, Cockayne and Fountain. John Gunson, basically unassuming and conscientious, never sought publicity—even favourable publicity. Now, sadly, he found himself in the glare of a critical searchlight.

What of the company's directors? They were in an extremely difficult position, almost certainly facing a huge compensation bill and, of course, being responsible for the actions of their servants. They had also to consider the shareholders who, after all, financed the company and looked for bounteous dividends in return. For some days, the directors maintained public silence except to beg forbearance while they sought to clarify their situation. Inevitably, that angered some impatient potential claimants. Then a statement, dated 21 March and signed by William Smith (chairman), was circulated to shareholders. It began by mentioning that the company had existed for thirty-four years without any previous serious mishap and continued: 'It is hardly necessary to say that the principal object of regret to your directors is that the accident should have caused so much loss of life and so much human suffering. They regret also that a great destruction of property has been caused and that the prospects of the company are at present materially affected. They have to inform you that since the first confusion created by the accident has subsided, their best endeavours have been directed to ascertaining the extent and particulars of the damage sustained; they are also endeavouring to procure the best possible legal advice upon the question of liability of the company and as to the most practical mode of dealing with the affairs of the company under the circumstances in which they are now placed. The directors, in case they should find such a step desirable, will take the opportunity of calling the shareholders together before the ensuing general meeting; at present, however, there are no circumstances known to the directors which have not necessarily publicly transpired.'

It was noncommittal, yet little more can have been expected. The statement did not hold much encouragement for property-owners who, in their misguided way, might have anticipated an early and unchallenged settlement. To some, it appeared the company were scratching around for a legal loophole through which to leap, and they may well have been right. The directors were up against it and it was only natural that they wanted to strike the most acceptable bargain they could. They were unlikely to win a popularity contest at that moment. It was not all one-way traffic, however. Sympathy was expressed for the directors and shareholders who, it was held, were as saddened as anyone about the events and stood to lose a great deal of money as well. Sheffielders were urged, in their own interests, to stand by the company. One gentleman, apparently carried away by the tears being shed for the company, suggested that the voluntary subscriptions swelling the town's relief fund might prove sufficient to save shareholders from parting with a penny. There was confidence, mainly among some in the higher-income brackets, that such honourable men as the directors would do what was fair; all they needed was a little time. So, for a while, the company were not unduly badgered. On the whole, however, the deepest sorrow was reserved for the real sufferers—the poor.

William Leng, the editor of *The Sheffield Daily Telegraph*, left no doubts as to what he thought. With a characteristic touch of acid lucidity, he wrote: 'Our thought is, we admit, rather about saving life than about saving dividends, and we are more concerned for the lost inhabitants than we are for lost profits; but for this peculiarity in our preference we hope to be forgiven. The people who have perished are silent and cannot write letters to the papers —were poor, and have left behind them no influential friends —were trustful and did not dream of danger; yet if we must at this time sympathize with any of the sufferers by this accident, we shall certainly sympathize less with the shareholders than with them. Odd as one of our correspondents may deem the fact, we are more concerned at the sight of the rulley-load of coffins in the High Street than we are with the depreciation of property and more impressed with the falling of houses than with the falling of shares.'

Few people emerged with more credit in those early, critical days than Thomas Jessop. As Mayor, he devoted countless hours to the urgent task of relieving the most distressing cases and spent much of his day at the Town Hall, where he presided at meetings, listened to wretched souls seeking subsistence and generally organized arrangements to deal with the aftermath of the Great Flood. He was unable to direct much energy or time to his own business, although William Jessop and Sons had sustained appreciable damage from the waters. In fact, such were the pressures upon him, Tommy Jessop was close to having a breakdown in health. As treasurer of the fund, he was delighted to report that almost £23,000 had been received within the first five days. So desperate were some of the cases investigated by members of the sub-committees that it was decided to allow discretion in making payments on the doorstep without first seeking permission from the executive committee. So volunteers, making door-to-door inquiries in the worst-hit areas, adopted roles rather like the rent man in reverse. The responsibilities of the executive and sanitary committees, formed by the General Relief Committee, were assuming full-time proportions and they agreed to meet daily until the worst of the crisis was over.

While officials and helpers from the town's relief committees, as well as those from the Poor Law organizations, toured the districts, work went on almost non-stop to clear the rubbish from the streets.

Thousands of cartloads were taken away and dumped. A week after the failure of the dam, Dr John Charles Hall was able to report to the Health Committee of the Town Council that in The Wicker, at least, things were getting back to something like normality so far as the state of the road and pavements was concerned. The common sewers had been nearly freed of mud and most of the cellars in the immediate neighbourhood had been pumped dry. He said a few bodies were still being recovered, often from under debris heaped against the bridges. In many streets, houses remained flooded and conditions in Harvest Lane (not far from the Don) were described as 'most awful'.

From Dr Hall's report, which related to the whole of the affected area from the town to Malin Bridge, it was obvious that a great deal had yet to be done. Hundreds of houses were in a dreadful state and, as some residents were too old or too poor to clean them, the doctor recommended that notices be served on landlords to have the work carried out. Dr Hall said he would not advocate the disposal of liquid mud into the river in normal circumstances but, in view of the danger to health, it was preferable to leaving it squelching in the streets. He was particularly concerned about the presence in such a populated area of a slaughter yard—'kept by a knacker named Holt'—in which were deposited horseflesh and pig carcasses. The Health Committee, it seems, had great faith in the powers of lime and chloride of lime, for they ordered further large quantities to be distributed.

News of the Dale Dyke disaster reached far beyond the shores of Britain and, such was the interest in it as an engineering showpiece from which lessons might be learned, a number of professional men travelled from overseas to inspect the damage. Among them was Monsieur A. Mille, the French Government's chief engineer of bridges and causeways, who, in the company of Rawlinson and Beardmore, examined the site shortly before the inquest was resumed. Another distinguished engineer to cast a qualified eye over the fractured embankment was John Fowler, a forty-six-year-old Sheffield man, who was destined for even greater prominence and also a knighthood when he was associated with Benjamin Baker in building the Forth Bridge. Fowler was born at Wadsley Hall, on the outskirts of Sheffield; from this stately home the family now gave help, food and clothing to those in the district made destitute by the flood. But for the charitable acts by them and others before the relief organizations got into full stride, there could well have been deaths from starvation and exposure.

By this time, John Fowler was firmly established as a highly reputable engineer. The list of works upon which he was engaged was extensive, his offices and London home being at 2, Queen Square Place, adjoining Birdcage Walk. He was a considerable landowner in Scotland and his financial state was comfortable. Fowler had enjoyed a happy childhood at Wadsley Hall where his father, John Fowler, a respected land agent and valuer, now eighty, lived with his daughter, Annie. The young John Fowler had long since left the family home, becoming a pupil at the age of sixteen to none other than John Towlerton Leather. He had, therefore, a special interest in the dam disaster. Fowler learned a great deal about civil engineering from Leather, whom he regarded as his *pater secundus*, and from Leather's uncle, George. He never forgot their kindness and tuition, recalling that 'my early training was exclusively waterworks and hydraulic engineering'. To that, Fowler was to add a vast knowledge of railway engineering which began when he left the Leathers to enter the employ of John Urpeth Rastrick, one of the great engineers of his time. Thus impressively equipped, Fowler went into business on his own account in 1844 and profitable it had proved. He was an undoubted success.

Now Fowler was inspecting a failure—a reservoir and embankment designed by his early mentor, J. T. Leather. The pupil had returned to pronounce upon the work of the master. Just what went through his mind we can but guess but, later, in company with four other top engineers, Fowler put his name to a report which set out to absolve Leather and Gunson from any suggestion of faulty planning or incompetent construction.

Sheffield continued to present an unprecedented free show for the thousands who arrived daily to feast their eyes on the sad spectacle. For most of them, it was just an exciting day out—a chance to view a real tragedy, with real people filling the principal acting roles. The poor sufferers, already dazed and tattered, must have felt like caged animals at a zoo, to be discussed, inspected and pitied. There was nothing much they could do about it, however, as the intruders trampled over the bruised ground, ferreted in the rubble or guffawed when one of their number got stuck in the mud. Happily, it seemed, they wended their winding way up and down the Loxley Valley, some joyfully carrying mementoes

of the occasion. On the whole, the intrusion was tolerated remarkably well and there were only a few reports of minor incidents—
usually amounting to no more than an overheated argument. Some
people appeared in court for stealing from abandoned houses and
damaged shops, but they were Sheffielders who, not unreasonably,
regarded their small hauls in the category of 'finders-keepers'
rather than as unlawfully come by. The sentences were light. Much
more heartless were instances of profiteering by a few traders who,
taking advantage of a desperate situation, put up the prices of
food. Sadly, those who stooped to such measures contravened no
law.

There were, of course, rumours of worse crimes (such as large-
scale looting) and the correspondent of the London *Daily Telegraph*
drew upon himself the wrath of Sheffield when he allowed his
colourful pen to write that 'wholesale pillage has added a repulsive
horror to what was in its own nature purely tragic. Felon hands
have been busy at the pockets of the dead and the land rats of
Sheffield, which is plagued with those vermin no less than any
other large town, have made known to an inland place of industry
the old devilish practice of wrecking'. Certainly a case or two of
stealing from corpses had been referred to (in the local newspapers),
but the journalist's exaggerated generalization was going too far.
He later apologized for his references to plundering and malicious
damage, but felt unable to retract his statement regarding the
'depravity of the crowds in the streets at night, as well as the
unseemly conduct of many people visiting the field of the inundation by day'. Again, he overstated his case by maintaining that
some of those outside the public houses were 'as loud and shameless
in their expression of brutality as any mob I have watched in front
of the Old Bailey on the unhallowed eve of a hanging', but the
police explanation that the noisy night scenes were due to temperance workers attempting to convert the boozers seems an equally
overstated exercise in whitewash. Something midway between the
extreme views was probably nearer the truth.

Drunkenness was not peculiar to Sheffield; it was rife throughout mid-nineteenth century England. The lordly and the lowly
drank to excess and the working man was often considered socially
inferior by his colleagues if he could not put away copious draughts.
For those sweating in the heat of steel furnaces, daily doses of ale
became necessary restoratives. An idea of the popularity of drink-

ing as an almost required pastime can be gauged from the fact that in Sheffield in 1864 there were something like five hundred hotels, inns and taverns, and a similar number of beerhouses. The effects of alcohol offered a brief escape from the unpleasant realities of some industrial areas. Sadly, it was no answer and, in too many cases, drinking too much was regarded as being synonymous with depravity and degradation. Sheffield had its share of squalor in the 1860s, there is no denying that, and it was not an aspect of which to be proud any more than it was a matter to be glossed over. Sheffield was no worse in that respect than other sizeable centres of industry however, and, what is more, could point with justification to the fact that a higher proportion of their working classes were better paid, better clothed, better housed and better fed. Nevertheless, parts of the town were positively primeval.

It is equally true the working man did not only drink. He enjoyed walking and running, relished gardening, went fishing and became a member of a choir or brass band. An increasing number also read. A free library opened in Sheffield in 1856 (Yorkshire's first) and, such was its popularity, in the first full year nearly 105,000 book-issues were recorded in the lending section and about 9,400 in the reference department. The Sheffield worker was not without education and recreational facilities, but the unvarnished fact remained that drunkenness was a real social problem. Mary Walton, in her splendid book, *Sheffield, Its Story and Its Achievements*, referring to a slightly later period, wrote that 'Sheffield was roughly divided into two classes, those who drank too much and those whose views on temperance were fierce.'

For years, Sheffield had nurtured a sense of independence. The Great Flood opened the town to inspection from outside. First-time visitors cannot have been overjoyed by the sight of blackened houses or of the Lowry-like figures tramping from work, the grime of labour in the lines of their faces. An uneasy rapport existed between rich and poor and, if one did not look too closely, it appeared to work well enough. The opposite social poles came closer together at the time of the flood and, in some cases, met in real friendship. Some of the wealthy felt a genuine sympathy for their poorer sufferers and enthusiastically supported the cause, working long hours and making many sacrifices. One also gets the impression that some men of 'substance' flamboyantly showed the flag

with no more feeling than they had done what was expected of them
—in public.

The Times were having a field-day at the expense of the Sheffield
Waterworks Company. The daily cornerstone of upper-crust
England told their readers 'what magnificent effects can be produced in water as well as fire, which is generally selected as the
best material for display. Clever and enterprising engineers, at
great expenditure of the town funds, had prepared a grand surprise.
They tell you at Chatsworth that every display of the Emperor
fountain is computed to cost £100. This exhibition has cost at least
half a million, but then it has been terribly more effective. By
throwing, we can hardly call it a dam, but a light screen across
some deep valleys above the town, they backed up a world of waters
—more than two million tons weight. Suspended, as it were, in
the hills above the town, there it hung as in a vast cistern. One
would not sleep with even a charged shower bath above one's bed,
but here was water enough to float all Her Majesty's Navy, only
waiting, as it were, the pull of a trigger, and just held together by
a little loose rubbish'. The article was bizarre and biased and could
have no effect but to prejudice a jury and a waiting public.

Other newspapers and journals published their 'findings' long
before the official verdict was returned. *The Builder* attributed the
failure to water filtering into 'the loose and porous embankment,
which caused the disrupture of the puddle wall'; the *Saturday
Review* speculated at some length upon the 'suspect' quality of the
workmanship, adding that 'earthwork cannot be done rapidly and,
at the same time, safely'; the *Daily Telegraph*, of London, surmised
that the 'evil will be traced to some neglect or omission'. Other
sections of the Press weighed in with their conclusions, some of
which were basically correct. By the very law of averages, they had
to be. Almost every aspect of the dam's construction was analysed
and the harassed directors of the waterworks company must have
felt the roughness of the rope around their necks.

The assumptions and criticisms were voiced not only by the
newspapers: many other pundits clambered aboard the buckling
bandwagon to put in their fourpence-worth. One civil engineer,
upon reading a report of the disaster with 'my professional eye',
concluded that the Dale Dyke dam had been constructed entirely
of clay and went on solemnly to explain why that would never
do. He announced with some self-satisfaction that he would have

used 'gravel soil, some clay intermixed with rubble stones, and the whole braced together at intervals with bundles of brushwood, made up into what is termed *faggots*. If the reservoir embankment had been constructed with these materials, and with proper external retaining walls, it would have resisted 10 times the pressure of the present clay embankment.' Writing from his home in Cork, another worthy had no hesitation in stating that 'this reservoir was not constructed on sound principles'. He declared that the 'earthen and sand wall' could not possibly have held back 115 million gallons (in fact, the reservoir capacity was 712 million), but he had a point when he commented that 'engineers are at fault in their method of constructing these vast reservoirs, as they form them now precisely the same as they were made a century ago, when only small dams and ponds were required'. Among other theories advanced was that in an article appearing in the *London Review* that the dam had been built across an inclined plane of clay— 'rather like the *Great Eastern* when that vessel was ready for being launched broadside first'—and leakage through fissured rock put the whole slope through a 'soaping process', thus preparing the embankment for a slip.

Many agreed the dam had been built up, in effect, with 'so many wagon loads of loose earth tipped down at the entrance to the valley'. Some explained that the structure would have been stronger had it been curved in a semicircle, with the convex side towards the water. Sheffield's own Dr Henry Clifton Sorby, distinguished scientist, archaeologist, chemist, geologist and metallurgist, re-examined the ground in the immediate vicinity of the dam—an area he knew intimately. After careful study, he concluded that 'the bursting of the reservoir was not occasioned by anything connected with the arrangement of the subjacent strata'. In other words, he ruled out a landslip. That is worth remembering in view of later developments. He also thought there was insufficient clay of suitable texture available in that region to build a strong puddle wall of such dimensions. His opinions, modestly expressed but based, as they were, on extensive local and technical knowledge, were worthy of attention. They appear not to have been taken up in any official sense, however.

A certain W. D. Allen, tongue in cheek, suggested that the waterworks company might care to finance the painting of tide-marks on the walls of some houses to show future generations how high the flood had risen and 'how large a supply of water they delivered to the town in less than an hour'. (A number of markers —not donated by the waterworks company, one suspects—still exist in Sheffield. One is about eight feet from the ground on the building of the Hallamshire Steel Company, where Neepsend Lane, Bardwell Road and Boyland Street meet, and getting on for 18 feet above the normal height of the nearby River Don.)

A gentleman, using the pseudonym 'Reservoir Banks', confessed to being highly amused at the ideas on dam construction put forward by amateurs and appealed to 'such meteors of engineering science' to come forth and 'give us the particulars of the great works your masterminds have conceived—not in the air, mind you, but in reality—and then we must say adieu! Yes, adieu, ye Fowlers, Hawkshaws, Leathers, and all ye little pigmy fellows; your occupation will be gone, and never more will our engineers hold communion with you; that is, if our banks do not give way before they are commenced, we mean—on paper'. Everybody, it seemed, wanted to get into the act and were not above devising the most trivial reasons for doing so.

The disaster also prompted a surfeit of poetry from budding Byrons. A lot of it did not attain the standard demanded by a schoolboy editor of a fifth-form magazine, but it was all honestly conceived from the heart. One example was composed by no less an academic than a Master of Arts, one Richard Fielder, of Ely, and succinctly entitled: *Ballad on the Lamentable Bursting of the Dale Dyke Embankment, Sheffield, on Friday night, March 11, 1864*. It began:

> Come listen to the tale I bring,
> Ye lads and lasses all;
> A sad catastrophe I sing—
> Concerns both great and small.

After no fewer than 36 more similarly trite verses, it ended:

> And when the embankment they restore,
> Let's hope the builder man
> Will make it stouter than before
> And on a sounder plan.

The author dated his work 'March 18th' and it was probably no more than a coincidence that the *Sheffield and Rotherham*

Independent published it on All Fools' Day.

The last pre-judgements were made, opinion being weighted heavily against the waterworks company, and the inquest looked like being little more than a formality. The jury had yet to hear the evidence, of course, and to digest the conclusions reached by Robert Rawlinson and Nathaniel Beardmore. Rawlinson had exercised diplomacy and striven to avoid any skirmishes preceding the main battle. It seemed he had been the soul of discretion. Or had he? Following the dam failure, there were widespread fears (many of them imaginary) about the condition of other reservoirs in the British Isles and, naturally enough, Rawlinson had been among those approached for advice.

He received one anxious letter from Sir John Gray who, among various other claims to recognition, was chairman of Dublin Corporation's waterworks sub-committee. As a young man of twenty-seven, Gray had been indicted with three others for conspiring against the Queen. That was twenty-one years earlier. Since then, he had become 'respectable', was proprietor of the influential *Freeman's Journal* and destined to be M.P. for Kilkenny City. At the moment, however, he was worried about the state of Dublin reservoirs. Rawlinson was consulting engineer to Dublin Corporation and consequently knew all about their dams. In a letter dated 18 March he assured Gray as to their safety and unwisely added they had 'nothing in common with the Sheffield failure. You are sound in stratification, in material, in design and in execution'. Rawlinson probably expected his comments to be treated in confidence, at least until after the inquest; if he did not, then his reference to Sheffield was ill-advised and certainly ill-timed. In fact, it wasn't even necessary.

A copy of the letter appeared in newspapers a few days afterwards. The implications were obvious. By the morning on which the inquest was resumed, the jury—and the public—had no doubts about Robert Rawlinson's opinion of the broken dam on Bradfield Moor.

6 'Then, it's the Eighth Mistake'

John Webster entered the court-room in Sheffield Town Hall at precisely ten o'clock on the morning of Wednesday, 23 March 1864. As he did so, the animated chatter died away, barristers made final adjustments to their wigs, reporters smoothed out notebooks and everybody stood up. The Borough Coroner briefly surveyed the scene, nodded his acknowledgement and sat down. At his side were Robert Rawlinson and Nathaniel Beardmore. To John Gunson, understandably apprehensive and enduring the biggest crisis in his life, that trio must have seemed more magisterial than investigatory and, as things turned out, there were grounds for such fears.

In a number of ways, the resumed inquest was a curious affair. Only five witnesses were called during the two-day hearing—all were professional engineers of whom only one, Gunson, was at the dam when it failed. Not a single contractor, navvy or local resident who had inspected the fatal crack in the embankment on that stormy night was asked to give his story; not a solitary soul who lived in the shadow of the works and who must have known something of events during the years of construction was invited to testify. Samuel Hammerton, the farmer, one of the first to examine the fissure, was present for some hours on the first day of the inquiry, but was then released. The inquest developed, therefore, into a kind of forum for experts and also provided a platform from which the coroner launched some extraordinary verbal rockets. In view of the widespread interest in the event, very few members of the so-called general public attended. The Mayor, other members of the Town Council and, of course, directors of the waterworks company, were there in some force.

Webster formally explained that the jury's task was to discover 'how and by what means' Thomas Elston and others had met their deaths, adding it was unlikely that much more would be heard about the victims during the proceedings. In fact, nothing else was heard. The information subsequently adduced was from men who, because of their official attachments and loyalties, were unlikely to reveal more than they had to. Clearly the two engineers responsible for the dam would be restricted by factors of self-interest and, indeed, professional self-preservation.

First to give evidence was John Towlerton Leather, the consultant engineer, who displayed a mixture of confidence and reserve. Dale Dyke, he said in answer to the coroner's questions, was one of three reservoirs forming the Bradfield scheme, and the building contract for it had been let in 1858. Originally, the intention was to set the embankment farther down the valley, but because of disturbances in the strata discovered by trial bore holes, he had re-examined the ground and altered his plans to meet the requirements of building the dam on the present site. A puddle trench to a depth of 10 feet below ground level was first envisaged, but, as it proved impossible to find a solid foundation, it was necessary to go down to as much as 60 feet below the surface to ensure a watertight base. Water had filled the trench during building operations, but was pumped out. As the puddle wall itself became higher in the early stages, the water rose with it and percolated round the sides, though not through it.

Under examination, Leather conceded he had seen the puddle trench once in 1861 and the puddle wall on one occasion two years later. He confessed he had not been there during the actual puddling of the trench, at all events not when it was at its lowest point, but the puddled clay he had inspected was of good quality. So far, Leather felt comfortable; he had been able to answer truthfully, without difficulty, and hoped he had impressed the jury by his undoubted authority. He now imparted a few vital statistics. There would be no challenge here. The embankment across the valley, he said, was 418 yards long, 500 feet thick at the base and 12 feet thick at the top. Both the inner and outer slopes had an inclination of $2\frac{1}{2}$ to 1 and the highest point of the dam was 95 feet above ground level; the puddle wall was 4 feet thick at its apex and 16 feet thick at the bottom, which was up to 60 feet below the surface of the ground and measured, therefore, a maximum height of 155 feet. The surface area of water in the reservoir covered 78 acres and the total that could be impounded was estimated at a little more than 114 million cubic feet (712 million gallons). The water gathering-ground spread over some 4,300 acres.

Material for constructing the dam, Leather continued, was excavated from within the reservoir and, as a result, rocks had been bared. The embankment was made up of stone, clay, shale and earth, but he could not say just how the material had been conveyed or put into it. He explained that Gunson, who had superintendence of the works, was not his servant although occasional consultations took place between them.

CORONER: All the plans are yours?
LEATHER: The plans are.
CORONER: And he [Gunson] could not deviate from those plans without your permission?
LEATHER: No; he would never think of such a thing.

The engineer then described the nature and positioning of the outlet pipes which ran in a straight line from within the reservoir and, at an oblique angle, underneath the embankment to the outside. Rawlinson showed keen interest at this stage, listening intently to Leather who said there were two pipes, each being 18 inches in diameter, about 500 feet long and made up of 56 nine-foot sections. These sections were joined by sockets 'in the ordinary way that you see in streets' and the joints made with lead. The pipes were wrapped in an 18-inch covering of puddled clay and laid in a trench about nine feet below the level of the ground. The valves were on the outside of the dam and, that being so, Leather conceded that in the event of a burst pipe it would be difficult to locate and repair a fault in the pipeline. Leather found himself being pressed into admitting that had there been a pipe fracture at Dale Dyke it would 'most likely' damage the embankment, which might collapse before the source could be traced. He was quick to add he had never heard of a case like that. He persisted that the pipes used were doubly strong and thought it unlikely there would be uneven pressure upon any part of them. Water mains in streets, he suggested, seldom gave way under external pressure; he had never known a joint to yield to such pressure. It was, he volunteered, 'impossible'. Rawlinson, who had apparently come to terms with his conscience about his role at the inquest, now put a few questions. There was more than a hint of self-confidence in his voice.

RAWLINSON: Is it not a common thing for a new line of mains tried for the first time in the town to have blemished places discovered, and leaking joints?

LEATHER: Not to my knowledge, certainly, because all pipes before they are laid down by the waterworks company ought to be, and I believe in this case are, severely tested.

RAWLINSON: I saw the testing machine in your yard, and I have no doubt they have been tested; but notwithstanding, I think the question a proper one to ask, because I am bound to say my experience is on the other side.

LEATHER: Well, my experience extends over thirty years, and my experience is that defective joints are rare.

Before he had time properly to reflect on that little exchange, Leather was replying to the coroner that he had 'never' heard of a bank falling after water crept along the trough where pipes were laid. The engineer also disagreed with Webster that it would have been better to have laid the pipes in a culvert. He had to admit he had not the calculations with him to say what was the pressure on the valves when the reservoir was full. 'Can you tell us, Mr Gunson?' the coroner asked, but before the resident engineer could reply, Rawlinson had chipped in with the answer: 'Between four and five tons on each valve.'

Leather was now about to experience the cut-and-thrust of John Webster's power of interrogation. The coroner leaned forward. 'One valve took half an hour to open,' he said, 'and, during that time, there was a great shaking of the pipes and apparently a great strain upon them during the opening, which was not perceived before opening or when fully open.' Not a jot of evidence on those points had been even hinted at so far but Webster, quite unperturbed, asked: 'What was the reason for that?' Leather explained that although there might be greater disturbance and noise as the valves were opened, the pressure on the pipes and valves would, in fact, diminish. The pipes would run off about 10,000 cubic feet of water a minute, at which rate it would take about eight days to empty the reservoir—not taking into account further water running into it. To more questions, Leather replied that he had foreseen no necessity for having other than outlet pipes and a bye-wash to let off water in case of emergency. He added, perhaps to his regret, that to discharge water suddenly and too rapidly could be serious. The coroner needed no prompting. 'Yes, but it would not be so serious as discharging the whole reservoir at once?' he inquired with some triumph.

'Of course not,' responded Leather, 'it is a question of degree,' and, attempting to retrieve his position, he strove to satisfy the coroner and jury that he had done everything he considered necessary to ensure the safety of the dam. If Leather thought that was an end to the matter, he was sadly mistaken. The coroner, sensing a weakness in the engineer's hitherto self-assured attitude, clung on like a limpet.

CORONER: I do not see the object of employing an engineer, except to minimize the danger?

LEATHER: That has been so.

CORONER: No, it has not. There has been no attempt here to minimize danger, none at all. I want to know from you, as a practical engineer, whether it is not desirable to have other means of reducing or lessening the danger, even on suspicion of danger, than has been adopted here?

LEATHER: Whether desirable?

CORONER: Whether not absolutely necessary?

LEATHER: I don't know of any such means.

CORONER: Well, I think I could devise means. I ask you as a gentleman concerned in drawing plans for waterworks—suppose you placed on the hills, at a considerable height, an immense body of water, put up an embankment and, when there was suspicion that it would give way, you have any means of avoiding its all coming down in one body?

LEATHER: I cannot conceive of any means.

CORONER: It appears to me very strange. Did you never think of a mode?

LEATHER: No.

CORONER: Then you mean to say as a professional man that you cannot conceive of any mode of relief for a dam in case of danger?

LEATHER: I cannot conceive of any other mode than what has been adopted.

CORONER: Now when I was there the other day, I saw on the south side of the reservoir a large cutting, apparently to take water away. Could not that cutting have been made available?

LEATHER: Not under these circumstances, it could not.

CORONER: Could you not have made a cutting something similar which might have been of use?

LEATHER: No; the water ought to have been taken from the reservoir, or nearly so, to relieve it.

CORONER: Could not that have been done?

LEATHER: I know of no means by which it could have been done.

CORONER: I am very sorry I am not an engineer, that's all; I would do it, or I would not be an engineer.

The consulting engineer felt uneasy and frustrated by the coroner's imputations and may well have considered that here was an ignorant amateur trying to tell a professional his business. For his part, Webster was irritated by what he saw as an aloof and evasive manner by the witness, but already he was beginning to overstep the mark. Having survived the first round of the coroner's questioning Leather was probed by Rawlinson (who again drew attention to the possibility of fractured pipes) and by some of the jurors before reaching the comparative sanctuary of examination of Perronet Thompson, counsel appearing for the waterworks company. Leather began to regain some of his composure. Yes, he said, he had been consulting engineer for all the reservoirs built by the company and there had never before been an accident. The plans for the Bradfield reservoir and for those which had stood safely for years were 'precisely the same' in principle; there was also a 'great similarity' in the kind of material used in some of the dams. Leather stated modestly (and he was a man who shrank from publicity of his own achievements) that he had utilized all his professional experience in designing the dams and had done all he possibly could to secure their stability. In his judgement, the workmanship at Dale Dyke was good throughout. Shortly afterwards, the coroner asked him point-blank: 'Then what, in your opinion, was the cause of this embankment bursting?'

Leather replied, 'Well, I really don't know,' but must have realized immediately that an answer like that was not going to satisfy the persistent Mr Webster.

CORONER: If you don't know of your own knowledge, will you tell me your conjecture?

LEATHER: I have very great difficulty, indeed, in forming an opinion; exceedingly so. I have no opinion worth any reliance whatever, but I can form a conjecture and so can anyone.

CORONER: I only want a conjecture.

LEATHER: And that is not worth much.

CORONER: It will not be worth much if it is worth no more than what we hear in the town.

LEATHER: There is the possibility of a landslip. A landslip under the side of the bank may have produced it. I do not believe the embankment itself slipped, but the stratification beneath the bank might have slipped.

CORONER: Then you do not ascribe the bursting of the reservoir to unsound principles of engineering or to bad workmanship?

LEATHER: Certainly not.

Further pressed by Rawlinson, Leather thought it possible a landslip might have been produced by water (that which naturally percolated into the strata) getting between the face of rock and the bed of clay resting upon it, thus causing the superincumbent mass to slip off. Water emanating from fissures inside the reservoir would be cut off by the puddle and, in the unlikely event of its managing to get below the wall, would probably find its way to a spring lower down the valley.

For the time being, Leather's ordeal was over. He returned to the body of the hall and it must have been a diffident John Gunson who now stepped forward to give evidence. After outlining the method of laying the outlet pipes and describing the construction of the puddle trench and wall, he related in some detail how the embankment itself was made. It was, he said, built up in layers (or 'tips') of between three and five feet in depth, carts (two and three-wheeled), barrows and wagons being used in the work. He denied that material was taken indiscriminately from inside the reservoir; indeed, he emphasized it was carefully selected. To prevent the embankment from slipping upon its surface, the outer bank was faced to half-way up its height with special stone, for which an extra 3d per cubic yard was paid. Less coarse material was next to it and the material got progressively finer until only the very finest was in contact with the puddle wall itself. He considered all the material to be of good quality.

The coroner took Gunson back to the question of the pipes and was told that special precautions had been taken where they passed through the puddle trench. The iron pipes, encased in puddle, were laid in a trench of 'perfectly water-tight, strong shale' about nine feet below ground level. About two lengths of pipe actually crossed the puddle trench, the bottom of which was between 40 and 50 feet deeper. Gunson said his fear was that if the puddle subsided, the pipes at that point would not and the weight of the embankment above could fracture them. To guard against that possibility, it was necessary to get a 'long equal bearing' for the pipes and it was decided to extend the puddle from the bottom of the trench (beneath the pipes) at a flat slope to points 100 feet either side of the puddle wall. (This meant that about 200 feet of twin pipelines, 30 inches apart, were resting on nothing more substantial than puddled clay—a practice Rawlinson was later to condemn). Whether that arrangement was on Gunson's own initiative or with Leather's permission was not clear. Gunson added that steps had been taken to prevent water from creeping along the outside of the pipes; the connecting sockets were firmly locked but, being socket pipes, there could be a small deflection in the line without danger.

Gunson then gave details of the rainfall in the area of Dale Dyke, explaining that the smallest flow of water down the stream was in summer and amounted to half a cubic foot per second for each thousand acres of the watershed and the maximum some 150 cubic feet. He saw nothing 'hazardous' about baring rocks inside the reservoir in the course of extracting material for building the dam. During early stages of construction, he said, surplus water was diverted via an artificial cutting (subsequently partly destroyed). In June 1863, water was allowed to accumulate in the reservoir and, due to heavy rain, had risen to about 50 feet in two days. After closing the valves of the outlet pipes, some water was seen running on the outside of the dam, but Gunson was convinced it was from rocks outside and not from within the reservoir. Exactly where it had originated, he did not know. Then he had an argument with the coroner, who maintained that Gunson had said water came from rocks and through the embankment, and the engineer remaining adamant that he was referring to rocks outside. 'They mystify me,' snapped Mr Webster. 'I have been told twenty times that water could not get through rocks below the embankment, and now I am told it comes out below the embankment, and through the bank.' Even Robert Rawlinson confessed that he did not understand just what was going on. Mr Webster was clearly annoyed, but he let the matter drop and asked Gunson if the Agden reservoir embankment was designed on the same principle as the Dale Dyke dam.

GUNSON: Yes, the principle of construction is the same.

CORONER: And I suppose the principle of destruction is the same?

GUNSON: I hope not. If I thought it was, I would run away from it.

CORONER: Suppose it does burst, what will become of it?

GUNSON: The same as you have seen, but I don't anticipate it.

CORONER: But I do.

Webster was again on the attack and, in that frame of mind, had already demonstrated that he could be withering with his comments. Rashness and emotion could well take over from logic and impartiality. He suggested to Gunson that there should have been easier means of getting at a possible fracture in the pipes and repairing it than had been the case at Dale Dyke.

GUNSON: Some say we might have increased the pipes but, if we had done so, we should have increased the danger.

CORONER: I didn't say anything about increasing the pipes, but I am looking at the possibility of the pipes being broken, or so injured, as to cause a crack, and I say it would be better to have precautions to get to the fracture and so repair it, in the original construction, than to have to devise means to get at them.

GUNSON: Perhaps it might.

CORONER: Is it not unreasonable to suppose so?

GUNSON: If you suppose that anything had happened.

CORONER: No, I don't suppose anything had happened, but that it might happen.

GUNSON: We suppose it cannot happen.

CORONER: I say you have no right to suppose that, but to construct the dam on the assumption of every conceivable danger and to take precautions against these dangers. Don't you think you ought to take steps to meet them, rather than wait until an accident happens?

GUNSON: I didn't apprehend the slightest danger.

CORONER: There is the fault of the whole proceeding; neither you nor Mr Leather would look before you.

GUNSON: This is the eighth reservoir on the same principle ...

CORONER: Then, it's the eighth mistake.

PERRONET THOMPSON: Surely these are not proper observations to make before the jury.

CORONER: Oh, yes, they are, and I shall make them again. It is not a question of criminality, but I want them [the engineers] to think of some means to avoid the danger and to speak like rational men. The whole plan is that there will be no danger, and everybody else sees that it is full of danger. There is not the slightest precaution against danger.

PERRONET THOMPSON: Not when they go sixty feet down?

CORONER: No, not when the water runs down and they don't know where it goes to. It is a very serious matter. We have lost 250 of our fellow inhabitants and no man can go away without seeing it might have been avoided. They are constructing another dam on the same principles and we shall have the same mischief repeated.

The court-room was charged with tension and suppressed anger registered on the faces of the engineers and directors of the water-works company. Webster had gone well beyond the normally accepted bounds of judicial propriety, but he believed (not without some justification) the 'experts' were trying to put one over on him or, at any rate, to conceal or play down the whole truth. Certainly Leather and Gunson were volunteering as little as possible at times and Webster, who seemed overburdened by preconceived notions and hearsay evidence, found it impossible to control his personal feelings.

The hearing continued in something of an embarrassed atmosphere as Gunson went on to recount his movements on the day of the disaster. It must have been extremely painful to him as he recalled only too clearly that stormy night, the drama of the crack and the unsuccessful attempts to reduce the pressure of water before it leapt through the dam and into the valley. He said that on 10 March the water was 2ft. 3in. below the level of the bye-wash and 1ft. 3in. below on the afternoon preceding the disaster. He did not apprehend any danger at any time before the collapse.

CORONER: There is a tale in the town, Mr Gunson, that you had remarked during the day something about this embankment falling. Is that so?

GUNSON: Never.
CORONER: About bursting?
GUNSON: Never.
CORONER: Made no remark whatever?
GUNSON: Nothing whatever.

Questioned by Perronet Thompson, Gunson declared that he had superintended the construction of the dam with the utmost care and had done everything within his knowledge to render the embankment safe. He conceded, however, in the light of lessons to be learned from the failure, it would be advantageous to have better facilities for releasing a greater quantity of water in case of emergency. 'I believe,' he added, 'that in this case no means of that sort, carried to any practical extent, would have been of the slightest service.' Gunson went on answering questions put to him by the coroner and Rawlinson, during which time he praised the standard of workmanship on the dam and also the quality of the puddle used in the core wall.

Before the end of the first day's hearing, Rawlinson presented some general statistics. It had been ascertained, he said, that the total fall of the river from the dam to Owlerton was 450 feet, or 72 feet per mile. The advance of the flood was calculated to be 18 miles an hour ($26\frac{1}{2}$ feet per second) and cross-sections showed that 40,170 cubic feet (251,062 gallons) of water was passing every second. At that rate, the reservoir would have been emptied in about 47 minutes. 'The velocity was something awful,' he concluded dramatically. 'After the dam broke, a Derby horse could not have carried the information down the valley in time to have been of use.'

Newspapers gave full coverage to the inquest and, although they varied a little in what they selected to report, none missed the outspoken comments made by the coroner. Because of Webster's ill-timed salvoes, there was some feeling for Gunson and Leather who, some thought, had been unfairly treated. Others, of course, believed the engineers had got no more than they deserved; after all, it was prematurely argued, it was their fault and they jolly well ought to pay for it. When the hearing resumed on the Thursday morning, a wary eye was kept on the coroner for any signs of peevishness. There was an air of expectancy that further indiscretions would be committed by the irascible Mr Webster.

Thomas Matthew Bullock Jackson, a civil and mechanical engineer, who lived in Sheffield and once worked for Robert Stephenson, told the jury of his wide experience as consultant to important reservoir projects in Australia. He had visited the Dale Dyke dam four times since the failure, he said, and thought the quantity of material in the embankment ample, the slope sufficient and the puddle 'decidedly good'; neither did he have any fault to find with the bye-wash. He was critical of the use of railway wagons for tipping, particularly on the inner bank where he believed layers should not have exceeded two feet a time. Such wagons, travelling on the same line, emptied their loads in a manner which tended to consolidate the bank unequally. It was obvious 'tips' of more than two feet had been used; ideally, he would have recommended layers of only six inches in depth, ensuring that each was properly compacted before another was added. He had seen work in progress at Agden, where one layer was not completed before the next was started. If the method of construction at Dale Dyke was similar (which he believed to be the case), there would have been unequal settlement and the danger of a slip—particularly as the pipes ran underneath the embankment. There could result a 'springing' at the pipe joints, causing a leak. He had little doubt that that had happened.

Jackson was offering no more than a professional guess, perhaps influenced by the fact that a similar fate had befallen one of the dams he had supervised at Melbourne. The big snag at Dale Dyke, however, was that the pipes were buried under the embankment and beyond the reach of even a cursory examination. If they were unearthed and found to be broken, who was to prove that the damage was caused before or after the fatal subsidence?

The coroner had shown himself consistently fascinated by the theory of a fractured pipe and, as though reminded of the fact by Jackson's opinion, he commented generally: 'We are endeavouring to find out every possible fault in the construction of the dam. According to the description of Mr Leather and Mr Gunson, the work was so perfect that it was impossible to improve upon it. Now, in my opinion, there must have been something fatal either in its design or construction or it certainly would not have burst.'

Ralph Blakelock Smith, for many years legal adviser to the waterworks company, remarked: 'It would appear from the evidence of Mr Leather and Mr Gunson yesterday that the bursting of the bank might have been caused by a natural slip of the ground.'

CORONER: Your evidence yesterday was that the work was perfect.

SMITH: As perfect as human work can be.

CORONER: Your witnesses went for rather more than human perfection, I think, and I am now trying to test their work.

There was a lengthy discussion as to whether or not the inquest should be adjourned while the company, at their own expense, excavated the pipes for inspection by the jury. In the end the matter was shelved, although the company were urged to have the pipes examined in the near future in view of the fact that other reservoirs in the area were being, or were to be, constructed on the same principle.

SMITH: We want to know what the cause of the accident is and are as much in the dark as anybody else and we must take means for ascertaining that. But our question now is as to criminal responsibility.

CORONER: If you wish us to do so, we can soon find Mr Leather guilty of manslaughter and then it can go to York.

SMITH: That is for the jury, I submit.

CORONER: The jury have made up their minds to find no one guilty of manslaughter.

Webster, who intimated that the cause of the accident was too remote to involve criminality, again appeared to have jumped the gun. At least two men in the astonished courtroom must have breathed more easily. The verbal brickbats were by no means over, however, and Gunson, unexpectedly recalled just before the lunch-time adjournment, was in another clash with the coroner. He was questioned about deviations he was alleged to have made from the specifications (notably with regard to the puddle wall and to the depth of 'tips') and explained it was not always practicable to carry them out to the letter because of various circumstances that could arise on the site.

CORONER: Then, am I to assume that the specification is really worthless?

GUNSON: No, sir.

CORONER: What is the good of it, then?

GUNSON: As a guide.

CORONER: Then your answer is that a specification is a mere guide?

GUNSON: Which can be deviated from under peculiar circumstances. May I further say that when that specification was made, Mr Leather knew nothing at all about the material that was inside the embankment and which had to be worked.

CORONER: That has nothing to do with it. I have come to this conclusion, that a specification is a thing to mislead. There is not a particular specification for the Agden reservoir. You are making it on the same principle?

GUNSON: Yes, it is carried out something similar to that.

CORONER: You will remember, gentlemen, that it is made in precisely the same way as the one that is broken. [Jury handed a plan of Agden].

A JUROR: Is it on the same principle as this at Bradfield?

GUNSON: Yes, exactly.

CORONER: And that is directly in opposition to the terms of the specification?

GUNSON: I have no specification for that particular work.

CORONER: You say it is made in the same way as the Bradfield one; if so, it is in direct opposition to the words of this specification.

The inquisition continued and Gunson, who must have felt uncomfortable and somewhat bewildered, appears to have become less positive with his answers. He was asked about his consultations with Leather during the progress of construction work at Dale Dyke and replied that 'whenever anything has occurred of any consequence, my practice has been generally to go over and consult with Mr Leather'.

A JUROR: How many times in each year did he come to view the works?

GUNSON: I cannot say whether it was above twice or six times

A JUROR: Are you sure he came once a year?

GUNSON: I think he did.

A JUROR: He thinks he has not been once a year.

GUNSON: Yes, I think more. He was necessarily bound to come once a year in order to report to the directors the state and condition of the works, so as to appear in their report.

The editor of *The Sheffield Daily Telegraph:* William Leng

One of the twenty engravings, from photographs, offered at a penny a time by Samuel Harrison, editor of *The Sheffield Times.* The whole collection (printed on two large sheets) could be bought for 10d.

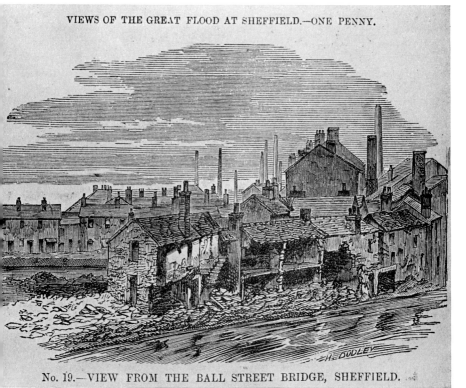

VIEWS OF THE GREAT FLOOD AT SHEFFIELD.—ONE PENNY.

E. H. DUDLEY

No. 19.—VIEW FROM THE BALL STREET BRIDGE, SHEFFIELD.

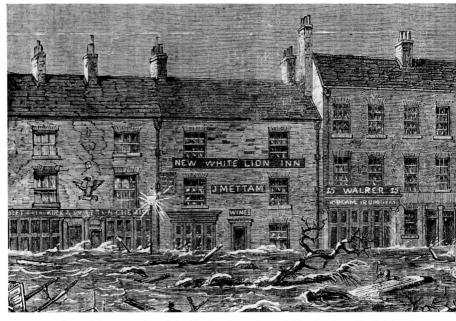

An artist's impression of the flood rushing through The Wicker, Sheffield, where (said one observer) there was sufficient water to float 'a ship of the Warrior class'

Part of Waterloo Houses, Sheffield, in which surprisingly there was only one death—that of an eighty-seven-year-old woman, Ann Cooke, believed to be the flood's oldest victim

CORONER: He is the consulting engineer and that means that he is an ornamental officer. He really knows nothing about it at all.

Then the luckless Gunson was asked if he was adhering precisely to the specification's requirement in building up the puddle wall *simultaneously* with the embankment at Agden which, as had been established, involved the same principle of construction as that adopted at Dale Dyke. He replied that, in the specific circumstances appertaining to the site, it was 'impossible'.

CORONER: I don't believe in impossibilities, and you must not talk in that way in a case of this kind. The lives of hundreds of people have been lost. How far below the embankment is the puddle wall at Agden at this moment?

GUNSON: I cannot say to a foot or two, but perhaps ten feet.

CORONER: Is that anything like the fact, Mr Fountain?

FOUNTAIN [one of the contractors]: Yes, something like the fact.

CORONER: Now, being ten feet below the embankment, there is the possibility of stones and other things falling into the puddle?

GUNSON: Yes, there is, and they do frequently.

CORONER: Was this plan followed at Bradfield?

GUNSON: The puddle wall was occasionally lower than the embankment.

CORONER: Is that not an improper mode of proceeding?

GUNSON: No, I don't think it is.

CORONER: What I apprehend is this. A specification drawn out in a formal manner like this is the result of experience and points out the best and only mode in which the works should be conducted. We have been told in the process of this inquiry that the puddle wall is the most important part, and must be the most carefully made.

GUNSON: So it is.

CORONER: The specification directs that the puddle wall must be carried up simultaneously with the embankment, and I find that that portion of the specification is absolutely thrown on one side—not the slightest attention paid to it.

GUNSON: It has been impossible to carry it out.

CORONER: I don't believe in impossibilities. Mr Leather would never put it there if it was impossible.

GUNSON: You had better ask him.

LEATHER: He does not mean impossible.

CORONER: Yes, he does; he says so.

There was no holding Webster now. He had hit on what he regarded as the nub of the matter and Gunson's failure to follow the specifications in every detail was revealed in the worst possible light. Gunson, of course, argued that the variations he made were slight and by no means dangerous. Nevertheless, he must have felt vulnerable under the constant questioning of the coroner, to whom the specifications became something of an obsession. Stones falling into the puddle, he maintained, could be 'mischievous'.

CORONER: Can you guard against it when you make your embankment in that way?

GUNSON: Certainly, I did.

CORONER: Is that a proper and satisfactory mode of carrying out an important work like this, upon the perfection of which depends the lives of hundreds of people in the town of Sheffield?

GUNSON: To my own mind, I have done nothing but what is satisfactory. I have had from the commencement of the work, the greatest anxiety, knowing that though we have constructed many before, this is of far greater magnitude, and that has kept me alive to everything where I thought danger existed. Whenever I have seen danger, I have been allowed to use everything to avert it; the money question has never been taken into consideration at all.

CORONER: I never imputed motives to you or to the company. You may have exercised the best of your judgement, but I must say it is bad judgement.

LEATHER [in answer to the coroner]: Of course every precaution is taken to provide for contingencies and that is endeavoured to be done to secure the stability of the work.

CORONER: If you take my advice, when you do it again, have no specification and then it will not mislead me and the jury, or the public. It is not intended perhaps to mislead, but it does so. You think, gentlemen, that the specification is intended to be carried out?

SEVERAL JURORS: Yes, certainly.

CORONER: Here is one made expressly to be carried out and it has not been carried out. I am out of all patience. If the work at Bradfield has been carried on in the same way as that at Agden, they are very much to blame; they will not admit a single error and entirely destroy confidence in them. If they would admit something, I should have more confidence, but they think everything is perfect.

GUNSON: Not perfect, but perfect so far as our knowledge will admit.

CORONER: Then I am sorry you have so little knowledge.

GUNSON: It is a great misfortune.

CORONER: My notion is that if you had carried out the specification the accident would not have happened.

Later in the proceedings, Webster expressed his view that the company's directors did not interfere with the work of the engineers and 'if there be any fault, it is not that of the directors'. He also offered his opinion that 'the whole system of engineering appears to be bad'. He thought the consulting engineer should attend the site more regularly and insist on his specifications being carried out. 'But the engineer is really a gentleman who lives at a distance,' added the coroner, 'and knows nothing about the work, but rests on the report of a sub-engineer for his own report to the directors and that is the end. In the middle of the night, we are all hurried into eternity without warning.'

HENRY PAWSON [jury foreman]: Will you say in how many instances you did refer questions to the consulting engineer during the progress of the Bradfield reservoir?

GUNSON: Perhaps half a dozen during the progress of the works.

CORONER: Did you consult him and ask permission to make the puddle wall in the same way that you are making it now at Agden?

GUNSON: Certainly not, but he has seen it.

CORONER: And has not found fault with it?

GUNSON: No.

CORONER: Then he ought to be ashamed of himself.

Gunson volunteered the information that James Simpson, the

celebrated engineer, had seen the Agden embankment the previous August and 'is in a position to say how these works at that time were being constructed and carried out'.

CORONER: He may say what he likes, all the engineers in England can say what they like; you have no right to hoodwink the public with specifications and never carry them out. They are made to be carried out for the safety of the owners of property and the public, and ought to be carried out to the strictest letter of the law. I do not care what engineers may say to the contrary. There is a specification saying do the work one way, and you do it quite contrary; when destruction comes upon us, you dare to say the work is perfect. It won't do at all.

Everybody was taken aback by this uncontrolled outburst and even a juror felt constrained to say: 'I think, Mr Coroner, you should take it more deliberately.'

Webster was not to be shaken off, however, and commented: 'It is difficult to do so. They have not constructed the work in a workmanlike manner; they have destroyed nearly 300 of our fellow citizens. It is no use having specifications and plans if they are to be departed from at will, no use at all.'

Blakelock Smith said the company were prepared, if required, to call some of the most eminent engineers in the world. The company welcomed the fullest possible inquiry into the cause of the disaster.

CORONER: Can you tell us the cause of the breakage?

SMITH: We cannot, nor can any of the witnesses.

CORONER: If you cannot point out a reason for the embankment breaking, we have a right to assume that it has failed from bad workmanship.

SMITH: I demur from that. It has been suggested that it is not bad workmanship, but a natural failure in the ground which human foresight could not prevent.

During the afternoon session, Leather was recalled and said he had not objected to the contract taken by the company on the ground that too little money was being paid. Of the seven tenders submitted for the building of the Dale Dyke reservoir, two were below his own estimate, and that of Mr Craven, which was accepted, was £900 above. Blakelock Smith said the original contract price was £27,469, to which £1,000 was added when the site of the embankment was altered. Extras had cost upwards of £6,000 already and were continuing.

Robert Rawlinson then took the oath. Although his views were on anticipated lines, they were listened to intently. An engineer, he believed, should be master of his work, not the work master of him, and he said he was generally against laying pipes underneath embankments because the practice precluded examination or repair. He preferred the provision of a tunnel, or culvert, through the solid stratification on one side of the valley and perfectly free from the loose earth of an embankment; within this tunnel outlet pipes were laid and a method provided for closing them on the *inside* of the reservoir, not on the *outside*, as at Dale Dyke.

Referring to the mode of laying the pipes at the failed dam, Rawlinson expressed himself surprised to learn that where they crossed the puddle trench they had not been supported as if in solid ground. 'In place of this being done,' he declared, 'an artificial trench had been excavated at a flat slope from the bottom of the puddle trench, until at the surface line it exceeded 200 feet in length; that this had been filled with puddle to a depth of 30 feet in the puddle trench, thinning itself to 18 inches of puddle on the solid at either end, leaving upwards of 200 feet (i.e. 20) pipes in 9-foot lengths, with no bottom support other than the puddle beneath them which, in the centre, if I remember rightly, is said to be 30 feet deep, and this would be in that portion of the embankment where the greatest possible weight would be brought to bear—under the apex.'

Even if the vulnerable sections of piping had slipped into the artificially formed compressible substratum without fracturing or 'drawing' a joint, a cavity would be left in the extended puddle trench above it. The inference was that as the water rose it would penetrate the inner bank, which appeared to have less watertight material in the top half of it—the higher the water, the smaller became the intervening space between it and the puddle wall—and seek out the weakest point. The water could then find its way down the inside face of the puddle wall to the cavity which had been caused by slipping pipes. 'The first top water,' said Rawlinson, 'has been described as coming over in sheets and waves of foam. That water did not flow down the slope of the bank, but was absorbed vertically into it, showing that the material of the bank was of the openest possible character.'

That dramatic observation was followed by one even more sensational. 'Having seen the Agden embankment,' Rawlinson continued, 'and seeing the mode of tipping the wagons now in operation day by day, and the material tipped, I have no hesitation in coming to the conclusion that the substance of that bank is as porous as a sieve.' He waited until the shocked murmurings had died away before he proceeded: 'The specification which has been alluded to, gives the height of the tips as not to exceed three feet; the tips at present in work are at least double that height. This method of working rolls the largest stones continually to the foot of the tips and makes, in fact, a rubble embankment, open and porous in layers.'

John Gunson must have felt professionally naked at that time as Rawlinson, quietly and precisely, made point after point. It was far more shattering than being shouted at by the coroner who, after all, knew very little about the practicalities of building a dam. Rawlinson was a different matter. He knew what he was about and, even if his were no more than theories, here was a professional (in the capacity of a Government inspector) stating firmly that faulty construction existed at Agden which, as Gunson himself confirmed, was being built on the same principle as the dam at Dale Dyke. The jury would undoubtedly go for what Rawlinson had to say— and he had by no means finished.

Rawlinson thought it 'most objectionable' to take material for making the Dale Dyke dam from within the reservoir and below the water line. Several acres of surface and many square yards of fissured rock had been bared; into that rock, surface water flowed easily without pressure. How much greater, with pressure, would be the discharge of water into those rocks? No engineer, according to Rawlinson, could tell just what would become of it. The water might waste itself harmlessly below, but there was a possibility of its communicating with fissures beneath the external slope of the embankment. He was also critical of the bye-wash, which he considered too small for the job it was intended to perform; neither was it and the outlet pipes combined adequate for discharging sufficient water in case of danger. Rawlinson believed there should have been a watercourse independent of the dam and said he was 'astonished the engineers destroyed the one they had made [to divert water when making the dam] and did not keep it for this purpose'.

After what must have been an agonizing afternoon for all those connected with the waterworks company, Rawlinson ended by saying it was 'humanly impossible' to come to any positive conclusion as to the cause of the failure. (The coroner did not, on that occasion, say he did 'not believe in impossibilities'). There could have been one or more of a number of reasons, including fractured piping, a blown or drawn joint, the sinking of pipes, a landslip resulting from undiscovered fissures or springs, or a creep along the main pipes. In his judgement, the 'most fatal mistake was to lay 200 feet of piping in the centre of the embankment upon an artificially formed compressible material'.

Nathaniel Beardmore told the inquest he agreed substantially with what Rawlinson had said, which surprised nobody. Nevertheless, he thought the puddle wall reflected 'most excellent workmanship and I think that the immense depth excavated must have removed danger from springs'. He was also inclined to the view that the method of laying the pipes was the most likely source of the trouble.

Blakelock Smith said if the jury had decided no criminality was involved, it would waste time if he were to bring forward further evidence which would be of a theoretical nature, although of equal value to that produced by the other side. The jury's foreman announced that they wished to retire just to settle the point of personal responsibility but, when they returned some fifteen minutes later, the coroner said they had reached a verdict and it was unnecessary for him to sum up. 'I am rather glad it is so,' he commented, 'for had I summed up I should have spoken more strongly than some people would like and would have expressed my feelings in such language as, in many people's opinion, might not be fit from this bench but which, in my opinion, the case would justify.'

The foreman, Pawson, rose and delivered the following:

We find that Thomas Elston came to his death by drowning in the inundation, caused by the bursting of the Bradfield reservoir, on the morning of the 12th of March instant; that, in our opinion, there has not been that engineering skill and that attention to the construction of the works, which their magnitude and importance demanded; that, in our opinion, the Legislature ought to take such action as will result in a Governmental inspection of all works of this character, and that such inspection should be frequent, sufficient and regular; that we cannot separate without expressing our deep regret at the fearful loss of life which has occurred from the disruption of the Bradfield reservoir.

So there it was. The official conclusion of the jury would remain forever on record. Legal representatives gathered up their documents, newspaper reporters hurried off to tell the world and little groups of men, in quiet conversation, gradually dispersed. The room, which had staged a national drama, emptied and went back to being just another room.

John Webster went home to Broomhall Park in the knowledge that he had startled a few skeletons in complacent cupboards. By his outrageously unconventional approach he had swept aside some of the restrictive decorum usually associated with court procedure and, as a result, had achieved some success in extracting additional information from reticent witnesses. In that strength lay also his weakness: by blurting out his personal feelings, the emotional Mr Webster had managed to produce the opposite effect to that he had intended and his indiscretions had sparked off a wave of sympathy for the company's engineers. Nevertheless, it is difficult not to admire the man who, exasperated at what he saw as evasion, pressed vigorously in an attempt to bring out the whole truth. There can be no doubting his sincerity nor the fact that he had expressed in public what many people thought privately.

Travelling back to his country seat at Leventhorpe Hall, near Leeds, John Towlerton Leather was perhaps still smarting from some of the coroner's sharp-tongued remarks. He had been crudely described as an 'ornamental officer' yet, in a sense, it was true. As consultant engineer, he had prepared plans and, occasionally, presented reports, but he appears to have done little more. Nothing more, perhaps, was expected of him. He undoubtedly deeply lamented the widespread misery caused by the failure of the dam but, for years now, Leather had concentrated his attention on his successful business as a contractor and given less of his interest to his role as engineering consultant. He was currently engaged on supervising the construction of sea forts in Spithead to protect the naval dockyards at Portsmouth; other commercial projects and outside activities also claimed much of his time. Leather, who was nearly sixty, owned extensive estates and was already wealthy enough to be thinking in terms of devoting more of his life to their development and management. Before he withdrew from business affairs completely in the latter half of the 1870s, he had large holdings of land also in Northumberland, where he had another grand country seat at Middleton Hall, Belford, about three miles inland from the coast which looks out to Holy Island. He was to be Deputy-Lieutenant of Northumberland and, in 1875, the High Sheriff. As one of the landed gentry, Leather moved easily in high circles and it was unlikely the inquest verdict would affect his reputation as a first-rate contractor or interfere in any way with his social standing. He was a man of position and would survive without difficulty.

With John Gunson, it was different. He had been responsible for supervising the actual construction of the Dale Dyke dam and, as he left the Town Hall, he must have felt mentally drained. A lack of 'engineering skill and attention' the jury had said, an all-embracing phrase with a ring of finality about it. If only he could have convinced them of just how much time and attention to detail he had put into that work, he may have mused, but verdicts are cold and calculating and often do not take into account the honest endeavour and fallibility of man.

Gunson would never forget that ghastly night on the storm-swept moors, nor the sight and plight of the sufferers. For all practical purposes, he was the one upon whom much of the official blame appeared to have settled. To their credit, the Sheffield Water-works Company stood by Gunson and he remained in their employ for the remainder of his days. A cynic might say that to have released him from his duties would have been interpreted as an admission of guilt by the company, but that seems unfair. Indeed, the company never conceded the collapse of the dam to be any more than a pure accident beyond anyone's control. There were a number of examples of Gunson's being singled out for praise by his seniors, both before and after the disaster, and it is doubtful if the company had a more devoted and conscientious servant during the whole of their 57-year history.

Nevertheless, there had been errors in the building of the Dale Dyke dam. A jury had said so.

7 Twenty-five per cent

Almost the only common factor to emerge from the proceedings at the inquest was one of dissatisfaction. The verdict was considered vague, the hearing limited in approach and much of the evidence not really evidence at all. Most people already accepted that constructional defects existed at Dale Dyke, but there was regret that no specific reason for the dam's collapse had been proved. For their part, the directors and engineers of the waterworks company rejected any suggestion that human error was involved and were also dismayed by the unbridled comments made by the coroner. Indeed, there was widespread concern, and even some hostility, about the manner in which the inquiry had been conducted.

It was argued strongly in some quarters that all but one of the witnesses had witnessed nothing. Of those on the spot when the embankment fell apart, only Gunson was called upon to give an account and it was highly improbable that a servant of the company, particularly one so closely associated with the dam, would volunteer information likely to compromise him with his employers or, more significantly, incriminate himself. On the other side of the controversial coin Rawlinson and Beardmore, recognized as first-rate engineers, were also bound by an allegiance—in their case, the government. As it turned out, they had been unable to do more than speculate upon what might have occurred. Rawlinson made much play on the possibility of fractured pipes being the reason for the disaster and had put forward a convincing case but, at best, it was only professional guesswork. The pipes remained buried under tons of embankment. They could have been damaged in the collapse, in which event it would be difficult to prove the point one way or the other and, even if they were found to be intact, there was nothing to say they had not 'settled' in the puddle, with fatal results, *before* the dam fell.

Nevertheless, some critics felt the company should have been ordered to excavate the pipes and the inquest adjourned until a thorough inspection had been made. It was also contended that a full cross-section of the embankment should have been revealed so that the 'tips' could be more closely examined. A bigger fuss centred around the absence of independent witnesses, however. Certainly it is hard to understand why the coroner did not summon to give evidence some of those employed in building the dam and a few local residents as well. Neither Samuel Hammerton, the farmer, nor Joseph Ibbotson, the corn miller, had anything to gain by not telling the truth about what they had seen. Was it not possible a layman, unrestricted by loyalties, could have thrown some useful light on the state of the dam during construction or at the time of its failure? A company employee, whose identity was not disclosed, said he had seen a 'hollow' where part of the inner bank had subsided some weeks before the burst, claiming it was at approximately the spot where the water first broke through. Whether or not he was a reliable witness, or his testimony accurate, could easily have been established in court. There must have been others. The omission to bring forward such witnesses seems seriously to have reduced the scope of the investigation. Without them, how could other than a partial (in both senses of the word) story have been told? It is just possible Rawlinson had some say in the matter, for we know from his confidential letter to the Home Secretary that he was worried by the thought of 'all sorts of evidence' being given. On the other hand, one cannot imagine the coroner being pushed into anything which he disapproved.

Whether the limitation resulted from a deliberate decision or poor judgement, anyone reading the newspaper reports could have been forgiven for thinking the inquest on the deaths of nearly 250 men, women and children (for that is what it amounted to) was basically a technical discussion between engineers, enlivened by peppery inter-round summaries by the coroner. Despite the censure hurled at them by John Webster, both Leather and Gunson were considered by many lucky to have got off so lightly. There was no doubt in numerous minds that it was their carelessness which had led to mass deaths and that they should have been punished for it. The view of others was that had the coroner exercised more restraint and summed up in a logical, yet incisive, manner, the effect upon the two engineers would have been far more salutary. The proceedings leading up to the verdict were anything but well received and Webster came in for a cascade of criticism even he could not have envisaged.

He was assailed from nearly all sides. Correspondents wrote to the Press condemning his 'unmeasured expressions' and the newspapers themselves, while acknowledging a coroner's duty to elicit the facts, decided he had far exceeded his powers and acted without the impartiality incumbent upon him. *The Leeds Mercury* referred to his 'unseemly conduct, his violence and his insolence', while *The Morning Star* thought his behaviour 'can only be characterized as presumptuous, overbearing and arrogant'. This paper went on to say the evidence was 'not sufficient to justify a criminal prosecution, nor so severe a censure on the engineers and contractors as would leave them under the intolerable odium of moral culpability for the deplorable loss of life and property that has ensued. But we must say that those gentlemen owe their escape from that unhappy position chiefly to the resolute moderation of Mr Rawlinson and Mr Beardmore, the Government engineers. If it had been left to the coroner and jury to frame a verdict according to their own notions, it would evidently have been one of manslaughter'.

The sturdy *Manchester Guardian* declared that the inquest must have been 'a very painful spectacle to all who were present, and its records will have been read with deep mortification by all to whom the honour of English justice is dear. It is not agreeable to know that in a room which, for the time being, was a court of justice, the only person who suffered himself to be overcome by irrational passion, and who behaved with such undignified impropriety, was the officer who presided in the name of the law'.

Not all the criticism was reserved for the coroner. For instance, the *Daily News* commented: 'The verdict is terrible even in its vagueness. Nobody in particular is condemned—neither the directors of the company who owned the reservoir, nor the consulting engineer who planned the work, nor the acting engineer who superintended the construction. Nor is the precise cause of the failure assigned.... In such works, nothing should be left to chance. Perfect security is attainable by known methods and there should be some means of insisting upon their adoption. No individuals, whether severally or in association, should be allowed to accumulate carelessly the elements of destruction above the heads of a helpless population. The public will probably agree with the jury that constructions of this order ought to be treated as public works and executed under inspection'.

The Observer reflected soberly: 'The inquiry, however, was necessarily restricted and, through a mass of theoretical evidence, clothed in technical phraseology, the jury have arrived at a sensible and moderate verdict.'

Those few examples were representative of reactions to be found in the general Press whose readers, in the main, were unfamiliar with many facets of civil engineering. It is interesting, therefore to see what *The Engineer*, a weekly devoted to the sayings and doings of professionals, had in mind. Predictably, it emphasized that the jury's verdict did not impute 'any special negligence or incompetence' to the engineers or contractors. The writer went on to defend Leather and his work and pointed out that 'hundreds of engineers who, seeing the Bradfield dam in progress, would have been satisfied with it simply because, from all the evidence given, it was made as scores of large reservoir embankments are known to have been made. It might have been better made, no doubt, and so might everything ever made by human hands. No member of our profession, on reading the evidence adduced before the coroner's jury, will fail to sympathize with Mr Leather. There are a number whose position, and the weight of whose authority, would have enabled them to insist upon and to obtain a better class of work in a large reservoir dam, but even those must be aware that in many cases other engineers cannot obtain the sanction of their clients for works of the expensive quality corresponding to the highest standard of possible safety. In such cases, an engineer must do the best he can and, although he may wish to provide better and more ample work, he must, so far as he conscientiously believes himself to be well within the limits of safety, sacrifice something to economy'.

The writer added that, whatever the public feeling, there was 'no evidence' as to the cause of failure—a fact, he said, that remained unaltered by Robert Rawlinson's views. 'Although employed by the Government,' he continued, 'Mr Rawlinson is not an authority above all others in matters of engineering. He is no doubt a very good engineer in his way, but the nature of his position compels him to be censorious. What he says goes far with the public, but it counts for nothing with the engineering profession, the members of which judge for themselves.' There followed a shift of emphasis. Having sympathized with Leather, believed that 'hundreds' of engineers would have approved of the dam during its construction and shown some contempt for Rawlinson's opinions, the writer concluded: 'That the Bradfield dam was lamentably defective no one can doubt.' He explained, however, that if the materials and work were bad, it was not from negligence or incompetence but because of 'a defective system, too generally followed, we fear, in the execution of most large modern works'.

A week later, *The Engineer* had another stab: 'We believe that so far as designs go, those for the Bradfield dam were sufficiently good to secure entire safety had they only been properly carried out.... The whole failure resulted, we have no doubt, from a departure from the specification and from haste and negligence in making the upper part of the dam.... It is to be regretted that Mr Leather was in a position where he was compelled to depend upon the co-operation of others for the faithful execution of his plans. If he committed any error it was, we apprehend, in not having exercised sufficient authority. As for the failure it arose, we believe, from the haste and neglect of those who actually constructed the work from Mr Leather's designs.' The journal for the professionals would not have gained first prize for consistency.

The inquest verdict did little to assuage the passions generated by the disaster, the cause and effect of which continued to be top priority in the columns of Sheffield's newspapers, the corridors of the Town Hall and the offices of the waterworks company. It was also a chief topic of conversation in the elegant mansions of Ranmoor and the humbler dwellings beneath the smoke. The arguments, allegations and recriminations went on for months. There were, too, some more pleasant aspects: by the end of March, the relief fund totalled more than £26,000 and some of it was being put to immediate use. In addition to obvious cases of destitution there were many sufferers who, with a little assistance, could usefully get back into harness. In that category were manual workers who had lost the tools of their trade. The most urgent claims were dealt with speedily and, in the first instance, over £600 was expended on replacing the tools for men upon whom 57 women and 182 children depended. It was noted with satisfaction that applicants had put reasonable values on the tools they required and that there had been no attempts at extortion. In most cases, the recipients signed a document surrendering any corresponding claim they would make against the waterworks company to the Relief Committee. The 'transfers' were made out in favour of the Mayor, as treasurer of the fund, and the wisdom of such a move remained to be seen. It was a gamble, but committee members feared the company might not pay up if they knew claimants had been wholly, or partly, reimbursed from another source. The company, it was felt, should be given no chance of evading their responsibilities.

The company were moving warily (cunningly, in the opinion of some) and announced they had not yet been legally advised as to what form of compensation they were liable to pay. Meanwhile, the Relief Committee went on dispensing goodwill and donations (not generously enough, according to some people, considering the huge amount in hand) and took as a simple yardstick those deemed to be most in need. It was a massive job, which needed to be continuous and conducted with the utmost care, vigilance and tact. After satisfying as best they could the most dire cases, the committee decided to buy furniture for distribution and, in many instances, the sufferers received items far superior to those they had lost. Two weeks after the flood, Mayor Jessop reported: 'The committee are not at the moment able to say what amount will be required in order to extend immediate relief to all who cannot afford to wait for it. But, as far as they can at present calculate, they sincerely believe that the amount already subscribed will very far from suffice to enable them to give full relief to all who come fairly within that description'. As it turned out, the committee overestimated how much money was wanted and, in the end, a great deal had to be returned. They could not be expected to foresee the future, however.

Despite commendable efforts to clear up, it was a slow process. Streets were still covered with mud, houses and shops badly affected by water and filth. Even now, the magnitude of the disaster was difficult to comprehend. Measured merely by the cartloads of sodden rubbish taken away, it was enormous—and that was only part of the picture. Battered homes and factories remained, some for months, as grisly reminders of that terrible night. Tables, chairs, cooking utensils and other domestic articles swept out of homes by the flood were deposited at centres, awaiting collection by their owners. It must have been impossible to know if the claimants were *bona fide* and, after a time, the items were auctioned or consigned to the scrap-heap. In some districts, it proved impossible to pump out cellars for, due to overfilled drains, the water just flowed back. The discovery of another body was an almost daily occurrence. Decomposition and disfiguration made the identification of some quite out of the question and, for the same reason, rapid burial was essential. An unparalleled horror had hitched itself to the everyday life of Sheffield and, although the national spotlight had dimmed and moved on, the sorrow and destruction remained.

It was noted by one journalist that 'a persevering and very zealous effort has been made in this town to gloss over the late accident, to praise up the ruined embankment, to eulogize the engineers who planned and executed that fearful failure, and to cry down all who may have officially expressed any degree of censure on those on whom rests the responsibility of the great work which has so ignominiously and with such disastrous consequences broken down'. That sharp pen can have been wielded by none other than William Leng.

Nevertheless, there prevailed (chiefly among the wealthier element) a genuine sympathy for the directors of the waterworks company who, it was argued, had run into a bad patch and deserved all the support they could get. Support was fair enough but, accompanied by attempts to exonerate completely the engineers and to free the board from all blame, smacked too much of special pleading to attract a majority view. The motivation for such tactics, it seemed, sprang from private, and not public, interests. 'Let's stand by the directors, who will then play ball with everybody,' appeared to be the crux of the campaign. The directors were men of the strictest integrity, it was pointed out, and indeed they were. They would act nobly, fairly and generously towards all interested parties, it was asserted, and doubtless (within limits) they would. What seems to have been overlooked was that the directors, however honourable, were hard-headed businessmen out to obtain the best possible deal they could for themselves and the company's shareholders. There was nothing wrong in that. After all, it was business.

The directors' rating was confirmed in the eyes of their supporters (and even rose a little in the estimation of their critics) when, two days after the inquest, they announced a halt to further work on the Agden reservoir until the 'best possible advice' as to its future had been obtained. The decision looked thoughtful and highly responsible, even magnanimous. Here were the directors doing their best to co-operate with widespread opinion, although they disagreed with it; now they were surely showing their true colours. Such a move was bound to be popular. It was also unusually well timed. It was more than a coincidence that, four days later, the directors received from the Home Secretary what amounted to an official request to cease operations at Agden. Grey's letter reminded them of 'the very serious responsibility which the Sheffield Waterworks Company will incur if, after the failure of the Bradfield reservoir, and with the knowledge of the opinion expressed by eminent engineers, as well as by the coroner's jury, as to the errors committed in its construction, the company continue to construct the reservoir at the Agden embankment on the same plan and without adopting proper measures for preventing similar consequences to those which are alleged to have produced the catastrophe at the Bradfield reservoir, attended by such a fearful loss of life, as well as destruction of property'. No amount of soft-soap or whitewash was going to expunge that weighty warning from Whitehall. Or so it appeared.

Rawlinson had lost little time in acquainting the Home Secretary of his views on the two dams. In a letter, he stated unreservedly that 'everything objectionable at the Bradfield embankment, which has failed, is now in the course of repetition at the Agden embankment'. Before returning to London after the inquest, Rawlinson had revisited the Agden site. Not only did the directors know that, but they probably also had an idea of his intentions. Indeed, it is likely that he told them. Anyway, they had beaten the Home Secretary to the punch and, in their reply, were able to tell him they had already made their decision before getting his letter. The directors also made it known they were anxious to dispel any uneasiness that might exist about the condition of the company's other reservoirs and had appointed Thomas Hawksley and J. F. Bateman to investigate. The two men, from the nation's top-drawer of civil engineers, reported the Rivelin reservoirs to be in 'a most perfect and satisfactory state'. The reservoirs at Redmires, they observed, were 'generally speaking, in good condition, but a few ordinary repairs are needed'. (Gunson was straightway sent to arrange for the 'ordinary' repairs to be carried out. A town councillor, Isaac Ironside, who visited Redmires five months later, said he saw the largest reservoir had been emptied to allow repairs to the embankment, part of which had 'given way'). Hawksley and Bateman concluded that the company's reservoirs had stood the test of 'many years, during which they have undergone no important alteration' and there 'ought not to be the occasion for any doubt or apprehension'.

What else had the directors in mind? How were the company to meet a great demand for compensation and, at the same time, retain the confidence of shareholders? The plan upon which the directors eventually embarked promptly put them out of favour with most of the town. Less than twenty-four hours after the Town Council had agreed to postpone discussing important motions concerned with the dam failure, liability and a take-over bid, in order not to exacerbate the situation, the company issued their annual report.

The council's apparently reasonable attitude was prompted by the Mayor, who had made himself ill by his recent exertions. From his sick-bed, Tommy Jessop sent a message (by Alderman John Brown) in which he indicated to his civic colleagues that the company's report, including the directors' keenly awaited proposals, would be of such a character as would be acceptable to the town. He was either misinformed or had misjudged the position and later found reason to change his tolerant tune. The report revealed that the company were to seek Parliamentary permission to raise additional capital of £400,000 to meet their liabilities. Few people would object to that. What they also sought, however, was sanction to make a 'moderate' increase on the water rates they were currently entitled to levy. In other words, the company wanted to obtain from their consumers extra money to help pay debts incurred by the failure of their own dam. That, of course, did not go down well, although it was noted that the proposed rise was to be 'moderate'. In addition, the company wished legally to be released from their obligations under the 1853 Act to guarantee compensation water to the millowners in the Loxley Valley which, it was claimed, would enable 'the company to fully supply the requirements of the town more rapidly than would be practicable under the existing system'. The directors expressed themselves in disagreement with the publicly stated alleged causes of the Dale Dyke failure and also with any suggestion that the Agden embankment was unsafe; accordingly, they had called in top engineers, including Hawksley, Bateman and James Simpson, to examine both dams and report.

On the face of it, the company had presented a reasonable case. General liability had been admitted—a strong point in favour of their image, although they can have had no alternative. They had

confessed to being unable to raise the necessary money from existing funds and were prepared to get the extra capital by creating
preference shares and by mortgages. They had offered to provide
quickly an improved water supply to the town if they could un-
saddle from their backs the burden of providing compensation
water. Had the directors not also exercised good judgement by
suspending building at Agden? Finally, they recorded their 'deep
thankfulness' for the charitable contributions to alleviate immediately some of the suffering. 'Whatever may be the ultimate extent
of the liability of the company,' it was stated in the report, 'it is
obvious that the situation of the company renders impossible any
attempt to offer immediate relief to any case or class of cases, however hard they may be. It must be, therefore, a source of satisfaction
to the shareholders to know that the magnificent fund raised in every
part of the country for the assistance of the sufferers must, in many
instances, have averted that ruin which, in the absence of such a
provision, would have involved many of those persons whose
property was injured by the inundation.'

To those who could afford the luxury of waiting, the company's
proposals might well have been seen in an advantageous light. It
would mean an increased water rate, of course, but also the benefits
of a better service. That was one way of looking at it. For the less
well educated and poorer sections of the community, who would
more readily appreciate a short-term solution, there was the promise
of compensation—a chance to collect. That was another point of
view. Initially, therefore, reactions were moderate, even optimistic.
Then came a bombshell: in published details of their proposed
Bill, the company revealed that the 'moderate' addition to the
water rate was to be a recommended 25 per cent. The news was
greeted with dismay and anger.

Even the shrewd William Leng, who had earlier thought the
company's case 'reasonable', was not now so sure. He was caught
in mid-stream, but began paddling steadily towards the opposite
bank from where he was later to assail the directors. For the present,
however, he told readers of *The Sheffield Daily Telegraph*: 'We
feel great sympathy for the shareholders but, as no one ever
proposed that they should pay over for the benefit of the town any
of their surplus profits, so they can only ask the town to assist them
in their extremity as a favour and not as a right.' Advocating
public ownership of the water undertaking, he maintained: 'In

other towns, a better and more constant supply of water has been secured by transferring the waterworks from trading companies to the municipalities. We don't see why Sheffield should not enjoy the same advantages. At all events, the option of securing them in the future should now be obtained.'

The Mayor was in a quandary. Complying with a requisition, he called a meeting at the Town Hall on 5 May to discuss the company's Bill upon which subject, he said, there was 'great diversity of opinion'. He thought a 'strong desire' existed in Sheffield to do what was right by the company and also in the best interests of the town. Personally, he found much difficulty in reaching a decision and, in view of his position, begged to be excused from expressing any specific view. Like other leading citizens, the non-plussed Mr Jessop had friends on the company's board of directors and, as Mayor, he was expected to be impartial. So, for the moment, he squatted uncertainly on the fence. There were many in that crowded hall of property owners and occupiers not shackled by such obligations, however, and the directors came in for some severe criticism. One resolution adopted was that, while pleased to learn that liability to pay compensation had been accepted, the meeting expressed surprise that 'a wealthy company should attempt to tax the town for the reparation of the damage caused by the failure of their own works'. There were still misgivings about certain aspects of the inquest and the resolution's proposer, Michael Beal, claimed that anyone who went to Dale Dyke 'might get more information from a poor navvy in reference to the bursting of the reservoir than from the whole of the evidence laid before the coroner's jury'. His view was not an isolated one. The meeting also agreed a petition opposing the Bill be forwarded to John Arthur Roebuck for presentation to the House of Commons. In addition, a committee (including the Mayor) was elected 'to oppose the said Bill in such manner as they may deem best for the interests of the public'.

Not all the Bill was condemned. The company's proposal that commissioners should be appointed to adjudicate on compensation claims was welcomed in principle (though not in all details, including the suggested members of such a tribunal) by the meeting. (In the event, an independent commission met in Sheffield, thus eliminating any need for claimants to appear at ordinary civil courts which would have involved much time, expense and travelling). No, what really stuck in the gullet was the 25 per cent clause which, according to some speakers, would put the company in an even sounder position than at present. It was considered 'monstrous' and, while the accident might be unfortunate for the directors, it was their problem to solve without calling upon the town. There were cries of 'dishonest', 'preposterous' and 'unfair' and calls of 'sell to the Town Council'. One incensed gentleman said on the morning before the disaster that the company, according to the share list, was worth £549,000 so that, even now, with their estimated liabilities, they were a comparatively valuable asset at £150,000. Shareholders realized that, he added, and, after a slight initial panic, had clung tightly to their shares.

The Sheffield Waterworks Company knew exactly where they stood with one important cross-section of the community. They, too, were preparing a strong case and assembling a powerful posse of supporters to chase objectors off the range of increased rates. The company were backed by 380 shareholders and also had influential allies among prosperous traders and manufacturers. Other meetings were held before the Bill reached a Select Committee of the House of Commons. Millowners had reason to rejoice when the company withdrew all proposals to rescind their legal duty to supply compensation water along the Loxley. For whatever reason, the company had appeased one considerable body of known opposition. The hope of a quicker and improved water supply to the town presumably faded as a result. With so many of the inhabitants against it, the Bill was not given much chance of success. Surely, it was argued in effect, the innocent would not be made to pay the debts of the guilty.

For a time, attention was diverted from the clashing factions after a report of an outbreak of fever at Owlerton. The story soon gained currency, for still frighteningly fresh in some minds was the visitation of cholera in August 1849, and the far more devastating epidemic which had swept through Sheffield in 1832, when the disease killed more than four hundred, including John Blake, the Master Cutler. Now, in the wake of the flood, the danger of some killer contagion was real enough; the whole situation was ripe for it. Happily, it was a false alarm, the 'epidemic' turning out to be a few cases of illness—no more than the average for that time of year. Nevertheless, Sheffield's record of health (or, more accurately, the lack of it) did not inspire confidence. While other large towns had actively heeded warnings by such reformers as the pugnacious Edwin Chadwick, secretary for the Poor Law Commissioners, that fever was often traceable to bad water supplies, poor sanitation and ineffective sewage disposal, Sheffield dithered. Less than four years previously, the Town Council thought it 'not expedient at the present time' to consider improving sanitary conditions. So the stench and slime continued to be endured and 'abominations' went on being tipped into choked rivers. Despite some improvements during the rest of the 1860s, a hygienic Sheffield was a long way off.

In his *Victorian Cities*, Professor Asa Briggs wrote: 'The relatively high earnings and standard of comfort of the Sheffield artisans, except in periods of bad trade, kept them uninterested in large schemes of municipal reform for most of the Victorian age. Their trade societies were often societies complete in themselves and it was not until the twentieth century that they became an active force in municipal government.' By adopting the Local Government Act in 1864, the Town Council had the opportunity of implementing a number of urgently needed public schemes, but it remained to be seen if they would do so. One thing the council did do, with rare alacrity, was officially to oppose the waterworks company's Bill electing a sub-committee to prepare a suitable case for presentation (through counsel) to the Select Committee. The decision was by a substantial majority (objections being confined mainly to councillors with an interest in the company) and, on the whole, Sheffield applauded what was being planned by the civic authority. Opposition to the Bill grew and, on paper, it looked as if the company's brainchild would be crushed at birth.

Robert Rawlinson and Nathaniel Beardmore meanwhile had completed their official report on the failure of the Dale Dyke dam, dated 20 May, and it was 'presented to Parliament by Her Majesty's Command'. It appears not to have been readily available until early June, however, by which time the Home Secretary had received letters from Sheffield's Town Clerk and from the waterworks company inquiring anxiously for copies prior to the opening of the hearing before the Select Committee. In one such message William Smith, the company's chairman, said the directors wished to know of Rawlinson's conclusions because it was 'imperative to get on with the works to meet the requirements of the population'. They all had to be patient.

The document, incorporating appendices of a transcription of evidence at the inquest, a list of the dead and missing, a map of the flood's course and plans of the reservoir, contained few real surprises, but it was couched in plain language. There was criticism of the bye-wash and outlet pipes, which would together discharge some 19,000 cubic feet of water a minute whereas, in extreme flood, about 30,000 cubic feet per minute would be flowing into the reservoir. Leather and Gunson, it seemed, had not done their homework. Commenting upon the actual bursting of the dam, the authors of the report stated that 'the greater portion of the mischief was effected in from 15 to 30 minutes, in which time 92,000 cubic yards of material were swept away'. On the siting of the reservoir they had this to say: 'We did not notice any landslip at the site of the Dale Dyke embankment to lead to the conclusion that such contingency had caused the failure.' For most practical purposes, the findings of the two engineers were in the report's final paragraphs:

An examination of the pipes will not now be evidence against them, as it may be said the rupture disturbed and injured the pipes rather than that the pipes originally were the cause of the failure. Destruction so rapid and so entire requires, however, adequate power for its accomplishment. The facts stand as under: the puddle trench was unfavourable; the outlet pipes were laid in a most objectionable manner so as, in fact, to ensure a fracture somewhere; the puddle wall is much too thin and the material placed on either side of it is of too porous a character and was placed by railway tip-wagons, which is the worst manner of constructing a watertight embankment.

No puddle wall should ever be placed betwixt masses of porous earth, as puddle under such conditions will crack and is also liable to be fractured by pressure of water. A wall of puddle 16 feet thick at the ground line and 95 feet in height could not remain entire in the midst of such material; any injury to any part of it would be permanent and, if exposed to pressure of water, could be dangerous. A puddle wall needs to be backed up, on both sides, to at least double its own thickness, with fine-selected material, so as to prevent direct pressure of water from inside or any drying and consequent cracking on the outside. Six feet in depth of water will puncture 12 inches of sound

puddle, if laid hollow over rubble stone and loose earth like this
bank; so that 16 feet of puddle would be liable to be punctured
by a head of water of 90 feet if the least flaw existed in any
part, and the full pressure could act upon it.

The objectionable mode of laying the outlet pipes most probably fractured the puddle wall at the point of crossing. The loose
state of the material at the top of the bank let in the water. As
it rises in the reservoir, this water had most probably found its
way down the face of the puddle to the fracture in the puddle
wall above the outlet pipes, and hence the destruction so swift
and terrible in its effects.

Cast-iron pipes ought never to be laid under such conditions
as these were. A culvert of masonry, with an inner valve-well,
as in the Bradford reservoirs, should have been provided. The
culvert should have been on one side of the valley, and in
solid ground, free from the loose earth of the embankment. The
lower 20 feet of any reservoir, formed on the plan as this at
Dale Dyke, may, if required, be drawn by syphon arrangement,
and the valves may be in reach for examination or for repairs.

The bye-wash arrangement at Dale Dyke was inadequate for
the drainage area. The length provided, 64 feet, ought to have
been not less than three feet for each 100 acres of drainage area,
or 129 feet, and extra power for lowering flood water during a
storm should, even with such a length of bye-wash, be provided.
The embankment was not properly designed. The material and
mode of construction were all alike—defective.

The following recommendation of the jury—'That, in our
opinion, the Legislature ought to take such action as will result
in a Government inspection of all works of this character, and
that such inspection should be frequent, sufficient and regular'—
has received our serious attention. We cannot, however, recom-
mend it for adoption. Any approval of plans or casual inspection
of waterworks cannot ensure ultimate safety in such work. The
responsibility must remain, as at present, with the engineer and
persons immediately connected with the works. Magistrates have
jurisdiction under clauses inserted in recent Waterworks' Acts.
In our opinion, a longer period than is usually inserted in such
Acts for the construction of works of this character should be
allowed, and arrangements should be made gradually to test the
strength and soundness of the work. For this purpose, ample

means to draw the water down should be provided, considerably below the permanent full-water level.

The report may have contained no major surprises, for Rawlinson's views were already well known, but it packed a powerful punch and can have brought no comfort to the company's directors and engineers. Indeed, it was a weighty indictment, scarcely any part of the dam's construction escaping criticism. After such condemnation, it might have been naïve to ask just why that particular dam had fallen down. Yet the significant fact remained that Leather and Gunson were not newcomers to the game and, having collaborated successfully on building other reservoirs for the company over a period of thirty years, it was strange they had apparently made such a terrible mistake with Dale Dyke. They claimed to have used basically the same principles of building throughout and it is, perhaps, both flippant and unfair to suggest their other embankments were not subjected to such close scrutiny simply because they stayed up. Is it possible that Gunson was pushed to expedite operations at Dale Dyke which were known to be well behind schedule? Certainly he gave no intimation this was the case, although he could hardly be expected to 'sneak' on his employers. Possibly the choice of site for the large structure was a mistake?

Reservoir embankments were becoming bigger and it appears likely that therein lay the truth of the matter. What had sufficed for smaller works, perhaps, no longer applied. The margin for error was substantially reduced. Even so, that did not entirely explain why there was not a crop of collapsing dams in the country. Engineers differed on exactly what went wrong at Dale Dyke. Nevertheless, the tragedy served as a fearful warning. In his excellent book, *Victorian Engineering*, L. T. C. Rolt said the disaster 'prejudiced engineers against the earth dam and subsequently nineteenth-century dams were massively built of masonry in accordance with a theory of construction propounded by the celebrated Professor Rankine of Glasgow'.

By the time the Rawlinson-Beardmore report appeared, Thomas Hawksley and his colleagues felt they had investigated sufficiently to express an interim opinion that the Dale Dyke failure resulted from a landslip and was an unavoidable accident. These engineers were retained by the Sheffield Waterworks Company, of course, and unlikely to favour a burst pipe or a porous embankment as probable causes any more than Rawlinson and Beardmore were expected to attribute the fault to some mischievous gremlin. So it seemed at the time. Anyway, the academic *pros* and *cons* meant little to those who had borne the brunt of the flood's onslaught as it crashed through Damflask, Malin Bridge and Hillsborough on its route to further destruction in Sheffield. Fate or fault did not matter to them. Whichever won, they had been the losers.

8 'Property Protects Property'

Sheffield Waterworks Company got the Bill through the House of Commons with an ease that must have surprised the directors almost as much as it did their opponents. They were required to make a few minor amendments to some clauses, but the main objectives had been achieved. Subject to ratification by the House of Lords, the company were empowered to raise extra capital of £400,000 and to increase the water rate by 25 per cent in perpetuity; for their part, they were legally bound to furnish a continuous supply of water to Sheffield within five years. Efforts by the Town Council to purchase the waterworks ended in dismal failure. In fact, what had looked 'impossible' at one stage had happened: the company, while admitting liability to compensate sufferers, had got their way.

Dress rehearsals were all very well, but when it came to the real thing the company showed themselves better equipped to face the Select Committee of the House of Commons. Their legal representatives were fully briefed, their witnesses well disciplined, their case cogently argued and, of course, they had plenty of facts and figures at their fingertips. The opposition, though considerable and vociferous, appeared to lack a co-ordinated plan. They were unable to make much headway despite the fact that, numerically, they had the backing of much of the town. Sadly, from their point of view, the persuasiveness of influence, social position and substance counted for rather more than numbers.

The company had faltered occasionally. For instance, some of their key witnesses had not had an opportunity of reading the report of Rawlinson and Beardmore, copies of which, for some reason, were not to hand until just before the hearing began. An astute barrister successfully filibustered until the main points had been digested, however, and then smartly capitalized on the situation by assuring the members of the Select Committee that the company had eminent engineers available to refute the conclusions reached by the Government inspectors and to say the failure of the dam was due to an unforeseen accident—a landslip. The Town Council's representatives would have warmly welcomed a chance of the disaster's cause being debated, for they had at their disposal the reports of no fewer than nine of the country's leading engineers all of whom, independently, concurred broadly with the findings of Rawlinson and Beardmore. Counsel for the company was again quick off the mark, however, and persuaded the Committee it was unnecessary to go into the question of cause as his clients fully accepted liability although, he added, they repudiated any suggestion that negligence was involved.

It was submitted on behalf of the company that they were excellently organized and properly maintained, their shares being so reliable as to be known locally as 'Sheffield Consuls'. Now they faced a crippling bill for damages and, at the same time, were engaged in an ambitious programme of works to benefit the people of Sheffield. Counsel went further. 'The suffering of the company,' he said, 'is hardly less than that of those directly injured by the flood.' (Councillor Ironside later remarked it was a kind of 'pity the sorrows of a poor old man speech'—but it was impressing the Committee). After declaring that 'the company must either be sacrificed or some means of meeting the claims upon it must be found,' counsel claimed that even the cost of restoring the Dale Dyke dam (estimated at £40,000) could not be met by present resources. Flood damage to property, goods and stocks, as well as consequential damages for loss of time etc., had been assessed at a total of £327,000, to which had to be added considerable expenses and the payment of claims for loss of life and personal injury. The company listed the result of the disaster as follows: 111 buildings destroyed, 293 seriously damaged and 4,267 slightly damaged or flooded; material loss had been sustained by 990 owners of property and 5,550 occupiers.

Counsel's opening speech lasted about three hours. It covered every possible point upon which objection might be forthcoming and was followed by a formidable array of witnesses. William Waterfall, an aptly-named director of the company and a bank

manager by profession, went into infinite financial details and concluded that the water rate should have been increased years before.
The latest balance sheet showed a surplus in 1863 of £18,260
which, after deducting the amount due to mortgages, was reduced
to £9,281. No dividend had been declared at the last annual meeting; the surplus fund was £12,311 and that had been employed as
capital. Asked why the company had not pursued their intention to
purchase the water rights of millowners on the Loxley, Waterfall
replied simply that there were now insufficient funds to do so.
John Gunson, the troubled resident engineer, assured the Select
Committee that the recent catastrophe had not affected water
supplies to the town and that present storage represented enough
to last for 134 days. He pointed out that the water rate in Sheffield
was lower than that in other provincial towns (naturally he did not
mention it was higher than in many of those where the water was
controlled by the corporation). He spoke of rebuilding the Dale
Dyke dam farther up the valley and also of plans to complete the
Agden and to start work on the Strines reservoir. John Towlerton
Leather told the committee the cost of the Agden reservoir would
be about £30,000, the Strines, £33,600, and the new Dale Dyke
works an estimated £28,750. The Agden, he forecast, might be
completed within three years; in fact, it took five. Leather said he
was still retained by the company and, despite the disaster, had no
reason to think that the directors had lost confidence in him.

The hearing, which began 6 June, lasted several days. Specialists were called to say how well the company had discharged their
duties during the thirty-four years of their existence; opposing
specialists imputed negligence and accused the company of failing
to provide an adequate service. There were conflicting views on
whether or not the Town Council should take over the water
undertaking, but the directors flatly rejected any offer to buy them
out.

Then there was the drama of the telegram which came to light
when Mayor Jessop was giving evidence. Sheffield's chief citizen
had turned back-somersaults in an effort to remain impartial, but
it had proved impossible. He finally decided his duty was to serve
on the sub-committee of the Town Council and to oppose the Bill,
believing perhaps that he had a moral obligation to go along with
the majority opinion of the town. In doing so, he lost some friends,
but he won more support and respect for his courage in taking

positive action. Even so, it was a delicate matter because not all councillors were against the Bill; indeed, some had made it perfectly plain they were in favour of it and a few had travelled to London to say so.

The Mayor attempted to persuade the Select Committee that the company should be purchased by the corporation, he criticized the 'poor water supply' and added that there was an 'almost universal feeling' in Sheffield against the proposed 25 per cent increase.

Then Mr Riley (for the company) asked him: 'Did you telegraph from London that the council must either agree to the 25 per cent increase or buy the works?'

MAYOR: It was not expressed in that way exactly.
RILEY: How was it expressed then?
MAYOR: I do not remember. The Town Clerk can tell you.
RILEY: Was it 'Are the deputation to submit to an increase of 25 per cent'?

Although Vernon Harcourt, for Sheffield Corporation, protested that it was a 'privileged communication', a copy of the telegram was produced by order of the committee's chairman, Henry Seymour. The Mayor admitted he had 'cognizance of it' and, on his authority, had been sent by the Town Clerk to Sheffield. The council, whose guidance he sought, had met the previous day and had passed a resolution confirming the desirability of purchasing the waterworks 'on terms hereafter to be agreed upon' rather than agree to the 25 per cent increase. Further questioned, the Mayor conceded that only 34 of the 56 councillors had attended the meeting, that no notice had been given that the subject of the waterworks was to be raised and that newspaper reporters had been excluded. Jessop also said that, while no official moves had been made by the company's directors, there had been verbal indications from two or three of them favouring a deal.

CHAIRMAN: Did each member of the council receive the usual notice of the meeting on Wednesday?
MAYOR: Yes, it was the monthly meeting of the council and every member had a printed notice sent to him.
CHAIRMAN: Was it held on the usual day?
MAYOR: Yes.

CHAIRMAN: But no notice was given that this matter of the purchase of the waterworks would be put forward?
MAYOR: No.

It was all rather embarrassing. The Mayor and his colleagues on the sub-committee had plenary powers to act as they saw best and, it was revealed later (though not at the hearing), they had been strongly advised by their own counsel that unless they had terms to offer and a 'distinct expression of the feeling' of the Town Council to back them, there was no chance of succeeding before the Select Committee. Reluctantly, and not unanimously, it seems, they accepted that legal advice and, as a result, the telegram was dispatched. One also imagines the company's directors did not take kindly to Tommy Jessop's suggestion that two or three of them (he had named William Smith and Samuel Roberts) were willing to sell the waterworks to the corporation. It was most likely true, but it was a different matter announcing in public what had been whispered in private.

In summing-up for the opposition, the legal representatives turned in a capable performance. They pointed to the fact that the Relief Committee had received to date something like £30,000 to alleviate suffering and claimed that if the company were not called upon to repay the amount expended it was, in effect, added to their existing assets. A handsome offer by the Town Council to purchase had been rejected by the company which, contended Mr Mundell (for a body of ratepayers), 'has done so badly in the past'. Vernon Harcourt, recalling the company's opinion that work on the dam was 'faultless', declared that 'perhaps it was not Mr Leather's fault; perhaps it was not right to trust such extensive works in the hands of Mr Gunson. But, on the evidence given before the jury and the verdict of the jury, it is impossible that the other side can say that the work had been performed in a proper and satisfactory manner; neither was any reason made out why the burden of that great disaster should be saddled on the consumers'. If it was considered the damage could be met without increasing the water rate, commented Harcourt, then 'let that increase be in the hands of the corporation by enabling them to purchase the works for the town, so that the profits arising from the works can be enjoyed by them'.

The Select Committee were unconvinced by the objectors and unanimously decided to allow the Bill to go forward. So the first round went decisively to the company, but their opponents were already re-grouping for a more effective attack before the matter reached the House of Lords. Fresh enthusiasm was whipped up, the company's directors were again roundly denounced and there appeared to be growing support for the Town Council in their bid to acquire the waterworks. The sale could be effected only with the consent of the company, however, and there seemed little likelihood of that. Compulsory purchase in such circumstances had never been known.

A special meeting of the Town Council on 27 June carried resolutions vigorously objecting to the Bill and advocating municipal ownership of the waterworks, but it was noted that only 31 councillors attended. The report of the sub-committee appointed to organize opposition against the Bill was presented and Isaac Ironside, renowned for his radical views and plain speaking, had plenty to say about the Commons Select Committee hearing in London. A parliamentary committee, in his judgement, was 'a glorious uncertainty in the superlative'. While he did not complain about the committee in question he remarked, with a hint of sarcasm, that he thought the chairman, though intelligent, had little idea about what had been going on. Another member went along apparently to sleep, two others seemed more concerned with answering personal mail, so that only the chairman and one of his colleagues showed much interest in the proceedings. It had been impossible to know just what the committee were likely to do, Ironside added, and 'what will happen at the Lords is anyone's guess'.

Several councillors lashed out. The millowners, said one, had gone to London with an outward display of pretending to oppose the Bill but, in fact, had supported it and were 'doing all they can to saddle the town with the 25 per cent clause' as well as 'being guilty of an attempt to take money out of the pockets of the ratepayers and put it into their own'. There was also astonishment that so much sympathy existed for the company and so little for the poor ratepayers. Thomas Jessop was praised for the 'upright and manly way in which he has done his duty' which, considering his recent minor misdemeanour, must have given him unexpected comfort. In truth, the Town Council were badly shaken by their defeat in London and members were trying desperately to convince themselves all would be well when the battle was renewed before a

The Sheffield Coroner
John Webster

The Mayor of Sheffield
Thomas Jessop

In Remembrance of

Albert Mrs., aged 45; and 3 children.
Appleby John Coartos; mother and sister.
Armitage (Stag Inn,) Eliza, 70; with her son William and his wife and six children ; Elizabeth Crownshaw, servant; James Frith and Henry Hall, lodgers ; and a relative.
Armitage Greaves, 28; with wife and child.
Atkinson Morris, 15; William, 12.
Atkinson George, 42, with wife ; James, 40, with wife ; and William.
Barrett George; wife and child ; a sister and a lodger
Bagshaw James, 20; and Mary his wife.
Bates Thomas, 45; with wife and three children.
Bedford George ; wife, child, and William Waters, lodger.
Bethnay William, (Limerick Wheel.)
Bennett Mrs.
Bisby George, wife and six children.
Booth Walter, and Joseph Gregory, (Harrison's tilt)
Bowers John.
Bradbury William.
Bright Mrs., 50; Alfred, 4; two grandaughters; and Edward Cross, a lodger.
Bullard Thomas, 49; and wife, 46.
Burkinshaw Henry
Chapman Daniel, 31; wife, 23; 2 children ; John Bower and George Clay, apprentices; Frederic Chapman and Alethea Hague,
Chapman William, 15.
Coggans Alfred, 18; Eliza, 8; William, 6.
Cook Ann.
Colton Christopher, 46; wife, 30; Joseph, 4.
Crookes William.
Crapper Jph.; Elizabeth, his wife, 40; Joseph, 14.

Cramp Mary, 70; Samuel, 38.
Dawson, child of Walter.
Denton Joseph; and Thomas.
Dean Joseph.
Drabble Isaac, his wife, and two children.
Dyson Joseph, 40; wife, and two children; Richard Snape, apprentice, and Samuel Senior, lodger.
Elston Thomas, 34; wife, 33; and child.
Etchell Mrs., a widow.
Fairest Thomas, 47.
Foulds Isabel and John, (children of Paymaster-Sergeant Foulds.)
Gannon John, 50; wife, 45; and 6 children.
Glover John, 35; Sarah Ann. 35, (wife)
Green Mrs.
Goddard Joseph, 66; Sarah his wife, 70; with a daughter and two grandchildren.
Gill Thomas, 48.
Hakin Alfred; wife; and neice.
Hazlehurst Richard, 70.
Heaton John, and Kezia, his wife, 51.
Hudson John, 40; wife, and two children.
Ibbotson John Platts; Charles and King.
Jepson George, 74; and wife, Harriet, 68; a daughter-in-law and a grandaughter.
Longley William ; wife and two children.
McLaughlin Denis, 68.
Mappls Eliza, widow.
Mayor John ; wife, and daughter.
Midwood John ; wife, and 3 children.
Mills George 62, and wife.
Mount Ann, a widow, 40.
Needham, boy and girl.
Peacock John Thornton, 62.

Petty Thomas, 34; wife, 34; and 3 children.
Peters Jane, 20; Julia, 4; Christopher, 1.
Pickering William ; wife, sister, and a lodger.
Price Charles, 50; and wife, 50; their son Edward and wife, with their two children; (twins) Hannah Hill, 3; and Walter Damms, 20.
Rolley Edward.
Ryder Robert, 11.
Sellars William, 60; and Caroline his wife.
Snape George, 55, and wife ; Richard, 20.
Sparks Mrs, 47; and two children.
Simpson William.
Spooner Hannah, 64 ; Benjamin, 75; Jonathan, 47; Sarah Ann, 7.
Taylor Charlotte, a widow, 42.
Trickett James, 40; wife and 4 children, viz. Jemima, 17; James, George, and a baby, Thomas Kay, and Joseph Barker, 27 ; with two men-servants and one maid-servant.
Turner Isaac, 40, and wife; two children ; and H. G. Marshall, son of Mr. Marshall, Westbar.
Turner Jonathan.
Turton John, 50; and wife.
Varney Sidney, 18.
Vaughan John, 61; and wife, 55.
Watson, Sarah Ann, 32 (wife of William Watson,) and two children ; and J. Oakley, father in law
Wallace Emma, 38.
Webster Peter, 29; wife, 34; and 2 children.
Willett Priscilla.
Winter Thomas.
Woledchohne William, 74; and Thomas and Selina Spooner with their seven children.
Wright George; wife, and Miss Johnson.

Who were drowned by the bursting of a Reservoir,

At Bradfield, near Sheffield,

ON MARCH 12TH, 1864,

BETWEEN THE HOURS OF TWELVE AND ONE IN THE MORNING, WHEN UPWARDS OF 250 LIVES
WERE LOST.

Soon the streams became as brooks, the brooks as rivers wide,
And all the valley one vast sea, lash'd up by angry tide.
High above the water's roar was heard the voice of prayer;
Man's agonising cry for help, his wail of wild despair.
The aged matron and the maid, the husband and the wife,
The grandsire, and the infant babe now struggling into life.

And children for their fathers wept, and fathers for their sons,
And mothers, scarcely mothers made, wept for their little ones.
The widow mourn'd the husband lost, the husband mourn'd the wife,
And everywhere was heard a wail for loss of human life !
These perish'd nigh three hundred souls beneath the boiling wave,
For tho' men heard their cries for help, men had no power to save.

A memorial card produced soon after the disaster

Lords committee. Alderman Saunders, one of Sheffield's busiest men in public life, was less optimistic. He was sure their lordships, like their counterparts on the Commons committee, would not hold the waterworks company responsible for the dam failure nor allow them to be 'wracked-up' to pay such losses. 'Property protects property,' he maintained, 'and the company will be protected to that extent by the men of property in Parliament.' He had a point.

Some Sheffielders felt they had been grossly misled by the company, whose proposals in the Bill were seen as repudiating the responsibilities they affected to acknowledge and provide for. Townsmen were aggrieved that the company had bought time by urging would-be claimants to delay action against them, thereby encouraging a belief that all would be well. *The Sheffield Daily Telegraph* took up the cudgels on behalf of the poorer inhabitants: 'The company's Bill may have the approbation of wealthy "sufferers" who may not care whose money they receive so long as the compensation is ample, and may be passed by one of those House of Commons committees whose sympathies are all on the side of vested interests, but it will never be approved of by any who remember how miserably poor are thousands of those upon whom its burden will fall ... that such persons should have their burden increased to reimburse and reward the authors of a work which has just been officially condemned seems, in our humble opinion, one of the strangest pieces of injustice ever enacted in the name of justice, and under the authority of Parliamentary law.'

Apart from the directors, other shareholders and some of the richer sufferers, virtually the whole town opposed the Bill. Even the Mayor, who had vacillated for a while, began to disguise his jolly nature with some hard-favoured rage and, now that he had nailed his colours to the flagship of the opposition, he stuck gamely by his convictions. At a public meeting, over which he presided, loud cheering greeted the passing of a resolution urging that the company 'ought, as they agreed to do by their Act of Parliament passed in 1853, to pay such damages out of their own funds'. The Select Committee were deprecated for their 'extraordinary' decision and hackles appeared to rise at the mere mention of the Sheffield Waterworks Company. One enraged citizen described the action of the directors as 'cold, heartless, indifferent and ungrateful', while another was applauded when he declared: 'Worse than all the floods have ever been is the flood of immorality which the water company have let loose, and I hope we do all we can to dam up the foulest stream than could ever flow.'

Daniel Doncaster, the steel manufacturer and a supporter of the temperance movement, showed much courage in expressing opinions unpopular to the overwhelming majority at the meeting. He thought the Bill was 'not as iniquitous as has been represented,' that the allegations against the directors were extremely unfair and that if action proposed by the meeting received legal sanction it would cause 'great hardship' to the shareholders. Like the biblical Daniel, he was in a lions' den and his statement prompted hisses and shouts of 'It's harder for the poor sufferers.' One has to admire his pluck. Isaac Ironside countered that the conduct of the company had been 'as cold as their water' and he wondered how 20,000 inhabitants, who had received relief, would have fared had the Mayor adopted the same attitude? Jessop, always anxious to be fair, commented that although the company had been legally unable to make a grant, 'the shareholders, particularly many of the directors, have behaved most liberally towards the inundation fund'. Because of the growing opposition to the Bill, there persisted a feeling at the meeting that the Lords committee would reach 'a more correct judgement'—a piece of optimism no doubt based on a belief of the Englishman's sense of fair play.

Sheffield's two M.P.s came in for a terrible towsing. John Arthur Roebuck and George Hadfield had not spoken against the Bill as it passed through the Commons, a silence which gave rise to wide-spread indignation. Roebuck had visited Sheffield recently and, during his stay, was acquainted with the views of the Town Council and supporters but, according to some of them, he had already been got at by the company's directors. They must have done a good job on him, for Roebuck was satisfied not only that the company were better qualified to control the waterworks but he was also convinced that the town should be called upon to contribute towards the cost of the disaster. Hadfield, a considerable shareholder in the company, was also castigated. It was not difficult for some to calculate that a 25 per cent increase on the rates would help handsomely to line his already bulging pockets. Soon forgotten, it seems, were Hadfield's years of parliamentary service to the town, philanthropic gestures throughout his lifetime and the fact that he was among the first generously to contribute to the flood relief fund. He had been elected to look after the interests of Sheffield, it was

said, and not his own. Many were certain that had Roebuck and
Hadfield spoken against the Bill, there was every chance of its
being tossed out.

'Surely,' wrote Samuel Harrison in *The Sheffield Times*, 'members are not sent to Parliament to speak when they can serve themselves and remain silent when they might serve the town.... Before
the Bill passed the Committee of the House of Commons, Mr
Hadfield's shares were only worth about £50 each and he must be
aware that if the 25 per cent clause passes, they will ultimately be
worth nearly £150 each.... Mr Hadfield was also aware that he,
as a shareholder, was legally and morally bound to make compensation for the damages caused by the flood and that the Bill in
question would practically transfer the liability from himself and
partners to the householders and poor people of Sheffield'.

The editor, who reckoned Hadfield had £15,000-worth of shares
in the company, could hardly level similar allegations of self-interest
against Roebuck, but he managed something just as startling. He
wrote: 'Even Tear-'Em, too, the self-styled watch-dog of England,
has become a dumb dog that cannot speak. He cannot plead as an
excuse for his silence that he is a shareholder. Perhaps he sym-
pathizes with Mr Hadfield. He ought to do so, for many a time has
that gentleman's purse cemented their friendship and proved, poli-
tically, a mutual advantage.' Harrison's story was that Roebuck had
been persuaded by company shareholders that the 25 per cent clause
was a good one and the Bill sensible, an opinion he represented to
members of the Town Council; on hearing the latter's views, however, Roebuck had replied that the council's wish was his command
and apologized for his name being on the back of the Bill, saying
it was purely a formality. 'The least he could have done,' Harrison
added, 'would have been to say that the people of Sheffield were
opposed to the Bill and, therefore, he could not allow his name to
appear on the back of it any longer.' Thus a watch-dog of the Press
denounced the watch-dog of England.

There was not much possibility that the Bill, which had been
given three unopposed readings in the Commons, was going to be
vetoed by the House of Lords. The objectors retained a semi-blind
confidence that justice would prevail, however. The company's
directors entertained similar sentiments but, in their case, having
got their Bill well on the way to becoming an Act, their self-assur-
ance was anything but blind. They could see the beckoning light

of victory. The hearing before the Lords Committee began on 18 July; the Duke of Buckingham was chairman, his colleagues being the Earl of Harrowby, the Earl of Malmesbury, Lord Saye and Sele and Lord Falmouth. This time the company were officially supported by the millowners, among others.

Much of the evidence was a repeat of that given before the Commons Select Committee just over a month previously. Counsel for the company admitted his clients had had 'severe censures' passed on them by the coroner's jury and by Rawlinson and Beardmore, but there was the 'best reason' to believe that the report of the Government inspectors was 'extremely erroneous'. The company, he said, had engaged Messrs Simpson, Hawksley and Bateman—'the first hydraulic engineers' in the country—as well as John Fowler and T. E. Harrison; the five had 'unanimously acquitted the company as regards the alleged deficiency in the employment of proper engineering skill', concluding that the accident had resulted from a landslip and 'not by any cause that could have been guarded against by human foresight'. Counsel also alluded to that telegram sent by the Mayor, remarking that the plain fact was the Sheffield Corporation had been for a long time 'greedy' for possession of the company's works and wanted to take advantage of a difficult situation to buy the property cheaply. If the council succeeded in their bid, he contended, they would certainly need to ask for far more than a 25 per cent increase on the rate. Finally, he made what was then a significant point—there was no instance where Parliament had forced a water company to dispose of their works.

John Gunson, who must have felt brighter now that the favourable 'findings' of the five engineers had been announced in public, told their lordships that under the 1853 Act the company were obliged to supply water to the town for twelve hours a day, an undertaking honoured with a few exceptions. Once, during the dry spell of June 1863, certain restrictions were placed on the use of water for cleansing the streets. Gunson maintained he had heard of no complaints about inadequate supplies for sanitary purposes which, on the face of it, seems an incredible statement. Then the proceedings were enlivened by a short clash between two of the lawyers, Mundell, for the ratepayers, and Burke, for the company.

MUNDELL: Whatever the company have done, they are responsible for the acts of their agents and servants.

BURKE: We don't dispute it and we are here to discharge our liabilities.

MUNDELL: But you seem to be here striving to create sympathy and to show that you have done all that could be expected.

BURKE: We admit our liabilities and are anxious to fulfil them.

MUNDELL: By making the inhabitants pay an increase of 25 per cent on their water rate?

BURKE: We say that we have been guilty of no negligence and that we are entitled to claim some consideration at the hands of the town and of Parliament.

Then Mundell tried unsuccessfully to shake the testimony of director William Waterfall who, true to form, remained adamant.

MUNDELL: Are you of the opinion that if the 25 per cent is not given, your shareholders will receive no dividend at all?

WATERFALL: That is my opinion.

MUNDELL: Then you don't think it a fair offer of the corporation to take your liabilities and give you two per cent besides?

WATERFALL: The position I take is this: I am unwilling to sell, more especially when the company have just suffered from so great a disaster.

MUNDELL: Do you hold that if you do not get your 25 per cent, you won't be able to pay your liabilities at all?

WATERFALL: That is my opinion.

John Towlerton Leather expressed the view that it would be impossible to guarantee a constant supply of water to Sheffield until the whole of the Loxley scheme was completed (by 1873, it was estimated), as storage facilities would be insufficient. That can hardly have given joy to the growing population of Sheffield who already endured long 'dry' periods because of the company's inability to cope with an escalating demand, but the company were gradually putting together a strong enough case to influence their lordships.

Land agents were called to present valuation assessments of the flood damage and property owners came forward to say they had no objection to the 25 per cent clause. In fact, J. F. Wright, a surgeon, declared he would be 'very glad' to pay the increase—a willingness, he added, shared by a 'great proportion' of the town's inhabitants. That was stretching credulity too far and, under cross-examination, he admitted there might be a 'great many' who would object. Another man of means, Samuel Butcher, as chairman of a committee of owners of damaged property, stated: 'I say that the Bill meets with our entire approbation and we have petitioned that it be passed unaltered.'

Asked why he objected to Sheffield Corporation buying out the company, he replied: 'We have experienced one calamity and I don't want to be inflicted with another.' When the laughter had died away, Butcher claimed he would have to pay 100 per cent increase if the town took over the waterworks, 'although,' he commented as an afterthought, 'I don't mean to cast any reflection on the council'. Butcher, a magistrate and part-owner with his brother of the Philadelphia Steel Works and the Rutland Works, estimated flood damage to his premises at more than £10,000 and saw the Bill as the only effective way of getting back his money. The same went for Edward Vickers, head of the steel manufacturing firm with premises in Sheffield and Brightside, who valued his damage at nearly £3,000. Like Butcher, Vickers was a JP and both were former Mayors of Sheffield. Vickers described the water supply to the town and trade as 'excellent'. He agreed that there was a 'great diversity' of opinion about the Bill, but held that the larger ratepayers were in favour of it. In saying that, he had hit on the truth and it seemed that influential men would again win the day.

Once more, the company were out-gunning their numerically superior opponents. In addition to an impressive range of facts and figures, commendably marshalled and presented, the company were able to produce 'quality' witnesses. Good breeding, respectability and financial and social status amounted to persuasive 'evidence'. Robert Younge, whose 120 houses in Sheffield brought him £3,000 a year in rents, told the aristocratic committee he favoured the proposed increase of 25 per cent and strongly objected to the corporation taking over the waterworks. He also spoke on behalf of other property-owning claimants and was asked by Mr Denison, Q.C., (for the corporation) if he approved of the commissioners recommended to assess damages.

YOUNGE: I do. I believe they are gentlemen.
DENISON: As they would have to assess your claim, what does

it signify whether the corporation or the company are the ultimate payers?

YOUNGE: So far as the claim goes, I don't think it matters a
great deal. I say again, so long as I am in the hands of the
company I know I am in the hands of gentlemen, but if I am
dealing with the corporation I know I am not in the hands of those
with whom I am safe [laughter].

DENISON: I can't go into the question of gentility at Sheffield
[renewed laughter].

YOUNGE: Well, you asked my opinion, and you must excuse
me if I am a little too candid. I have seen a great deal of them
and that is the reason I speak so positively.

DENISON: Do the other claimants approve of the commissioners?

YOUNGE: Yes, because they believe they are gentlemen.

DENISON: Well, that brings us round to the old point.

YOUNGE: Yes, it does, and shows the value of respectability.

DUKE OF BUCKINGHAM: You would prefer to have this Bill,
even with an increase of 25 per cent, rather than the corporation
should have the works?

YOUNGE: Oh, most undoubtedly.

EARL OF HARROWBY: You believe you would have to pay in
the shape of a borough rate more than you are now paying to the
company?

YOUNGE: Certainly.

DUKE OF BUCKINGHAM: Do you think the increase will press
heavily upon the poorer classes—persons in houses below £10
rental?

YOUNGE: I am sure it will not.

The company concluded their case by calling upon John Bateman and Thomas Hawksley, the engineers, who pointed out that
even allowing for a 25 per cent increase, the water rate in Sheffield
would compare very favourably with that in other large towns.
Hawksley, who said he was generally against corporations managing
waterworks, contended the company 'do not want to sell their
horse just at the moment he has broken at the knees', to which
Denison retorted: 'No, they want it to be cured at public expense.'

The corporation and other objectors to the Bill argued their
cause, but they had already an uneasy feeling it was all rather point-

less. The company appeared to have swayed their lordships, who showed few signs of being impressed by Mayor Jessop who told them more than thirteen thousand inhabitants had signed a petition opposing the proposals. Neither were they moved by his opinion that the company were acting contrary to the provisions of their 1853 Act by seeking the 25 per cent increase. Jessop also stated there had never been a good water supply in Sheffield, a view strongly endorsed by Councillor Ironside who also had a few sharp words to say on the subject of sewerage. Other witnesses spoke of the inadequate water service and also set out to show that the water rates in Sheffield were, in fact, higher than in many towns.

It was all to no avail. The noble lords had made up their minds and unexpectedly withdrew without even hearing any summing-up by counsel for the corporation. When they returned, the Duke of Buckingham said he and his colleagues approved the 25 per cent increase (limited to a period of 25 years, and not in perpetuity as the company had sought). The committee rejected any proposal regarding compulsory purchase of the company, Buckingham commenting that the corporation had made out a 'very weak' case.

Within a short time, the Bill received the Royal Assent to make it into an Act. Retrospectively, it seems surprising such a result was possible when the vast majority of Sheffielders were against what many of them regarded as dubious daylight robbery. Indeed, it was considered by some as a victory for privilege and position. Reaction in some quarters was bitter and there were calls for a further official investigation into the cause of the dam disaster. It was too late. No other inquiry was held. That did not prevent people from expressing their own feelings, however, and one severe critic of the company's directors asked: 'Is the town to be perpetually in fear of being drowned at any moment by these imbeciles?' Happily, his pessimism was ill-founded.

Although the attempt to destroy the Bill was unsuccessful, the opponents gained a few 'concessions'. For example, it would not be necessary for a claimant for damages in loss-of-life cases to prove negligence by the waterworks company, the Lords Committee having ruled them liable in any case concerning death or personal injury. The 25 per cent increase was to be levied impartially on all consumers, with the exception that water for cleaning streets or flushing sewers was to be supplied to the corporation at a reduced rate. It was also the company's legal obligation to give a constant

supply to the town within five years and to complete all works in
the Loxley Valley scheme by 1873. (It will be recalled that in
Leather's view the supply was dependent upon completion of the
Loxley Valley scheme.) For the privilege of getting those relatively
minor amendments, the cost to the town of opposing the Bill was
£3,426.

For the company, of course, the Act was an important achieve-
ment and provided a much-needed boost to the directors who,
despite insults and accusations hurled at them, adhered to the
difficult task of doing what they regarded as honest and fair. They
had lawfully established the company as the body fully capable of
controlling the water undertaking in Sheffield and had also won
some breathing-space in which not only to restore the broken dam
(and build new ones), but also to restore their tarnished image in
the eyes of so many of their critics. The company had been dealt
with favourably by Parliament and it was now up to them to carry
out their commitments.

William Smith was a worried man. He was also ill. As chairman
of the Sheffield Waterworks Company he had been under serious
strain during the past few months. His mind was heavily burdened
by the terrible effects of the flood and still filled with the recriminations and wrangles which had followed. It seems likely that
he was also at odds with some of his fellow directors, for it was
whispered that his private view was that the company should be
sold to the corporation. In reply to one question at the hearing
before the House of Commons Select Committee, he had indicated
as much when he said he believed 'all large towns ought to be
supplied by themselves, for the liability is so great'. Is it also
possible that he entertained a notion that the collapse of the dam
was due to faulty workmanship? If he did, he obviously could not
say as much in public.

Smith had been the company's chairman for twenty years, during
which time the administrative work and overall responsibility had
grown enormously. The Dale Dyke tragedy added to his problems
and, shortly after the new Act came into being, he resigned—
because of 'ill-health'. At a special meeting of shareholders in
August, William Waterfall was appointed the company's first
managing director, at a salary of £1,000 a year. He had left a
more remunerative position as manager of the Sheffield and Hallamshire Bank to take on the new responsibilities. George Hounsfield,

chairman of the Sheffield and Rotherham Bank, a wealthy and respected citizen, and considered a 'quiet, observant man of high honour and sound judgement', was to be the new chairman of the waterworks company. Less than a month after that special meeting his predecessor, William Smith, suffered a heart attack and died on 28 September, aged sixty-eight. Smith, a barrister by profession, was a Sheffield magistrate and a director of the Midland Railway Company, and his fellow directors on the waterworks company noted that their former chairman had always discharged his duties with the 'strictest integrity and the most conscientious desire to do what was right'. His home, in which he breathed his final hours, was called Dam House.

Meanwhile the General Relief Committee, headed by the industrious Mayor, found themselves in a strange position. More than £50,000 had flowed in from all over Britain. It proved too much. Having disbursed almost £30,000 to needy flood sufferers and spent another £1,500 on expenses, the committee still had about £19,000 in hand. That was not all; they reckoned on recouping (from the waterworks company) on 'transfers', issued in the Mayor's name to many claimants, and estimated that such moneys would swell the relief fund's surplus to something like £30,000—three-fifths of the total donated! It was by no means certain the company or, more important, the tribunal appointed under the Act to adjudicate in cases of disputed claims, would agree to reimburse the Mayor, as assignee of the Relief Committee. This committee had done a noble job in assisting the poorer flood victims at a time when confusion and indecision reigned; it was not known in those early days just what compensation the company would be called upon to pay. Now the committee had met all *bona fide* applications to date, so that the principal part of their work had been virtually completed. It was awkward, to say the least, to discover that, with or without the amount 'owing' to the Mayor, they had so much cash left over. What was to be done? Proportional sums could be returned to the donors, which would require considerable organization, or monetary gifts could be made to worthy causes in Sheffield which would need, of course, the permission of subscribers. It was decided to defer the matter until after the commissioners had outlined their rulings regarding compensation claims. What the Relief Committee did not want was that the company should benefit by even a penny because of the generosity of voluntary contributors. That, in their view, would never do.

The establishment of an independent commission was an important provision of the Sheffield Waterworks (Bradfield Inundation) Act, 1864. The three-man team, destined to sit for up to three or four times a week over a period of six months, were called upon to give judgement in a vast range of applications. They had an impossible job satisfying everybody but, on the whole, they emerged with credit. Tuesday, 4 October 1864, was the date announced for their first session, but before then. . . .

9 Engineers Versus Engineers

Robert Rawlinson may well have been displeased. His professional judgement, published by order of Her Majesty's Government, had been called into question. He was used to being challenged, of course, but somehow the manner in which the five engineers engaged by the Sheffield Waterworks Company had come out so blatantly against his considered opinions on the Dale Dyke disaster was irritating. He cannot have expected agreement, but the statement made by counsel to the House of Lords Committee that the report (prepared by him, with Beardmore's assistance) was 'extremely erroneous' was too much. Rawlinson, who prided himself upon his thoroughness, believed his opponents' conclusions to be based on the most tenuous of evidence. Although their findings had yet to be issued in detail publicly, those engineers were on record as saying that the failure was due to an unforeseen landslip and, what must have been even more unpalatable to Rawlinson, that the methods of constructing the embankment and laying the pipes underneath were perfectly sound. The engineers—and there was no denying their renown—had further intimated that the unfinished Agden dam was in good shape.

Rawlinson cannot have been delighted either by those references to him in *The Engineer* that 'he is no doubt a very good engineer in his way' and that his comments as an inspector appointed by the Government 'count for nothing with the engineering profession'. He remained steadfastly by his convictions, however, and published support (if, indeed, he needed any) was on the way.

Neither of the Parliamentary committees had deemed it necessary to go into the question of the specific causes of the dam failure, although the Sheffield Corporation had in their possession lengthy professional reports which backed up the opinions expressed by Rawlinson and Beardmore. The sub-committee, which had been elected to oppose the Bill, presented to the August meeting of the Town Council a review of their activities and appended (for publication) the 'unproduced evidence' of no fewer than nine top-ranking engineers they had enlisted to investigate Dale Dyke. It might not have been possible to get an 'airing' of the information in London, but the committee had no intention of allowing it to be buried in dusty archives. The documents ran to thousands of words and, to the committee's intense satisfaction, rated prominent coverage in the Sheffield newspapers. We are assured that the engineers reached their conclusions quite independently of each other, in which case their remarkably similar views add up to a powerful indictment of the dam's construction. Although the reports had lost some of their practical value when such evidence was ruled inadmissible at the London hearings, they were still important. (They were later incorporated into a parliamentary paper, as was one by Rawlinson when he replied to points made by the quintet of engineers retained by the waterworks company).

The engineers behind the corporation-held dossiers represented a glittering array of talent. James Leslie, at sixty-two, was currently engineer to the Edinburgh Water Company and among the top hydrologists in Britain. A fellow Scot, David Stevenson (1815-86), was an authority on marine engineering, rivers, docks and lighthouses; he came from a distinguished family of engineers and was an uncle of Robert Louis Stevenson. There was Henry Conybeare, noted engineer to the Bombay Waterworks and now of London. Peter William Barlow, the Woolwich-born son of a mathematics professor, had surveyed a number of railway routes in the Home Counties, was a Telford medallist, and, only recently had been engineer-in-charge of building Lambeth Bridge, opened in 1862. John Murray, who hailed from Kelso, was fifty-nine, and, as a young man, had been engineer to the River Wear Commissioners at Sunderland; he was a specialist in marine engineering and also in sanitation matters. William Lee, experienced geologist and expert designer of hydraulic works, was a native of Sheffield and thus well acquainted with the waterworks in the area and also with the terrain around Dale Dyke; in 1848 while employed by the corporation, Lee collaborated with James Haywood in producing a condemnatory report on sanitary conditions in the borough. Then there was Matthew Bullock Jackson of Sheffield, who had given evidence at the inquest; he was formerly chief engineer of Melbourne Waterworks and responsible for other similar projects in Australia.

Perhaps the two most famous of the nine were Sir John Rennie and Charles Blacker Vignoles. Rennie, in his seventieth year, was the renowned son of a famous engineering father, John (1761-1821), and younger brother of George (1791-1866), a celebrated mechanical engineer. Sir John is remembered chiefly for building London Bridge (designed and started by his father) and was knighted on the spot when it was officially opened by William IV in 1831. (That fine bridge was dismantled and shipped, stone by stone, to the United States where it was set up again in 1971.) There was not much Rennie did not know about bridges, railways and drainage. Less than a year after becoming a member of the Institution of Civil Engineers, he was president for three successive terms (1845, 1846 and 1847). He retired from business in 1862, but his views were still much respected. Vignoles was a name almost synonymous with railways and his work was to be seen in many parts of Britain as well as in a number of European countries, including Germany, France, Switzerland, Spain and Poland, so that he was well qualified to give opinions on building embankments. Between 1847 and 1853 (the year before the outbreak of the Crimea War), he was a frequent visitor to Russia where his outstanding contribution was the suspension bridge over the Dnieper at Kiev—then the longest of its kind in the world. Vignoles, who was born in County Wexford, was descended from a Huguenot family. He was employed by the Rennie brothers for a short while when he was in his mid-thirties. At this time he was seventy-one.

In essence, the engineers agreed with Rawlinson and Beardmore that the Dale Dyke embankment had been faultily constructed, that the outlet pipes and bye-wash were too small, the depth of 'tips' too great, that building materials ought not to have been taken from inside the reservoir and that the mode of laying the pipes was bad practice. A number of them believed that waterworks serving towns the size of Sheffield should be under public ownership, but that cannot be regarded as too surprising when the Town Council had engaged them to prepare reports. Even so, there was no ducking the fact that nine highly qualified professionals considered the dam a poor piece of work.

Sir John Rennie, for instance, was critical of the site selected for 'an embankment 95 feet high to sustain on one side of it a column of water nearly its whole height'. In view of the 'want of skill' exhibited at Dale Dyke and Agden, he thought the corporation had 'just reason to doubt the safety of the other reservoirs'. Barlow attributed the failure to the 'objectionable site and defective construction', while Conybeare submitted that the collapse was due to a leak in the pipes, 'creep' of water along the outside of them or to the insufficient thickness of the puddle wall or, indeed, to a combination of all three.

James Leslie felt that employing 'tips' of three-foot thickness, which could not be properly compacted, was 'in the highest degree objectionable' and contended that a bank so formed 'will not only sink or settle rapidly and unequally, but may continue to sink and subside for many years after its construction'. Stevenson had 'no hesitation in saying that any reservoir constructed in a similar manner to the one at Agden must be regarded as unequal to the important duty it has to perform, is not a sound engineering work and cannot be considered safe,' while John Murray stated that the dam should have been sited higher up in a 'more contracted' part of the valley and that the reservoir was 'defective in design and unsound in construction'. Jackson was certain the cause of the failure was 'water getting into and under the seat of the outside slope of the embankment, inducing a slip and settlement immediately before the burst'. He, too, thought the site was injudiciously chosen, the dam being placed in the 'immediate neighbourhood of ancient landslips, of strong springs and of suspicious indications of faults in the strata'. Like some of the other engineers, Jackson also suggested that not enough care had been given to examining the site before work began.

Particularly interesting was the report of William Lee, who was able to make use of his extensive local knowledge. He said there were numerous faults in the strata at the site of the dam, the puddle wall being on the flexure of one, while 'all the deep part of the outer embankment rests upon loose, crumbling and shifting shale, which may be picked in pieces by the fingers, while the two ends of the embankment rest upon rock'. He added: 'In fact, the inside site of embankment, and that of the two ends is millstone grit—the outside and deepest part, coal measures. The existence of those large springs flowing close to the foot of the intended inner embankment should have excited so much suspicion as to have caused the abandonment of the site; or, at least, a conviction that the work could not safely be commenced until a line or lines of borings or pits had been made along the lower part of the intended puddle trench, sufficiently close to each other to show an accurate section of the strata. Such borings and section would have proved the existence of a dangerous fault; at ten or twelve feet deep, the water of those great springs, which twenty horse-power [he was referring to the two pumping engines] scarcely sufficed to draw, would have gushed out to the surface of the ground.' His conclusion was that the reason for the failure was 'the adoption of an objectionable site and to defective construction'.

'In my experience and judgement,' reported Charles Vignoles, 'the system of construction adopted by the Sheffield Waterworks Company at the Dale Dyke and Agden embankments was, in many respects, erroneous; that the proper engineering experience was not brought to bear in the designs and specifications and that a great want of care and skill, together with evident deficiency of supervision, are manifest in the carrying out of the operations. For the future the town of Sheffield, and many other towns, the public in general and the Government want security against the possible recurrence of disasters such as that at Dale Dyke. This cannot be secured by trusting to the waterworks company, or to their officers, who seemed to have despised all experience not within their own limited range, which has consisted in repeating themselves, and, having hitherto the good luck to escape (if they have escaped) from serious accidents, would go on repeating the dangerous practices, if allowed by the Legislature.'

One wonders what effect such crushing condemnation would have had on the company's Bill had the reports been permitted as evidence at the Parliamentary hearings. The strong observations, particularly those by Lee and Vignoles, added up to a withering denunciation of the dam and those concerned with its design and erection. The Town Council's sub-committee also produced figures which, they claimed, showed it impossible now for the company to give a constant supply, but they were bound to provide it within five years under a penalty of no dividends on ordinary capital until they did. During the next twenty-three years the company faced a series of problems relating to finance, construction and water distribution, but they managed to resist further take-over bids before they were finally forced to sell out to the corporation.

An extremely difficult factor involved in supplying the town with enough water in the 1850s and 1860s, during which two decades the population increased substantially, was the company's obligation to provide compensation water to the millowners before a drop taken from the gathering grounds of the Loxley and Rivelin was permitted to be used in Sheffield. It was a crippling handicap and there were insufficient funds available to buy the necessary water rights. The millowners had said, in effect: 'Before you [the company] allow Sheffield residents to share from our streams, other than those running through the town, we will first have what we want.' Acts of Parliament backed the view of owners who, in practice, got not the annual average amount to which they had been accustomed previously, but the advantage of an all-the-year-round supply. Hitherto, the water-powered wheels had been dry and idle during periods of drought or little rain. Now, any deficiency in water supplies from the hilly areas of the Loxley fell upon the inhabitants of Sheffield, while the wheels of industry in the valley turned ceaselessly for six working days a week. So, with Dale Dyke out of action and the work at Agden halted, the company strove to keep faith with the fast-growing number of consumers. It was a continuous headache and, only a fortnight after the reports of the nine engineers were released, the company gave notice that for at least a week they would be able to supply water to the town only on alternate days.

As the *Sheffield and Rotherham Independent* fairly pointed out: 'The mills which, but for the reservoirs of the water company, would have been at a standstill for weeks, are able to work full hours day by day, while the supply to the town is reduced one-half.... Not only has the excessive expense occasioned by the pretensions of the millowners enhanced the cost of water and limited the sources of supply but, in times of drought, their unmitigated demands cause the scarcity to fall with an unfair and exclusive severity on the public.'

The smell from the rivers, which ran through Sheffield like large open drains, must have been almost unbearable in the sun. According to the *Independent*, 'thousands of water-closets now send down to the rivers streams of pollution which lodges in the river beds and makes them utter abominations'. Ways of eliminating the evil were suggested: one was to make deeper channels in the rivers to improve flow; another was to construct a large outfall drain to carry sewage 'some distance down the valley' to waste land, where the 'solid matter' could be utilized to fertilize the soil. Undoubtedly, something had to be done. The Town Council now possessed newly-gained powers to eliminate such an eyesore and, indeed, a nose-sore.

No less a person than Lord Edward Howard, Member of Parliament, touched on the subject a few days later when he spoke at The Cutlers' Feast, that annual gastronomic delight and sumptuous social function famed throughout the land. After consuming a gourmet's dream (the bill of fare included five choices of fish, eight of entrée, four of meat and a grand selection of game and poultry dishes), the cigar-smoking guests sipped their port and leaned back to listen to a list of speeches longer than the not inconsiderable list of wines. 'Certain things which strike the eye of a stranger coming into the town are certainly most necessary to be done,' said Lord Howard, 'and which I hope the Local Government Act will be the means of doing. I allude to what I saw of the state of your rivers, which ought to be a little cleaner'—at this understatement, some of those present found it dutiful to laugh and cheer. Thus encouraged, his lordship went on: 'There is unquestionably much thrown into the rivers which would be far better out.' Laughter or not, he had made an embarrassing observation. While Sheffield was among the most prosperous industrial centres in the world, the dismal lack of attention paid to municipal improvements reflected a shocking contrast.

Inside that elegantly decorated dining-hall, which echoed to a hundred 'hear-hears' and numerous platitudes, sat many living examples of Sheffield's prosperity. Some had deservedly earned their success and position after years of punishing competition; others had been just strong enough to hold on to the privileged plate upon which the prosperity had been handed to them. There they were: men of influence, men of property, men of inherited wealth, men of social standing. Outside, on that autumn evening, the reddish smoke rose in the north-east, the rivers struggled to ward off stagnation, families took their turn in communal privy middens and the steelworkers sweated at the mill. Down by the Don, damp-ness left by the flood still discoloured the parlour walls.

10 A Chance to Collect

On Tuesday, 4 October—207 days after the water had burst through the Dale Dyke dam—the three Inundation Commissioners took their places in a crowded room at Sheffield Town Hall to begin their unenviable duty of assessing damages. About 7,300 claims for compensation, ranging from small sums to thousands of pounds, and representing a total of more than £455,000, had been lodged with the waterworks company. All but around 650 were settled without recourse to arbitration. Nevertheless, the hearings of disputed cases occupied 51 days spread over a period of six months, during which time the commissioners listened to an incredibly wide variety of applications involving extreme hardship, drama, humour, dishonesty and downright stupidity. Beset by feuding factions, the commissioners (who sat as a court of equity and not as a court of law) were on something of a hiding to nothing. The Town Council and the Relief Committee alleged fraud by the company who, in turn, accused them of deliberately causing unnecessary friction; members of the public wrote abusive letters to the commission and there were substantiated instances of perjury and illegal claims.

It was sometimes no easy matter to distinguish between the genuine and the fraudulent and there can be little doubt that a few honest applicants suffered, while some ingenious rogues got away with money to which they were not entitled. The preparation of claims became a lucrative business; enterprising individuals touted for custom, making door-to-door canvasses to seek out flood victims who, due to ignorance, illiteracy or apathy, had not considered applying for compensation. Advertisements of offers to make out claims (at a fee, of course) appeared in the newspapers and, in the end, what might originally have been a reasonable request for a

small sum was sometimes outrageously translated into a much
larger one (in some cases, without the applicant's knowledge).
Numerous claims were of a grossly inflated nature and, because they
were properly challenged and argued in court, they greatly added
to the outlay of time and expense by the company. Many of the
awards allowed by the commissioners were well below the amounts
claimed and, when the semblance of a pattern began to emerge,
more and more cases were settled out of court.

Applications based on every conceivable ground were made. As
one observer put it: 'A cold or a sore throat within a month or
two of the flood became fever or chronic rheumatism, disabling a
man for life. Fabulous values attached to the humblest furniture
and a rickety hand-cart, which had cost a few shillings, rose to the
value of several pounds. One man broke his leg in gratifying his
curiosity to see the inundation and claimed compensation. A rat-
catcher said his living had been destroyed by drowning the rats
in the sewers and thought the loss should be made good to him.
Other people imagined a legal right to their customers and asked
compensation because the neighbouring population was diminished.'
One worker sought unsuccessfully from the company the sum of
£19. 4s. 9d. which, he said, was owed him by two of his mates
drowned in the flood.

The commission was headed by William Overend, Q.C., a shrewd
and alert individual, whose incisive questions were to leave more
than a few witnesses and claimants stuttering and at least one
legal representative floundering. Sheffield-born and now fifty-four,
Overend had been educated at the local grammar school before
being called to the Bar at Lincoln's Inn in 1837. He had aspirations to politics, having stood twice (in 1852 and 1857) as Conservative candidate in Sheffield, but on neither occasion was he
able to defeat Roebuck and Hadfield. He was returned as M.P. for
Pontefract in April 1859, but resigned less than a year afterwards.
Overend's colleagues on the commission were John Jobson Smith,
a stove grate manufacturer and a local Justice of the Peace, and
Mansfield Foster Mills, a Chesterfield estate agent. Overend was
the dominant member, however, and he soon made his presence
felt.

At the opening session the commissioners listened for five hours
to what amounted to 'test' cases; from them were determined
probable principles and policies to be adopted in applications of a

similar kind. Acknowledging that there were nearly four more weeks during which claims could be legally entered, Overend nevertheless expressed disappointment that the Mayor had not seen fit to put in his claims yet. The chairman understood many poor people had signed 'transfers' in favour of the Relief Committee and, as there could be doubt as to whether such an arrangement could be entertained within the legal powers of the commission, it could have been useful to have reached some conclusion that day. The final date specified for receipt of claims was 28 October and, with this in mind, the commissioners saw little point in sitting again until after then and accordingly adjourned until the second week in November.

When the hearings resumed, it was not long before the first clash occurred. It arose from an allegation by an old man, Francis Bullard, who said he had wished to claim only £24 and was astonished to find the amount filed on his behalf was £140. He had seen the company's managing director, William Waterfall, about the matter, saying he could not in conscience accept such a large amount and agreed to take £20 for the loss of tools, clothes and furniture. Bullard told the commissioners that he had made his initial claim through a respected Sheffield solicitor, C. E. Broadbent, who advised him to charge £40 for the loss of goods and £100 in respect of his son who drowned in the flood. He alleged he said he could not make such an 'extravagant' claim, for his son had never supported him in his old age, and all he wanted was enough to cover the funeral expenses and the loss of belongings. Broadbent, well known locally as a lawyer, told the court he thought the case had been withdrawn, as Bullard had decided to settle with the company, and was surprised to find it still on the list. For the company, Ralph Blakelock Smith said he had mentioned the matter because the facts 'astonished us'. Some heated exchanges followed.

OVEREND: You knew yesterday that it would come on today.

BROADBENT: I did not.

OVEREND: Yes, you did.

BROADBENT: I knew nothing of the charge this man was going to make against me.

SMITH: I make no charge against anyone.

BROADBENT: No, you make no charge, but you do worse than that, sir.

OVEREND: Mr Broadbent, Mr Broadbent; I cannot allow this, sir. I feel for you. You stand in a perilous position, but we cannot have this.

BROADBENT: It's a most disgraceful thing, sir; a most abominable, blackguard thing to think ...

OVEREND: Mr Broadbent, I must tell you I cannot allow this court to be made the place for such an exhibition as you are making. You are now upon your trial, for a very serious case of fraud is alleged and it is for you to meet it properly.

The flustered Mr Broadbent then found himself in the witness-box 'defending' himself. He agreed he had advised Bullard perfectly properly to claim for the amounts mentioned and the applicant was quite aware of the situation when he signed each of the two claims with a cross. Broadbent said he felt it was his 'duty' to assist as many of the poorer claimants as possible. He had sent in about 4,600 claims, of which about 500 had been already settled with the company whose officers, he declared, had shown the 'utmost vindictiveness'.

OVEREND: You tell us your desire is to assist the poorer claimants and that you have sent in 4,600 claims. Have you charged two guineas in each?

BROADBENT: I have made no charge, except in this case and others that have been settled with the company up to the present time.

OVEREND: But that is your charge?

BROADBENT: It would be about that.

OVEREND: I only want to know what the poor people get, if you get £9,200?

BROADBENT: Unless they settle with the company, they have not to pay me; other parties would have to pay me.

SMITH: I cannot allow that to go forward uncontradicted. The company do not pay the costs; they pay only taxed costs.

The chief commissioner recalled that in a previous case a claim for £50 had been forwarded by an agent of Broadbent's, whereas the applicant said he sought only £6.15s., although nothing at all in that matter reflected on Broadbent's character. Now here was a similar situation. At one point, Broadbent blurted out: 'I think the company have behaved as a set of thieves and my clients have a right to get what they can. They have had suffering enough to go through.'

OVEREND: You say your clients have a right to get as much as they can. Is that so?

BROADBENT: I think it is perfectly unprecedented for any person to be catechized in the way you are catechizing me.

OVEREND: We shall have to deal with thousands of claims you have sent in of large amounts claimed, thus throwing it upon the company to cut them down by calling evidence. If Bullard's statement is correct, your system of estimating damages is the most scandalous thing that can possibly be. The system pursued has been to claim most excessive and unlikely damages in the hope of getting more than the claimant was justly entitled to. It is an attempt to defraud; it is extortionate and unjust.

The Chief Commissioner, it was quickly appreciated, did not mince words. He said Broadbent had introduced a system of litigation into the town, the end of which could not be foreseen, and 'this inquiry is likely to become a curse to the town instead of a benefit to the public'. A much subdued Mr Broadbent assured the court he had honestly exercised his best judgement in making out the claims and he apologized if he had said anything offensive during the hearing. The result was that the case was 'withdrawn' which, ironically, Broadbent felt it should have been in the first place. Overend, it was further noted, did not bear malice. A few weeks later, when Broadbent was taken ill, he inquired anxiously about his health. During the ensuing weeks, Broadbent also established a happier relationship with the company, settling numerous cases out of court with their officials, who, he said, 'behaved in the most honourable way possible'.

The Relief Committee were having problems with the company concerning the settlement of amounts for which the Mayor held promissory notes from claimants. It was alleged that the company's staff often settled with these applicants by deducting from their claims sums already advanced to them by the Relief Committee. Furthermore, the directors did not recognize the 'transfers' to the Mayor as legal; nor did they concede his right to enter into such cases. A lot of heat was generated under the collars of the contestants and, after digesting lengthy arguments by opposing counsel, the commissioners announced their ruling on 22 November.

William Overend stated: 'We are of the opinion that in all cases the persons with whom the commissioners have to deal are the sufferers of the inundation. They are the only claimants whom we can recognize and no arrangement between them and third parties can dispense with the necessity of their appearing as the only claimants for compensation. The Mayor, therefore, not being a sufferer, has no *locus standi* before us, except that he has sent in a claim as agent for and on behalf of some sufferers. The sufferer, however, even in the latter case, will be the person in whose favour our order will be made.' He added that any payment or loan from the Relief Committee to such sufferers 'does not affect their right to ask for full compensation from us to the same extent as if no such gift or loan had been made'. Overend said the commissioners thought it outside their province to say whether or not money awarded by them to claimants should afterwards, wholly or in part, be paid to the Mayor. 'We wish at the same time,' he emphasized, 'to state that, by abstaining from giving any such decision, we hope that it will not be inferred that we desire to throw the slightest doubt upon their [the promissory notes] validity.' It was possible that such sufferers were legally liable financially to the Mayor.

The feelings of the Relief Committee members can be imagined and, understandably, though perhaps unfairly, the directors of the company became targets for additional wrath and one disgruntled soul suggested that 'a more disreputable set of men never sat in any board-room'. A number of cases was cited where the sum of relief paid to sufferers had been deducted from claims agreed with the company, but John Brown, the steel-maker, who was a member of the Relief Committee and also a director of the waterworks company, would have none of it. He believed his fellow-directors to be honourable men and quite unaware of the kind of practice now being alleged. If he found anything to the contrary, he promised, he would resign from the board. Mr Brown did not resign.

The commissioners' ruling was not, of course, an end to the matter. There followed more attempts to get the Mayor's claims heard, accompanied by accusations and refutations. Even the Town Council discussed the whole question, some members feeling that the Chief Commissioner had been guilty of improper comment when he once suggested that the Mayor had 'set a claimant in motion'. Thomas Jessop himself was put out. Why, he asked, did Overend, who refused to entertain his claims, inquire of claimants how much they had received from the Relief Committee? Tempers frayed, imputations of fraud by the company continued and there were retaliatory charges that certain parties were going out of their way to stir up trouble. The whole unpleasantness was miserably out of place considering that the basic purpose was to ensure that victims of a terrible event received ample compensation. Sadly, pride and prejudice were taking precedence over goodwill and tolerance.

Nevertheless, the legal wheels began to grind and the commissioners' decision was challenged when the case of Joseph Stones, a publican, was somehow thrust before them. It was stated that he had claimed £37. 10s. from the company, but received only £7. 10s. after being told by a member of the staff he had already obtained £30 from the Relief Committee. Stones said he had pointed out that he had entered into agreement to repay the £30 to the Mayor upon being compensated by the company. Henry Manisty, Q.C. (later to be a High Court judge), who represented Stones and the Mayor, alleged that similar cases involved thousands of pounds which were being withheld by the company, who knew perfectly well that the money ought rightfully to be returned to the Mayor. The commissioners, however, maintained that they had no jurisdiction to inquire into whether or not the agreement between Stones and the company was fraudulent or void; they also ruled that they had no power to award him more than the £7. 10s. and that, under the Act, they had no right to allow the Mayor to put in a claim for £30. Manisty gave notice of his intention to seek legal sanction to force them to do so and, on behalf of his clients and against strong opposition by the company, he succeeded in January 1865 in obtaining a *mandamus*—a writ from the High Court to an inferior court.

So the commissioners now had to investigate the case and the hearing occupied the whole of Wednesday 15 February. This time they found the agreement between Stones and the company void, decided he had suffered damage beyond the amount previously granted and gave judgement in his favour for £37. 10s. (This decision set something of a precedent for many of about five hundred similar cases later settled between the Relief Committee and the company.) Overend stressed that the commissioners had found 'no notice of fraud' in the case and hoped the public 'will not think the company have behaved ill. There may have been a mistake in respect of this claim, but I hope the public will not think there has been anything more'. Although pressed by counsel for both sides, the commissioners refused to offer an opinion as to the legality of the 'transfers'. It was, indeed, a long time before the Relief Committee were able to sort out those money matters, some claimants (and the company) refusing to recognize the validity of the promissory notes. Further legal battles ensued and, in the end, the committee recovered most of the money concerned in the 'transfers'. All in all, it was an unsavoury chapter and, undoubtedly, there were mistakes and petty vendettas on both sides.

The commissioners were called upon to deal with extraordinary affairs. Attempts to defraud, both cunningly and clumsily conceived, were winkled out with admirable perception, but it was patently obvious that the three men were going to satisfy only a small proportion of the applicants who came before them. Some awards looked puny against the original claims, which were often exorbitant, while, at the other extreme, some applicants were quite happy to settle for much lower sums than they had put in for. One of the most amazing agreed reductions related to a claim for £300 by Ellen Marriott for the loss of her father, a sixty-year-old carter, who had died on 20 March from an illness directly attributed to the flood. It seemed a reasonable amount. After some consultation, however, the lawyer for the applicant declared that £5 would be acceptable.

> OVEREND: It is really a very wrong thing. Here is a party claiming £300 and consents to take five. Yet the public say we are hard on people and don't give them enough.
>
> P. A. PICKERING, Q.C., for the company: And they say we are fraudulent.

No one seemed inclined to say much more and judgement was entered for £5, Ellen Marriott presumably going blithely on her way.

Less contented was a 'loquacious Irishwoman', Hannah Cooke, who asked for £500 compensation for the loss of her husband, Thomas, who, she claimed, had contracted cramp and ague from bailing water out of the cellar of their home and had died three months afterwards. She declared he had been healthy before the flood, being 'as wholesome, yer honner, as aver a fush that swam in the say'. There was amused confusion when the late Thomas Cooke's employer stepped forward to state that he had paid him for working during much of the time it was alleged he was confined to bed with sickness. The woman's solicitor, completely taken aback by the damning development, confessed to being 'highly indignant' at having been misled by his client. The Irishwoman, who had been so voluble, was crushed into silence as the case was dismissed.

There were, of course, many truly distressing stories told by sole survivors of large families, by the permanently crippled and by the orphaned and widowed. William Coggin, for instance, claimed a total of £350 for the loss of his three children, Alfred (aged 13), Eliza (nine) and William (six). It will be recalled that Coggin and his wife had been attending a family funeral in Wakefield and, on their return, found their children had been drowned. The elder boy, it was stated, earned eight shillings a week working for a skinner and a little more money for doing casual jobs. When the commissioners awarded only £25, the overwrought mother shouted: 'If that is all I have for my three children, I'll have life for it.'

An equally pitiful story was related on behalf of Selina Dyson, the only surviving member of the large family drowned at Hillsborough. She had been living with her grandmother at the time of the flood and now claimed £500 for the loss of her parents. She got £60.

The Chief Commissioner said that he and his colleagues were deeply moved by the wretchedness of such cases and explained that, much as they sympathized with the bereaved, they were empowered to award only the pecuniary loss sustained. If, for example, a father claimed for the death of a son, it was necessary to ascertain how much that son had been earning and how much financially he had benefited the father. In the case of Miss Dyson, who had lost her father, mother, three sisters and two brothers, the commissioners would have been 'very gratified, indeed, if we could have given her something for the anguish she has sustained, but the Act of Parliament prohibits us'.

And so it went on—a harrowing procession of claimants, many of them very poor, illiterate and simple, and most of them overawed by the official aura of the court-room. The painful story of Mrs Ryder whose son, Robert, was torn from her skirts while she clung to a lamp-post and to her small daughter will be remembered: Patrick Ryder, the father, said eleven-year-old Robert was earning 4s. 6d. weekly and was described by his employer as 'a sharp, intelligent lad'; he claimed £200 for the loss of his son, but accepted £20.

George Varney originally sought £2,000 for the death of his son, Sidney, whose horse had thrown him into the flood, but, on counsel's advice, agreed to take the company's offer of £150. The commissioners were of the opinion that the 'grossest possible perjury' had been committed by Natus Hobson, a file striker, who wanted £100 compensation for a 'sprained shoulder' which, he said, had been caused when he fell over some furniture when escaping from his flooded home and was aggravated that same night by catching a child thrown from the bedroom window of another inundated house. The case was promptly thrown out after the real child-saving hero, George Lawson, appeared in court and it was also proved that Hobson had injured his own shoulder at work.

John Harris, a grinder, of Penistone Road, did much better than Hobson before he was rumbled. He must have laughed heartily after being awarded his full claim of £500 on 9 February for head injuries which, he had convinced the court, resulted from the flood. His jubilation was premature, however, and he found himself back before the commissioners on 12 April for a new 'trial' which lasted eight hours. 'Bony' Harris, as he was familiarly known, appeared with a handkerchief tied round his head and told how he was sleeping on a downstairs sofa on the night of the flood. When the water rushed into his house, he tried to escape but the sofa toppled over and struck his head; his wife came downstairs and saved him. This time, Harris was closely questioned about his story. He admitted that during his employment grindstones had broken, flying fragments causing him injury; once he was hit on the face and body, on another occasion his chin was cut and some teeth knocked out while in yet another instance, a piece of stone had spun off and broken his nose. He strenuously denied, however, that he had damaged the back of his head before or after the night of the inundation. 'Bony' Harris had certainly had more than a fair share of injuries in his time and he confessed to being banged by an overhanging branch while travelling on the upper deck of a bus from Buxton to Sheffield. On that occasion, some hair got into the scalp wound to which 'a number of leeches were applied by a woman named Sylvester'. The treatment apparently did the trick.

Accident-prone 'Bony' also agreed that he had fallen down in

The Lancers public house after slipping on 'a piece of tobacco pipe'. Asked why he had not mentioned to anybody his accident in the flood, he replied that he never discussed his personal affairs at work after some of his mates had reported something he had said and, not being a union member, his machine-bands had been rattened. Harris denied that, having seen his wife and children were safe on the flood night, he went to Bridge Street to see if his mule had drowned. The court could not refrain from chuckling when he added that the animal was brought to him later that morning and 'I gave him something warm to eat'. Mrs Harris corroborated her husband's story—as did his two sons—but she admitted that when being treated in 1863 for rheumatism he always 'had his head tied up when he went out'.

Then came witnesses to challenge the Harris tale. The 'leech woman' said the wound she treated was in exactly the same place as that Harris claimed was due to the flood; a doctor said he had attended on Harris for rheumatism of the scalp; even Harris's son-in-law, Charles Edge, told of the claimant's earlier head injuries and that he had been in ill-health during the four years he had known him. Another witness said Harris told her he had been in bed throughout the flood and had not seen it, but that his wife got up 'to save the cats'. Then, for Harris, came the unkindest cut of all: his barber testified to having shaved the Harris head several times before the flood and that the injury on the back of it was plainly visible. The game was now over for 'Bony' who, concluded the commissioners, had perpetrated a 'great fraud' (reluctant admission he had 'conned' them at the previous hearing of his case) and dismissed the claim.

The court proceedings were not without light relief. The legal profession have a brand of humour all their own and judges, in particular, delight in affecting ignorance of slang terms. 'The court is not familiar with that phrase', they intone with childlike innocence, 'perhaps counsel could enlighten us?' Barristers appear just as bemused and reply, almost apologetically, 'Well, M'Lord, I am advised it refers to so-and-so'. Hearty chuckles all round. Still, it relieves the monotony. In the case of Henry Gray, a file cutter, who claimed £50 for contracting rheumatic fever and suffering permanent disability after 'getting wet' in the flood, all seemed thoroughly to enjoy the pastime of lofty pretence—with the possible exception of the claimant.

MR POPE [solicitor for the company]: Do you have a nick-name?

GRAY: I think I have.

POPE: What do you answer to?

GRAY: Owt they've a mind to call me.

POPE: Do they call you Tippler?

GRAY: Yes.

POPE: Why?

GRAY: I don't know.

POPE: Do you tipple?

GRAY: No, I wouldn't like to do. I don't because I can't.

CHIEF COMMISSIONER: What is tippling?

POPE: I don't understand it. I only know of it in the language of Acts of Parliament.

COMMISSIONER J. J. SMITH: Does it mean a tumbler or a drinker?

CHIEF COMMISSIONER: It means that he drinks out of a tumbler.

WILLIAM HALL [a friend of Gray]: I never see'd him tipple and don't know why they call him 'Tippler', but I expect he tipples if he wants to.

'Tippler' Gray, as bewildered by the questions as he was by the badinage which so amused the court, was awarded £15.

The judicial joke often passes unappreciated by the layman, who misses the point by mistakenly searching for some hidden gem of wit on a higher plane. The case involving Richard Nesbitt Ryan required no special insight; it was good for a laugh in almost everybody's book. It is unrecorded whether or not Mr Ryan laughed. The rest of the court was apparently convulsed, however. Ryan, formerly an actor for thirty years and now a poet, claimed £300 for the loss of manuscripts from his lodgings in Wicker Lane. He was no ordinary versifier, but a kind of English fore-runner of Scotland's William McGonagall and specialized in dedi-cating his works to 'various illustrious persons and families in Sheffield and neighbourhood'. Ryan's poems were good. We have his word for it. The waterworks company, unquestionably philis-tines in his view, had offered a cheeseparing £6 in compensation. Mr Ryan was deeply wounded by such cavalier treatment. Among the epics mentioned in his claim were *An Ode to an*

Anvil and *A Complimentary Address to the Proprietor of the Atlas Works*. His solicitor, Mr Barker, offered to illustrate Ryan's rare qualities as a poet by quoting a few verses, but the commissioners politely declined. Instead, Ryan willingly accepted an invitation to go into the witness-box from where he delivered a biographical peroration. Since his retirement from the stage, he said, he had earned his living by selling his poetry in printed or manuscript form. One such composition, extending to 40 pages of small type, was on *Sheffield General Infirmary* and 'eulogizes everything about it, doctors, patrons, patients and the cures there effected'. About 300 copies had been sold at a shilling a time during the first month after publication, some 80 more copies being swept away by the flood. What he must have considered his masterpiece (not then published) also went the way of the waters; it was *Life and Adventures of R. N. Ryan: Showman, Manager, Actor, Poet, Innkeeper, Etc.*, which would have amounted to 84 octavo pages of print and for which he anticipated a 'considerable sale'. It appeared there was hardly anything of local importance Mr Ryan had not committed to verse and he said the great John Brown himself had been enraptured by *Ode to John Brown's Great Armour-Plate*.

On the night of the flood, Ryan explained, he had made a fund-raising stage appearance at a minor theatre in Rotherham and, after taking his curtain calls, he had 'the great felicity of being arraigned for the first time in my life for performing in an unlicensed theatre'. By this time the court was rocking merrily as Ryan, in full dramatic flow, launched into further details of his chequered career. Mr Pope (for the waterworks company) wanted to know more about that performance at Rotherham, however.

RYAN: I played Hamlet, the Gravedigger and the Clown.
POPE: That is not 'utility' is it?
RYAN: It looks very much like it. You see I was manager.
POPE: And the manager can play anything?
RYAN: Yes, he is sometimes forced to do. I was raising money to print my life and I'm quite sure I could have sold ten thousand copies.

Producing a black-bordered document, Ryan declared it was *An Ode to the Great Flood*. If the commissioners cared to read a few lines, he suggested, they would see 'it is not the worst written thing in the language'. Again, the commissioners refused with thanks.

> POPE: How do you usually sell your poems?
> RYAN: Singly to parties who know me. I've never sold two copies to one party.
> CHIEF COMMISSIONER: You mean they have had enough with one?
> RYAN: They are satisfied with the first. I never wish to supply them to satiation.

When it was pointed out by Mr Pope that the claim was based on a fallacious estimate, Ryan replied that *Paradise Lost* was sold in Milton's own lifetime for £20. 'Five pounds,' corrected the chief commissioner. After some consideration, the commissioners announced that Ryan had made out a genuine case and awarded him £100.

John Furniss, who lived in Wicker Lane not far from where the poet lodged, had no pretensions to the arts—except, perhaps, that of self-defence—and claimed £150 for a broken nose which, he asserted, was sustained when he fell on a low roof at back of his home in escaping from the flood. He admitted, under cross-examination, that he had been in many fights in his time, but his nose was not damaged in any of them.

> CHIEF COMMISSIONER: What are you besides a bruiser?
> FURNISS: A scissor-grinder.
> PICKERING, Q.C.: On your oath, have you ever earned £10 at scissor-grinding?
> FURNISS: Yes, ten hundred pounds. I have not worked at it for two years; I've been assisting a butcher and doing odd jobs.
> MR SYKES [surgeon]: I have attended Mr Furniss and I think he will suffer some inconvenience beyond the loss of his personal beauty. I have attended him before; I think it was for rheumatism.
> CHIEF COMMISSIONER: What! In the nose?
> SYKES: No, sir.

Several witnesses were called to prove that the Furniss proboscis looked the same before the flood as it did afterwards. The claim was dismissed.

They could not be blamed for trying, perhaps. Most of those who attempted to put one across the commissioners were poor and saw a chance of collecting a few pounds from the company's coffers. They were more stupid than criminal and the majority of them made the same fatal mistake. They had reckoned without their neighbours. In such close-knit communities, very little escaped attention. How had William Tittcombe expected to succeed in his claim for £100 for 'illness' to his wife, who said she had contracted it after falling into flood water at Damflask, when it was 'the talk of the neighbourhood' that she had done no such thing? Did Harriet Bramwell, of Harvest Lane, really anticipate getting £50 for 'losing' her voice after catching cold from the flood, when it was common knowledge she had 'a throat disease of long-standing'? The commissioners dismissed that claim as 'impudent'.

Most of the claims were honestly submitted, of course, and mirrored the misery which followed the bursting of the dam. Week after week, the commissioners considered the cases of the destitute, the maimed, the righteous, the greedy, the forbearing, the simple and the cunning. It was not easy to detect a logical scale of values, however. For instance, the crippled William Elston, aged seven, who would 'never be able to earn his own living', claimed £500 for the loss of his father (drowned with his wife and infant son). The commissioners thought the company's offer of £100 was 'very liberal' and gave judgement for that amount. On the other hand, the commissioners awarded £487 (the company offered £178) to Walter Sykes for damage to property which included rare editions of 'the Bible, Shakespeare, Erasmus and Horace'.

Reviewing the work of the court, the *Sheffield and Rotherham Independent* had this to say: 'The proceedings under the Commission began with very active hostilities and many angry things were said. They have ended with volleys of compliments. The commissioners are complimented, and that most justly, for the skill and care with which they have treated the cases brought before them, and for the general satisfactory character of their decisions. The whole business has been conducted in a spirit of liberality to honest sufferers.'

Referring to the clash between the Relief Committee and the waterworks company, the writer commented: 'It is obvious that if one party goes so far as to charge another with fraud, there remains no alternative but to put it to the proof. And when that gross imputation is abandoned by those who made it, when an advocate can coolly get up and say, that not moral but only legal fraud was meant, fraud in a Pickwickean sense, we must think that the mode of getting out of the charge is pretty nearly as bad as the making of it. Whatever may have been said at the time, no competent person will dispute now that the company have been always ready to meet fairly the claims upon them, and they very naturally felt themselves entitled to expect from their townsmen a considerable degree of co-operation and sympathy ... we may now fairly say that by their own vigorous and able policy, which obtained the sanction of Parliament in spite of attempts to take advantage of their misfortune, which we shall ever regret, the water company have escaped from the jaws of ruin.'

The final hearing before the commissioners was on Thursday, 13 April 1865. Total compensation originally claimed from the company was more than £455,000, of which about £380,000 related to damage to property and the remainder to loss of life and personal injury. Settlements, withdrawals and judgements reduced that figure a great deal and, in the final analysis, the company paid out something like £275,000. Over 3,200 claimants accepted offers made by the company, nearly 1,400 settled by negotiated agreement out of court; of the cases which went before the commissioners for adjudication, about 420 resulted in judgement for the claimants and about 230 in favour of the company. More than 1,600 claims were withdrawn, suggesting that many of them were speculative in the first place and, upon consideration, untenable.

One wonders if the actor-poet, Richard Nesbitt Ryan, was moved to put all that into verse?

11 The Case of the Slipping Ground

Christmas is a time of reunion. It is an occasion when, according to tradition, children's eyes sparkle and grown-up offspring return home from afar to gather round the festive table presided over by a proud father. For too many Sheffielders, the Christmas of 1864 was an unhappy reminder of loss. There were empty places at the table. Memories of loved ones hurled into eternity the previous March remained painfully fresh, while legacies of destruction left by the flood were still to be seen in some streets. There was the added burden of being poor. It wasn't easy to enjoy His birthday in homes where wet walls peeled and draughts went through thin clothes. Do-gooders dispensed charity, Christians were encouraged to 'Love Thy Neighbour' (albeit for a few days) and sprigs of holly, well-stocked shops, plum duff, plump poultry and the thin-piping voices of waits all helped to create an illusion of prosperity. In reality, many of those bereaved by the flood (and thousands more who were not) could afford to do little more than stare and sniff from a distance.

The labouring classes of Sheffield were certainly better off than their parents had been. The financial fruits of a booming Victorian economy had filtered down to the lower echelons in the form of slightly increased wages, but existence on the bottom rungs of the social ladder was still no sinecure. After paying for some of life's necessities, little (if any) money was left for even a flirting taste of a few luxuries. Nevertheless, more working-class families were somehow managing an improved standard of living and sought to enlarge the scope of their activities. Among other things, there grew up a demand to be entertained.

Sheffield boasted a number of theatres and music-halls, ranging from the respectable to the disreputable and, presumably, all doing good business. At the Theatre Royal that Christmas, there was a chance to see a 'grand and glorious' pantomime, *King Diamond or High Low Jack and the Game*, during which Jack of Clubs 'slanders the Town Council' and 'makes a powerful incantation':

> By bets on the great St Leger lost,
> By what our town Improvement Act will cost;
> By Don and Sheaf and Porter's putrid smells
> And the pestilential Town Hall cells;
> By our Town Council's interesting jangles,
> By Highway, Watch and Health Committees' wrangles;
> By water, twenty-five per cent too dear,
> By Good Mr Necromancer, here appear.

The extract, however trite it may now appear, gives an intriguing glimpse into contemporary local opinion in 1864. Reference in the jingle to Sheffield's filth-laden rivers almost certainly prompted an ironic cheer from the audience and one can almost hear the derision that must have greeted the allusion to the increased water rates. It is difficult to conceive a more striking contrast between the town and its surroundings, while it is easy to see why rambling clubs became so popular. Not more than a mile or so from the fetid atmosphere of the industrial concerns was sweet-tasting moorland air, the blossoming smoke soon giving way to blossoming heather. Sheffield, it was pointed out by the industrialists, was a rich metal-producing town and, as such, could not be fairly compared with a Bath or a Cheltenham. Beauty and business did not mix. Health, it seems, took second place to wealth. It was the price of progress.

One must resist the temptation to judge by present-day values the conditions existing in the industrial towns of England in the 1860s. Social and economic climates and outlooks were utterly different and some of the traditionally accepted practices then would horrify us now. Even so, some abuses of labour aroused violent indignation in the second half of the nineteenth century when pathetic cases were 'discovered' by investigating officers dispatched into the field by reform-conscious commissions. The worst evils of child labour had been largely eliminated, but there remained many youngsters under the age of twelve who did a full day's hard work, often at the instigation of poor or lazy parents who saw in them supplementary breadwinners.

What sort of Christmas was it for the likes of William Crompton, aged ten, one of more than three thousand men and boys employed at John Brown's steel and iron works? His job, it was reported, was to stand in front of a furnace and to hold up the door each time white-hot metal was drawn out. He did a 12-hour shift (with a few breaks), either day or night, and of the five shillings weekly he earned for his labours, his parents allowed him to keep a penny. A representative of Cammell and Company was reported as saying it was impossible to prohibit night-work by young people because 'it would be tantamount to stopping our works'. To be fair to the bosses—at least, some of them—they were often begged by families to put young boys and girls on the pay-roll. The trade unions, to their credit, strove hard to discourage the employment of very young people in factories. It was said that among the most unfeeling of employers were fathers. One eight-year-old, William Henry Widdicombe, was set to work grinding cast-metal scissors on a dry stone. There was no fan to disperse the lethal dust and the boy, with 'a pale face and squalid dress', was found labouring alone by an inspector who believed the employer-father was out drinking. What kind of a Christmas would that lad have? Indeed, how many more would he see?

For all his comparative creature comforts, John Gunson could not have looked back over the previous ten months with any pleasure. As the waterworks company's engineer, he had been subjected to public and private criticism and, although he would never forget the tragedy, he may have derived some solace from the publication of the report of the five engineers retained by the company to seek the cause of the dam's failure. They had already given their opinion that the collapse was due to an unforeseeable landslip and now, just before Christmas, their detailed reasons were made public by the company. The document appears not to have won many converts, but at least an entirely different point of view was getting a good airing. Perhaps Gunson's Christmas was happier as a result.

It was a highly talented team which had examined the Dale Dyke embankment and the unfinished dam at Agden, about both of which structures Rawlinson and Beardmore had been so disparaging. The five men who now came up with different answers were James Simpson, Thomas Hawksley, John Frederic Latrobe Bateman, John Fowler and Thomas Elliott Harrison. In the first three, the company had secured foremost specialists in hydraulics. As long before as 1829 Simpson, then the thirty-year-old engineer to Chelsea Waterworks, had developed a technique for ridding water of solid impurities by filtering it through sand—a vital piece of pioneering which led to more advanced methods of water purification. Since then, he had constructed waterworks at Windsor Castle, designed and built the long pier at Southend-on-Sea and planned waterworks at Bristol. Hawksley, now fifty-seven, had no peer in the design and building of waterworks and gasworks and examples of his achievements were to be seen in many major towns. Bateman was a Yorkshireman. He was born just outside Halifax in 1810, was apprenticed at fifteen and was only twenty-three when he set up as an engineer on his own account; since then, he had been employed almost non-stop in the construction of waterworks and reservoirs for important towns all over Britain. He was much respected by his fellows and in 1867, in a paper written in conjunction with Julian John Révy, he proposed the building of a submarine railway, in a cast-iron tube, between England and France.

Sheffield-born Fowler and Harrison, who hailed from Sunderland, completed the quintet. Both had gained much experience in railway engineering, and hence a considerable knowledge of embankments, and Fowler, who was to gain fame for his part in the construction of the Forth Bridge, was currently engaged in the building of parts of London's Metropolitan Railway. Harrison, at fifty-six, was almost ten years Fowler's senior. He had assisted Robert Stephenson on a number of projects, including the London-Birmingham Railway and the high-level bridge over the Tyne to link Gateshead and Newcastle. He was engineer-in-chief of the York-Newcastle-Berwick line and, in 1858, had added to his professional laurels by designing and supervising the construction of Jarrow Docks. He was to follow that by planning the docks at Hartlepool. The Sheffield Waterworks Company had also invited John Hawkshaw, a top-class engineer who was to direct the building of the Severn Tunnel, but he 'declined to act'.

The views of any one of the five engineers merited consideration; in concert, their opinions deserved the closest attention. It could well be argued—indeed, it was—that they were unlikely to produce anything that could be regarded as detrimental to the waterworks company. It seems just as valid to say that none of the five was going to risk hanging his reputation on a slender thread. Nevertheless, there was room for manoeuvre. Rawlinson and Beardmore had reported confidently enough on what they considered to be serious defects in the construction of the dam, but there was some (though not much) scope for reasonable doubt. Nothing had been proved conclusively as the actual cause of the failure. In the event, the five engineers did no better. Their 'findings' were, in effect, contained in these paragraphs of the report:

... we are unanimously of opinion that the accident was occasioned by a landslip which occurred in the ground immediately on the east side of the embankment and which extended beneath a portion of the outer slope, involving in its consequence the ruin of that portion of the bank and producing the catastrophe which followed. [The engineers had stated that not only were tears and fractures to be seen in the lower part of the mass, but also that two cottages, 'both remote from the bank, give unmistakable proofs of the recent movement of the ground on which they stand. From the testimony of the occupiers of these cottages, this movement must have immediately preceded or been concurrent with the bursting of the reservoir'].

To this conclusion we severally came on our first examination, and every subsequent investigation, and the more intimate acquaintance we have since acquired with all the evidence and facts connected with the subject, have only the more firmly convinced us that to no other cause can the destruction of the reservoir be rightly attributed. We are moreover of the opinion that all the arrangements made by your engineers were such as might have been reasonably expected to have proved sufficient for the purposes for which they were intended and that, if the ground beneath the bank had not moved, this work would have been as safe and as perfect as the other five or six large reservoirs of the company which have been constructed in a similar manner and which have so long supplied the town of Sheffield and the rivers Rivelin, Loxley and Don with water.

We may add that, since the accident, the discharging pipes, the outer ends of which had been buried beneath the rubbish deposited by the flood, have been reached and carefully examined. They have been tested under a hydraulic pressure far exceeding that which they would have had to sustain in use. They have been inspected internally by a man passing through them and their lines and levels have been observed from without by means of candles of equal lengths placed centrally within them. In these several manners, the pipes have been proved to be accurate in their position, not having even bent under the pressure of the embankment, and perfectly sound and watertight. This is a state of perfection we never anticipated and speaks well not only for the mode of construction adopted by the engineers, but also for the excellent character of the workmanship.

Such a report might well have had a substantial impact some months earlier, but its appearance now gave it little chance in the minds of the public, most of whom were quite happy to believe that the failure resulted from incompetence. The evidence concerning the excellent condition of the pipes certainly destroyed the theory of a fatal fracture, but it did nothing to weaken the submission that the pipes had subsided into the puddle, thus creating a cavity through which water could permeate and undermine the embankment. Nevertheless, the engineers' emphatic conclusion that the whole trouble stemmed from a landslip seemed as difficult to accept as it was to disprove.

The company's directors of course were delighted and, armed with such encouraging information, lost no time in telling the Home Secretary that the engineers had also approved of the construction of the Agden dam, adding tactfully that operations would remain suspended if the Government thought another investigation desirable. Sir George Grey replied that, as the work on the Agden was in 'precisely the same state' as when Rawlinson inspected it in March, he saw no advantage to be gained by holding another inquiry or by having a further official examination. He reminded the directors that he had no power to interfere with any resumption of work, but stressed that any decision to do so would be 'upon the undivided responsibility of the company and without sanction, expressed or implied, on the part of Her Majesty's Government'. So it appeared there was nothing legally to prevent a recommencement of work at Agden.

It had been an intriguing clash of direct opposites. The Government inspectors had pointed to a number of faults in the construction of the Dale Dyke dam; the company-retained engineers found none (at least, they had not reported any). Rawlinson and Beardmore discovered no evidence of a landslip; the quintet based the whole of their case on such a reason. The 'porous' Agden embankment denounced by Rawlinson was 'passed' by the five. Public opinion was also divided but, as far as one can judge, few people regarded the latest report as a vindication of the company. Many saw it as no more than an exercise in exculpation. Rather unkindly, perhaps, it was suggested that men who could deduce a landslip from such sparse evidence 'would stir up Vesuvius to boil an egg or hire an earthquake to frighten away a fly'. To some, the arguments advanced by the five engineers held about as much water as did the Dale Dyke reservoir at that moment.

The Sheffield Daily Telegraph affected bewilderment. It was necessary to employ those engineers to locate a landslip, wrote their leader-writer (presumably Leng), 'seeing that unskilled persons could not find it and have never yet been able to find anything of the kind'. Then came a shaft of sarcasm; 'Unprofessional people reason in a vulgar way. They say that a landslip infers a slipping of the land, and that a slipping of the land involves a change of place and that a change of place means nothing less than a movement of the soil from one position to another. Arguing in this rude way, they contend that if the ground has moved or slipped other eyes than the eyes of retained engineers should be able to see some signs of the fact.... They cannot comprehend an alleged movement which has moved nothing, nor can they understand how a landslip can have occurred where the soil remains on the hillside, and where the grass grows upon the soil, without a crack or seam, just as it did before. But all that want of sight is, we presume, through lack of professional training, and it is hard to persuade them now that the soil first glided down into the valley and then, out of fear of the flood, climbed back up the hillsides and quietly resumed its place. But, perhaps, after all, the question is one of the meaning of a word.'

The newspaper was in agreement on one point: 'In the matter of the pipes, these engineers are probably right. We have always thought that Mr Rawlinson committed an error in placing too much emphasis on the pipes.' One thing is certain: Robert Rawlinson did not. He spent time in the following years defending his theories and, on the whole, modern opinion and assessment have supported him. As long after the disaster as November 1879, when he was sixty-nine, Rawlinson was still making his points during a discussion by members of the Institution of Civil Engineers on 'Tunnel

Outlets from Storage Reservoirs'. The debate included reference to the Dale Dyke failure and, predictably, Rawlinson spoke his piece. Just as predictably John Bateman, then in his second year as president, gave his version of what had happened. It must have been an illuminating clash.

Various views have been expressed over the years and, basically, they have boiled down to those advanced by Rawlinson and his supporters on the one hand and the five engineers and their sympathizers on the other. Mr Rolt, in *Victorian Engineering*, states concisely that the cause, though never established, was believed to have been due to 'the collapse of a large cast-iron supply pipe beneath the superincumbent weight of the dam'. In his book, *A History of Dams*, Norman Smith believes the collapse was 'initiated by the faulty positioning and laying of the outlet pipes. As the heavy bank settled, the pipes were probably displaced and water, percolating through the pervious embankment, began to wash away the puddled clay surrounding them. This undermined the core wall at a point where the pipes passed through it, and very soon a considerable volume of water was eroding away the interior of the dam. It is conceivable that at this point the central portion of the dam subsided enough to allow the already full reservoir to spill over the poorly constructed crest. Thus the centre of the dam was eroded from above and below and a collapse was inevitable.'

The recommendation, following the failure, that all dams and reservoirs in Britain should, by Act of Parliament, be subject to frequent inspections, was not taken up and, says Mr Smith, 'it took the Dolgarrog disaster of 1925 to bring about the Reservoirs (Safety Provisions) Act of 1930'. What the Dale Dyke calamity did do was to bring home the fact 'that the dam-builder has a considerable social responsibility. Well executed, his work is of great benefit to the community but, if it is not, a dam failure is perhaps the most serious man-made catastrophe likely to occur in peacetime. The rapidly growing literature on dams in the latter decades of the nineteenth century makes more and more frequent reference to this point, particularly because so many big dams were being built near cities in an effort to meet the ever-growing need for more domestic and industrial water'.

Not long after the report of the five engineers had been published, it was announced that Thomas Hawksley had been appointed the company's engineer-in-chief. It was a valuable capture because Hawksley, of Great George Street, London, had been long regarded as a top man in his profession. As a young engineer, he had been much impressed by the determined campaigning of Chadwick who believed fever was often directly attributable to bad water supplies and poor sanitary conditions. Hawksley pioneered a water scheme in Nottingham and, in 1843, confirmed that it had brought about a marked improvement in personal hygiene, cleaner streets and homes and, consequently, a noticeable falling-off of disease. Now, more than twenty years later at Sheffield, he succeeded John Towlerton Leather who had resigned, it was reported, 'owing to his numerous engagements'. With Hawksley at the engineering helm, an extensive programme designed greatly to improve Sheffield's water supply recommenced. Although he was able to devote only a comparatively small part of his professional time to the Sheffield Waterworks Company, Hawksley undoubtedly maintained a much closer liaison than had his predecessor. Work at Agden continued and, during the next few years, the new embankment of Dale Dyke was started (about a quarter of a mile upstream from the ill-fated dam) as was the building of the Strines reservoir (connected to Dale Dyke) and a larger project at Damflask. There were always problems, however, and it was a long time before some of those reservoirs were in continuous operation.

Following the Dale Dyke disaster, it was hardly surprising that there should be concern about the nation's reservoirs generally and particularly with regard to safeguards in the building of new ones. A Select Committee of the House of Commons, with none other than John Arthur Roebuck as chairman, was appointed to look into the whole question. After examining a number of leading engineers (including Rawlinson, Leslie, Bateman, Fowler, Hawksley and Murray) and carefully considering many aspects of the subject, the committee made certain recommendations designed to bring about some parliamentary supervision over the construction and maintenance of dams and reservoirs. In their report dated 23 June 1865 the committee stated that from the evidence they had taken 'it appears that the storing of water for manufacturing and other purposes in large reservoirs is always dangerous, and that sometimes great loss of life and great destruction of property have been occasioned by accidents to such reservoirs, and your committee therefore deem it the duty of the Legislature to protect the public, as far as circumstances permit, from the possibility of such mischief'. The committee emphasized that none of the suggested measures of inspection was intended 'to diminish in any degree the responsibility of undertakers' to pay any damage caused by the water.

The committee urged the Government to bring in a Bill, embodying the views expressed, early in 'the next session'. That, as it turned out, proved an unwitting piece of rash optimism. Appended to the committee's principal report was the report of the five engineers engaged by the Sheffield Waterworks Company together with some remarks upon it by Rawlinson. In a lengthy document, and quoting liberally from the reports of the nine engineers employed by Sheffield Town Council, he analysed the various opinions and, not unnaturally, summarily rejected the Dale Dyke landslip theory. He regarded the 'so-called tests and trials' as 'absolutely worthless in every respect' and the suggestion that the ground slipped as 'merely an assertion without proof'.

In general, Rawlinson welcomed official inspection of certain aspects of reservoirs, but 'I do not consider that it is the duty of Government to teach engineers their business nor in any way so to interfere with plans and modes of construction so as to remove the entire responsibility of the safe maintenance of the embankments and works from proprietors promoting and the engineer designing and executing such works.... Certain rules may be laid down with regard to modes of construction, which shall ensure strength and correct principles, without unduly fettering the engineer in his subsequent constructive operations. The test of gradually filling in reservoirs in stages, and under inspection, will, in my opinion, be an additional means of safety to the public.' In another appendix to the Select Committee's report, Rawlinson recommended some general principles to be followed in the planning and construction of reservoirs; to that were added a number of objections by John Bateman who, not for the first time (or the last), disagreed sharply with Rawlinson. As *The Engineer* commented: 'When engineers differ, who shall decide?'

Meanwhile, the Sheffield Waterworks Company were wrestling with their own problems. At a special meeting in April 1865, called primarily to discuss how to raise the money to meet demands, the company's chairman, George Hounsfield, took the opportunity to comment upon recent events. The directors, he said, had been 'abused up hill and down dale,' but he hoped that the spirit in which they had fought [regarding the compensation claims] had been a proper one and that they had 'not lost the respect of the people of Sheffield'. He and his colleagues absolutely repudiated any suggestion of any resemblance of fraud at any time in dealing with the claims for damages. In order to help to meet their heavy commitments, the company's directors successfully recommended the raising of £225,000 by creating preference shares and a further £175,000 by means of mortgages. In addition to paying out about £275,000 in compensation, the company also met claimants' costs, legal, clerical, commission and other fees as well as the expense of getting the Bill through Parliament. The company's total cost arising from the Dale Dyke failure (according to the annual report to shareholders in 1866) amounted to £422,380.

The company had not only to rebuild their broken reservoir but also, to some extent, their image and reliability as a sound investment. Indeed, the directors showed considerable courage for, despite obvious difficulties, they went ahead with their programme of works. But it was a struggle. The company were never able completely to shake off the heavy halter of the Dale Dyke disaster and, whenever they went to Parliament seeking new sanctions, their opponents could be relied upon to resurrect the tragedy. During the summer of 1866, for instance, the company presented to a House of Lords Select Committee a Bill which proposed to improve greatly and quickly Sheffield's supply of utilizing water from the Rivelin after purchasing the rights of the remaining mills (which would turn to steam-power). Thomas Hawksley referred to the 'existing and, occasionally, alarming scarcity of water in Sheffield'; it was further represented that the recommended scheme would result in raising the amount of water per head per day from about 12 gallons to 25 and that the sanitary condition of the town made the 'taking of this water an absolute necessity'. But for the Dale Dyke failure, it was claimed, a satisfactory supply would have been already in operation, Hawksley commenting that the Sheffield people were naturally 'very sensitive' about the progress of new reservoirs and the company had to proceed very slowly and cautiously with the work.

Details of the hearing need not concern us; suffice it to say that the Lords Committee ruled that the company could abstract water from the Rivelin, in accordance with their proposals, but for a limited period of four years (an almost impracticable decision that must have further frustrated the directors striving to satisfy increasing demands for water). What was interesting was that among the witnesses—this time as a member of the Commission on the Pollution of Rivers—was Robert Rawlinson. During his evidence he was invited to say 'a word or two' about Sheffield's reservoirs. He wasn't going to miss a chance like that. 'Well,' he was reported as stating, 'I should be very sorry to father the completion of the Agden embankment. I wouldn't do so for the whole fee simple of Sheffield. The bursting of Dale Dyke reservoir caused the loss of 250 lives in 15 minutes, and I shouldn't like to be in Sheffield the night the Agden reservoir is filled if it were filled with the base now existing.' Asked if the five engineers who had attributed the dam disaster to a landslip were not very eminent men in their profession, Rawlinson replied: 'None more so.' He was quick to add that he disagreed with their opinion, however, as did other engineers of 'equal eminence' to those engaged by the company.

The directors of Sheffield Waterworks Company undoubtedly had good intentions and, considering the problems under which they laboured, progress was surprisingly steady. Additional pipes were laid, new consumers were linked to the supply and work went ahead on major construction projects. From time to time there were cries for the company to sell out to the corporation and not a little criticism about other matters. The path was rarely smooth. It will be recalled that the company were legally bound, on the requisition of Sheffield Corporation, to furnish a constant supply of water to the town by 29 July 1869 (a condition of the 1864 Act). That they were unable immediately to conform probably caused no great amazement, but it did cause resentment and heated exchanges. The company explained that, because of faulty taps and fittings, a considerable amount of water was wasted when the supply was continuous. They were told in no uncertain terms that such defects were the result of nobody's failing but their own and that it was indisputably their responsibility to rectify the situation and to provide a round-the-clock supply as the law demanded.

So, once more, the directors found themselves in the centre of a vortex; old wounds were reopened and dark allegations again rose like a troublesome phoenix. It was strongly voiced (not for the first time) that vital facts relating to the Dale Dyke failure had not been revealed at the coroner's inquest and that no proper inquiry had ever been held into the precise cause of the catastrophe. In their issue of 10 December 1869 *The Engineer* declared: 'The Sheffield Waterworks Company have apparently fallen upon evil days. Their relations with the tax-payers of the town whom they promised to supply with an abundance of pure water are, to judge from the local papers, to the last degree unsatisfactory.' As though admonishing a naughty boy, the journal added that 'we have had occasion before now to criticize the proceedings of this company' and also revealed that they possessed some important facts about the dam collapse which had not been made public. Some years previously *The Engineer* claimed that the company had not carried out all the provisions of the 1853 Act under which the Dale Dyke reservoir was constructed in that certain storm channels specified in the parliamentary plans had not been built. 'Whether the existence of those channels of relief would or would not have averted the failure of the dam, we shall leave our readers to say,' commented the journal.

It was all too easy to criticize, of course, and the hard-pressed directors must have felt extremely vulnerable. Unquestionably they were men of integrity, with honest aspirations, and it does appear that they strove assiduously to do what was right by both their consumers and the company's shareholders. Whether or not they succeeded in what was, after all, an increasingly heavy responsibility is perhaps open to debate. They must have derived some consolation when Hawksley reported in April 1870 that 'the present stock of water, irrespective of the contributions from the streams and springs, is sufficient for the supply of the town and mills during a period of 150 days of continuous drought.... The system of constant supply at high pressure has been in uninterrupted operation in Sheffield from the 14th of December last and, although the waste has hitherto been very great, yet, as it is becoming gradually reduced in amount by the repair of leaky taps and cisterns, and the introduction of improved domestic arrangements and fittings, I feel justified in entertaining the hope and expectation that it will not again become necessary to limit the number of hours per day during which the supply shall be given'. He also stated that all the reservoir works were being carried out 'carefully and soundly and with every regard, consistent with stability, to the economical expenditure of the company's funds'. He added a tribute: 'In these matters my efforts have been ably seconded by Mr Gunson, to whose earnest and unremitting attention to his onerous duties I have much pleasure in thus testifying.'

At about this time there were suggestions that Sheffield Corporation should bid to take over the waterworks company if only for the side benefits of turning the land surrounding the reservoirs into public parks. *The Sheffield Daily Telegraph* waxed lyrical: 'In a great town like ours there is urgent need of accessible places where the pale mechanic can have leave to breathe. The sight of green slopes, crisp and shining shrubberies, and sheets of pure water, transparent as crystal, is good for the soul. Let the corporation possess the soil, and we will warrant it that generous citizens will be forthcoming to embellish it with fountains and statuary, and gifts of clean hardy shrubs.'

The suggestions came to naught and, despite some serious setbacks, the major works programme went on. The new Dale Dyke reservoir had a capacity of 486 million gallons (compared with the 712 million of its disastrous predecessor), the embankment was 80 feet high and measured over 900 feet across; this time, the bye-wash was 130 feet wide. Water was not drawn through pipes set underneath the embankment, but via a tunnel through rock at the southern end. Although completed in 1875, the reservoir was not brought into full use until the 'exceptionally dry year' of 1887. The Agden, which Hawksley claimed was among the safest and strongest dams yet built, contained 629 million gallons, impounded by an embankment about 1,500 feet across and more than 90 feet high. It was completed in 1869, the Strines (513 million gallons) in 1871 but the Damflask, by far the largest with a capacity of 1,158 million gallons, though built by the late 1870s, was not in constant use until 1896; the reason was that water, when it rose to above 30 feet, escaped through the natural strata at one end of the embankment and it was not until after the corporation assumed control that the problem was solved by the construction of a large, impervious wing trench.

Not only the waterworks company had troubles after the disaster. The town's Relief Committee also faced financial embarrassment, but in their case, it was not shortage of cash. They had too much. More than £55,000 had been subscribed to the fund and, after distributing relief to many poor sufferers (over £13,000 on 'transfers' was recouped from the waterworks company) and deducting administrative expenses, the committee returned about

£24,000 to donors (on the basis of half the subscription). Even so, with 'unclaimed' donations and also some money sent back by donors, there was still a credit balance of nearly £8,000 which it was decided to disburse as follows: Infirmary (50 per cent), Public Hospital and Dispensary (30 per cent) and Hospital for Women (20 per cent). In fact, only about two-fifths of the total subscribed was spent on the purpose for which it was originally sent. The response had been overwhelming and, at one stage, the Relief Committee were obliged to announce that no more money was required. The committee, whom some thought should have been more liberal in their allocations, held their final meeting more than two years after the failure of the dam.

12 The Final Enactment

Few of the original characters were on stage for the concluding act of the serial starring the Sheffield Waterworks Company and Sheffield Corporation. In 1887 while Sheffield, in common with city, town and village throughout the British Empire, prepared to celebrate the jubilee of Queen Victoria, the company were again before Parliament. They sought to extend indefinitely the 25-year period of the 25 per cent increase on the water rate (imposed under the 1864 Act and due to expire in 1889); this time, the corporation not only opposed the company's Bill but also introduced one of their own—for compulsory purchase. The hearing, before a Select Committee of the House of Lords comprising the Earl of Derby (chairman), the Duke of Leeds, the Earl of Arran, Lord Wimborne and Lord Alcester, began on Monday 7 March, and went on for nearly three weeks.

Much water had passed under the bridges of Sheffield since the failure of the Dale Dyke dam and, during the intervening twenty-three years, the overall memory of that calamity had gradually lost some of its stark clarity and bitterness. Nevertheless, though recollections may have become a little blurred at the edges, the event was far from forgotten. Sheffield Corporation still strongly contended that the fatal embankment had been 'imperfectly and improperly' constructed, while the company maintained (as they had done all along) that the collapse was in no way their fault. In fact, counsel for the company, Mr Pember, went further, telling their lordships that the result of the compensation after the 1864 disaster was that 'everybody benefited, except the people who lost their lives. For every old chair and table that was injured, the owners got a new one. For every old tumbledown house that was damaged, a new one was provided, and the corporation got the benefit because the rateable value of Sheffield at once went up'.

The waterworks company claimed that, despite heavy financial burdens incurred by the payment of compensation and also by the provision of a constant supply to the town, they had now established a system of works more than adequate to meet the needs of Sheffield, the water being both 'abundant and pure'. The company, indeed, were confident they had 'done their duty' and it was stated that during their 57-year history they had 'by the expenditure of something like two millions provided Sheffield with a supply of water as good as that of any town in the kingdom'. It was necessary, however, to obtain parliamentary sanction to perpetuate the right to charge the 25 per cent increase in the rate in order to help meet future commitments.

For their part, Sheffield Corporation expressed their conviction of being better able, and more economically, to control the existing waterworks and also to undertake any expansion that would provide more water. They felt, among other things, that as the body responsible for the sanitation of the town, it was desirable and logical that they should also have the administration of the waterworks. It was a duty they should be allowed to discharge with a 'due regard to the public benefit, rather than to private profit'.

The hearing, which produced thousands of words of evidence from a formidable array of expert witnesses, followed a not dissimilar pattern to that in 1864 and also to those in 1869, 1870 and 1872 when the corporation were again thwarted in their attempts to take over the waterworks. Now, after an interval of fifteen years, Sheffield Corporation were trying once more to achieve something unique—the compulsory purchase of a water company. In this, they were opposed not only by the company themselves but also, among others, by the Duke of Norfolk, Earl Fitzwilliam and various millowners on the rivers Rivelin, Loxley and Don. The corporation also had plenty of support for their Bill. Thirty-nine councillors had voted in favour of it, five were against and there were four abstentions. In addition, a public poll revealed a 22,037 majority in favour of the corporation's proposals, the figures being: for: 23,723 ratepayers and 1,918 owners; against: 3,016 ratepayers and 588 owners.

After listening for days to detailed evidence and the cut-and-thrust of legal argument, the members of the Select Committee

took only forty-five minutes to reach a decision. It was unprecedented. The Earl of Derby announced: 'The committee have come
to a decision that it is expedient that the works of the Sheffield
Waterworks Company and the control of the water supply should
be transferred to the corporation. They have come to this conclusion
on the grounds of public policy, but they do not consider there has
been any proof of mismanagement or failure of duty on the part of
the Sheffield Waterworks Company and they think, therefore, that
the terms of purchase should be not only fair but liberal'.

Although there was a little opposition during the third reading
in the Lords, the Bill became an Act. The purchase price was a
little over £2,000,000 and one effect of the deal, according to *The
Times*, was to lift the value of the ordinary shares (on which £100
was paid up) from £60 to £90.

Sheffield Corporation officially took possession on Monday, 2
January, 1888, but many of the men who had been closely associated
with the 1864 disaster were not around to see it. Ex-Mayor Thomas
Jessop, the good-natured son of a steel smelter, had died on 30
November, 1887, aged eighty-three, leaving personal estate worth
more than £663,000. John Towlerton Leather, wealthy contractor,
consulting engineer and landowner, was in his eighty-first year when
he departed on 6 June, 1885. The previous Christmas Eve had been
the last day on earth for William Overend, who had headed the
Inundation Commission; he was seventy-five. Mark Firth, who once
earned 20s a week as a smelter, died on 28 November, 1880, after
building up one of the world's largest steel-manufacturing organizations, becoming Mayor of his home town in 1875 and one of its
most generous benefactors; he was sixty-one and left about
£600,000. Sheffield's former M.P.s, John Arthur Roebuck and
George Hadfield, aged seventy-eight and ninety-one respectively,
died the previous year. The controversial coroner, John Webster,
also Mayor (1866 and 1867), alderman, magistrate and solicitor,
suffered latterly from heart trouble which defeated him on 28
June, 1878, when he was in his sixty-ninth year. Six years earlier,
life had ended for Nathaniel Beardmore, aged fifty-six, one of the
Government-appointed engineers who investigated the Dale Dyke
failure.

Some of the cast lived on: John Bateman until 1889 and Thomas
Hawksley until 1893; Sir John Brown, the steel magnate, died in
Kent on 27 December, 1896, at the age of eighty. In 1898, the

deaths occurred of Sir Robert Rawlinson (he was eighty-eight), Sir Henry Bessemer (eighty-five), Sir John Fowler (eighty-one) and Sheffield's Chief Constable, John Jackson, who was in his seventy-seventh year. Despite illness Sir William Leng, editor and part-proprietor of *The Sheffield Daily Telegraph*, laboured on and, when he became too feeble to hold a pen, he continued to dictate his articles in the comfortable privacy of his home. His death on 20 February, 1902 occurred about three weeks after his seventy-seventh birthday.

The little lamented demise of the Sheffield Waterworks Company was not witnessed by John Gunson, their most loyal of servants. He had died at his home—7, Clarkson Street—late on Sunday, 10 October, 1886, aged seventy-seven. This man, whose placid nature had been shattered by that living nightmare on 11 March, 1864, had been with the company for fifty-five years. Even when the infirmities of age prevented his regular attendance at the office, he did what work he could at home; colleagues frequently sought his advice and used his vast knowledge of the company's affairs. He had supervised the building of a number of the reservoirs in and around Sheffield, and Hawksley, in particular, had a high regard for his ability. An accolade from one so eminent was worth treasuring. When Gunson was forced, by age and health, to play a diminishing role in the company's activities, the directors might justifiably have bid him farewell, but they remained loyal to the man who had been faithful throughout a difficult period and whose principal interest in life was his work. One of Gunson's sons, Frederick, had become the company's distribution engineer; two others, Thomas and Charles, were mechanical engineers. That must have given pleasure to their father.

For 22 years Gunson, a person of a 'singularly retiring disposition', had carried with him the massive memory of the collapse of the Dale Dyke dam—an event which caused widespread death, destruction and misery, as well as financially crippling the company which owned it. 'The perils of that night and the terrible results of the catastrophe,' reported *The Sheffield Daily Telegraph*, 'were ever vividly remembered by him.' Was that disaster caused by unsound engineering or was it just wretched misfortune? Human error or act of Nature? The chances are that John Gunson died without even being absolutely certain of the real answer.

At the company's offices the next day, the blinds were drawn.

13 Reactions and Reminders

Considering the widespread damage and misery caused by 'The Great Inundation' (a phrase beloved by Victorian journalists), Sheffield returned to something like an even keel in a surprisingly short time, which says much for the resilience and courage of her people. Within a few days of the disaster, temporary bridges had been slung across the rivers and roads were made passable between piles of debris; the reconstruction of some factories and houses began soon afterwards, while laid-off workmen gradually returned to their labours. Of course, there were exceptions: a number of workshops did not reopen, some rebuilding did not get under way for months and other scars remained for years. Men wearily trudged the streets (or left the area) in search of other jobs but, on the whole, it appears that the failure of the Dale Dyke dam did not bring about such a high degree of long-term unemployment as might reasonably have been expected.

Even in the Loxley Valley, which suffered so cruelly, industry staggered to its feet remarkably quickly. At some 'Wheels' it was soon business-as-usual, although this was often conducted from the less damaged parts of the buildings while repairs were being carried out only a few feet away. For a while the valley, with its wide variety of manufactures (including steel tilting, rolling and forging; paper-making; corn-milling; cutlery grinding), must have been a depressed district, but it cannot be said that any specific trade was decimated at a stroke. Substantial capital expenditure was required to get the works fully operational again, however.

Some buildings in the valley today occupy the same sites as did those wrecked or seriously damaged by the flood. Indeed, a few relics of old watermills still exist although, as R. Hawkins points out in the *Sheffield City Museums Information Sheet* (No. 4), the 'surviving industrial remains in the river valleys represent only a small portion of the once extensive water-powered sector of Sheffield's industry'.

Very little survives also of the original Dale Dyke dam and a casual visitor (even with permission to inspect the area) could easily miss what there is. Weather-beaten marker stones, about four hundred yards apart on either side of the valley, bear the inscription 'CLOB' (Centre Line Old Bank); they are almost hidden amid trees and undergrowth. It would be intriguing to report that sections of the old dam are visible but, sadly, such is not the case. An overgrown mound or two can be detected, but these are now merely parts of the current landscape. One feels no sense of drama although, with the knowledge that here at least is the site, it is perhaps possible to 'recall' the scene of chaos, disbelief and fear experienced on the dam during that storm-tossed night of 11 March 1864. In truth, in that area of tranquillity and outstanding beauty, there are outwardly few signs to link the peaceful present with that turbulent tragedy of the past.

When he went to the site in March 1914 (fifty years after the disaster), 'Observer' wrote in the *Sheffield Daily Telegraph* that the dam was 'something of an outcast' and, although the Corporation had planted firs and larches in the vicinity, 'the old embankment has had the doors of beauty and attention barred and bolted against it.... There it stands now, pushed outside the Corporation care zone, its own monument to its own failure.... Man has shunned it and left it as it was'. There was no need to erect a stone or pillar, the writer added, for 'you know instinctively' it was the dam that burst.

Surprisingly, perhaps, there is no prominent memorial—either there or in Sheffield—to mark that calamity which, tragic though it was, is undeniably a major event in the city's history. Monuments commemorate the cholera epidemic of 1832 and pay homage to the dead of two World Wars but, to my knowledge, there is nothing significant to record the Great Flood. Not that nobody has thought about it. Samuel Harrison, the energetic editor of *The Sheffield Times*, was among the first to advocate such a memorial. 'The funds obtained for the relief of the distressed,' he wrote soon after the disaster, 'are more than sufficient, and it cannot be supposed that any subscribers would object to the appropriation of a small part of the surplus to so legitimate a purpose as the erection of a suitable monument of the Great Flood at Sheffield.' Similar recommendations followed and, even half a century later, his son, Councillor S. Gardner Harrison, commented in an article in the *Sheffield Daily Telegraph*: 'It is late in the day to suggest such a thing; nevertheless, would it not be well if some modest cenotaph were erected in some convenient place, say, in the General Cemetery, where many of the victims were buried?'

From time to time (notably on anniversaries and, occasionally, when a flood relic is presented to the museum) the story of the disaster is revived. In March 1964, on the occasion of the centenary, Sheffield newspapers produced special supplements, there were exhibitions at the museum and central library, a commemorative service was held at Bradfield Church and a party of engineers visited the ill-fated site of the old dam. Doubtless the 'Did-it-fall-or-was-it-pushed?' debates continue—albeit infrequently and in modulated voices—although they can be but speculative and academic. There remains the fascination of a mystery: no one can be more certain now than were the experts at the time as to exactly what happened to that embankment on the moors. In attempting to reach some sort of conclusion, however, one is bound to take into account the loyalties and personal involvements of the principal participants concerned with the event.

A number of melancholy 'reminders' of the flood are to be seen in cemeteries in and around Sheffield. For instance, tucked away in the graveyard of Loxley Chapel is a time-blackened headstone recording the fact that Eliza Armitage, aged sixty-seven, her two sons, their wives and seven children were drowned at Malin Bridge. Five of the youngsters were not found, but their names (with accompanying asterisks) are included in the inscription together with those of the other seven Armitages interred there.

Modern Sheffield has plenty of first-rate soft water. Until 1 April 1974 (when the Yorkshire Water Authority assumed control) the water undertaking was both owned and administered for eighty-six years by the Corporation, whose latest statistics showed that supplies to the city and district amounted to nearly 56 million gallons daily (an additional 16 million a day was provided as 'compensation' water to rivers). The area of direct supply covered about 240 square miles, the water reaching a population of about 750,000 via more than 1,800 miles of mains (bulk supplies to neighbouring towns increased that total to well over a million people). Progressive policies over the years enabled the Corporation to keep ahead of the ever-increasing demand for water and the large and complex undertaking included six treatment works, 41 service reservoirs and 37 pumping stations.

The 13 impounding reservoirs serving Sheffield have a total storage capacity of 6,760 million gallons. It is interesting to note that nine of them (the oldest, Redmires Middle, dates from 1836) were constructed by the old Sheffield Waterworks Company.

Principal Sources of Information

Books

Best, Geoffrey: *Mid-Victorian Britain, 1851-75*. Weidenfeld and Nicolson, London, 1971.

Briggs, Asa: *Victorian Cities*. Odhams Press, 1963; *Victorian People*. Odhams Press, London, 1954.

Bunker, Bessie: *Portrait of Sheffield*. Robert Hale, London, 1972.

Carr, J. C. and Taplin, W.: *History of the British Steel Industry*. Basil Blackwell, Oxford, 1962.

Coleman, Terry: *The Railway Navvies*. Hutchinson, London, 1965.

Gatty, Alfred: *Sheffield: Past and Present*. Thomas Rodgers, Sheffield, 1873.

Harrison, Samuel: *A Complete History of the Great Flood at Sheffield*. S. Harrison, *The Sheffield Times*, 1864.

Mackay, Thomas: *The Life of Sir John Fowler*. John Murray, London, 1900.

Pollard, Sidney: *A History of Labour in Sheffield*. Liverpool University Press, 1959.

Raistrick, Arthur: *West Riding of Yorkshire*. Hodder and Stoughton, London, 1970.

Reade, Charles: *Put Yourself in His Place*. Smith, Elder & Co., London, 1870.

Rolt, L. T. C.: *Victorian Engineering*. Allen Lane The Penguin Press, London, 1970.

Sheffield City Council (Water Committee): *The Water Supply to Sheffield and District*.

Smith, Norman: *A History of Dams*. Peter Davies, London, 1971.

Stainton, J. F.: *The Making of Sheffield, 1865-1914*. E. Weston and Sons, Sheffield, 1924.

Walton, Mary: *Sheffield, Its Story and Its Achievements*. S. R. Publishers and Sheffield Corporation, 4th ed., 1968.

Newspapers and Journals

The Sheffield Daily Telegraph; *Sheffield and Rotherham Independent*; *The Sheffield Times*; *The Times*; *Daily Telegraph*; *The Daily News*; *The Newcastle Daily Journal*; *Manchester Guardian*; *Leeds Mercury*; *The Huddersfield Chronicle*; *The Engineer*; *The Builder*.

Documents, Reports, Letters, etc.

The Public Record Office; Somerset House; The British Library Newspaper Library, Colindale; The Institution of Civil Engineers; Sheffield City Libraries (Department of Local History and Archives); Sheffield City Museums; Sheffield Corporation Waterworks.

Index